Leo Strauss

Leo Strauss

An Introduction

Neil G. Robertson

polity

The right of Neil G. Robertson to be identified as Author of this Work has been asserted in accordance with the UK Copyright, Designs and Patents Act 1988.

First published in 2021 by Polity Press

Polity Press
65 Bridge Street
Cambridge CB2 1UR, UK

Polity Press
101 Station Landing
Suite 300
Medford, MA 02155, USA

ISBN-13: 978-1-5095-1630-8
ISBN-13: 978-1-5095-1631-5 (pb)

A catalogue record for this book is available from the British Library.

Library of Congress Cataloging-in-Publication Data

Names: Robertson, Neil G., author.
Title: Leo Strauss : an introduction / Neil Robertson.
Description: Medford : Polity Press, 2021. | Series: Key contemporary thinkers | Includes bibliographical references and index. | Summary: "A non-partisan introduction to the ideas of the controversial political philosopher and classicist"-- Provided by publisher.
Identifiers: LCCN 2020053826 (print) | LCCN 2020053827 (ebook) | ISBN 9781509516308 (hardback) | ISBN 9781509516315 (paperback) | ISBN 9781509516322 (pdf) | ISBN 9781509516346 (epub)
Subjects: LCSH: Strauss, Leo--Political and social views. | Political science--Philosophy. | Political science--History.
Classification: LCC JA71 .R5853 2021 (print) | LCC JA71 (ebook) | DDC 320.092--dc23
LC record available at https://lccn.loc.gov/2020053826
LC ebook record available at https://lccn.loc.gov/2020053827

Typeset in 10.5 on 12pt Palatino
by Fakenham Prepress Solutions, Fakenham, Norfolk NR21 8NL
Printed and bound in the UK by TJ Books Ltd, Padstow, Cornwall

For further information on Polity, visit our website: politybooks.com

In memory of my parents, Ronald and Sheila Robertson
for their sustaining love and understated wisdom

Contents

Acknowledgments

This book is a culmination of the fascination with and critical admiration for the thought of Leo Strauss that I have had since first encountering him when I was an undergraduate, through the teaching of George Grant and of Robert Eden when both were at Dalhousie University. I have thought and taught and written about Leo Strauss for nearly forty years. I am so grateful for the teachers, colleagues, and students who have supported in so many ways my effort to understand this most evasive of thinkers. I must especially acknowledge two intersecting intellectual centers: the University of King's College and the Classics Department of Dalhousie University, together so fundamental to my intellectual formation, and the home for my thinking about Strauss.

There are specific colleagues and friends who have contributed directly to this book's composition by reading drafts of chapters and aiding and correcting my thinking and understanding of Strauss: Daniel Brandes, Eli Diamond, Susan Dodd, Mark Henrie, Ken Kierans, Simon Kow, David Peddle, and Henry Roper. I am also very much in the debt of the anonymous reviewers who gave such helpful corrections and suggestions to aid in the final reworking of the book. I am deeply grateful to George Owers and Julia Davies of Polity Press for the invitation to write this book and the care and consideration they have shown both it and me over its somewhat delayed emergence.

This book was made possible by six months' leave of absence from my work as Director of the Foundation Year Program at the University of King's College in Halifax, Nova Scotia. For the astonishing generosity of my colleagues, above all Susan Dodd who stepped in so graciously to take over my duties, I am deeply thankful: it is the most perfect affirmation of the collegiality in our little institution and in the program that is its heart. I am grateful as well to our President and Vice-President, and to the Board of Governors, for granting me this unplanned leave. The support of the University of King's College Library has also been an enormous help in the writing of this book.

However, the person who must be acknowledged beyond all others is my wife and the endlessly patient yet challenging editor of all the writing of this book. Whatever clarity, articulacy, or poise belongs to it is entirely due to her extraordinary care, skill, and talent with language. She has been aided in supporting me through this consuming task by my two wondrous daughters.

Neil G. Robertson
March 2021

Abbreviations of Works by Strauss

CM   *The City and Man*
CP   "Notes on Carl Schmitt, *The Concept of the Political*"
CT   "The Crisis of Our Time"
EW   *Leo Strauss: The Early Writings (1921–1932)*
FP   "Farabi's Plato"
FPP   *Faith and Political Philosophy: The Correspondence Between Leo Strauss and Eric Voegelin, 1934–1964*
GC   "Correspondence Concerning *Wahrheit und Methode*: Leo Strauss and Hans-Georg Gadamer"
GN   "German Nihilism"
HCR   *Hobbes's Critique of Religion and Related Writings*
IPP   *An Introduction to Political Philosophy: Ten Essays by Leo Strauss*
JPCM   *Jewish Philosophy and the Crisis of Modernity: Essays and Lectures in Modern Jewish Thought*
LAM   *Leo Strauss: Liberalism Ancient and Modern*
LC   "Correspondence: Karl Löwith and Leo Strauss"
LCM   "Correspondence Concerning Modernity: Karl Löwith and Leo Strauss"
LI   "The Living Issues of German Postwar Philosophy"
NL   "Natural Law"
NRH   *Natural Right and History*
OT   *On Tyranny: Corrected and Expanded Edition, Including the Strauss–Kojève Correspondence*
PAW   *Persecution and the Art of Writing*

PL	*Philosophy and Law: Contributions to the Understanding of Maimonides and His Predecessors*
PPH	*The Political Philosophy of Hobbes: Its Basis and Genesis*
R	"Restatement"
RCPR	*The Rebirth of Classical Political Rationalism: An Introduction to the Thought of Leo Strauss*
RLS	*Reorientation: Leo Strauss in the 1930s*
RR	"Reason and Revelation"
RSM	"Relativism"
SCR	*Spinoza's Critique of Religion*
SKC	*The Strauss–Krüger Correspondence: Returning to Plato through Kant*
SPPP	*Studies in Platonic Political Philosophy*
SSTX	"The Spirit of Sparta or The Taste of Xenophon"
TM	*Thoughts on Machiavelli*
TNRH	*Toward Natural Right and History: Lectures and Essays by Leo Strauss 1937–1946*
WIPP	*What Is Political Philosophy? And Other Studies*

Introduction

It is true of many important contemporary thinkers that they are controversial: often, what makes thinkers important is precisely that they say controversial things. What is especially challenging about Leo Strauss, however, is that the controversy surrounding him is often about what his position actually was. In both the secondary literature and the popular press, there is basic disagreement about what Strauss was in fact arguing.

Trying to provide an introduction to the thought and writings of Leo Strauss, then, is necessarily problematic. This is not an accident. The fact that commentators do not agree about what Strauss himself argued is itself a clue to what is most important in Leo Strauss. The most basic awareness a philosopher must have, according to Strauss, is the recognition of what he calls "the fundamental or permanent problems." At the very center of his life and thought, Strauss is calling upon us to recognize the deeply problematic character of human existence. It is entirely fitting that Strauss's thought should be inherently problematic.

But none of this makes the work of providing an introduction to that thought any easier. Strauss has generated dramatically varying interpretations. For his students and other admirers, sometimes called "Straussians," Leo Strauss is among the most significant scholars or philosophers of the twentieth century – in fact, perhaps *the* most important. For these, he is a figure who has revived political philosophy and classical thought, rediscovered old and hidden ways of reading, and made the very beginnings of Socratic political philosophy available to us once more. He has diagnosed with unsurpassed clarity the "crisis of our time," and yet has also recovered the nobility and validity of revelation and renewed the debate between Athens and Jerusalem. In so doing, this Strauss has helped free his readers and students from false and destructive ideological thinking or naive ambitions about the transforming possibilities of politics, and so has recovered political moderation and the need for statesmanlike prudence and restraint in our all-too-dogmatic political world. This Leo Strauss is a wise and sober friend to liberal democracy, and especially to American liberal democracy.

On the other side, Strauss has been greeted by his critics – of whom there are many – as the very opposite of that in almost every respect, often in strangely contrasting ways. On the one hand he has been portrayed as essentially an intellectual fraud, lacking in basic scholarship, or pursuing a scholarship that is perverse beyond the idiosyncratic: more a cult leader than a diligent scholar. Whatever claims he may have to philosophical insight are, from this perspective, entirely overblown: where he is not derivative, he is delusional. At the same time, other critics have portrayed Strauss as not so much an incompetent crank, more a kind of intellectual Moriarty, a spider weaving an insidious and hidden web that seeks to undermine liberal democracy. This Strauss seeks to effect a politics of lying and manipulation informed by the thought of Nietzsche or even by a kind of fascism. In this view, Strauss's all-too-superior "philosophers" are supposed to rule over all-too-human subjects. For critics in this camp, the role of Strauss's students in the "American right" (and above all the neo-conservatives who came to power in the White House of George W. Bush) reveals the inner truth of what Strauss has really been about behind the veil of traditional conservatism. For these critics, he is a false friend to liberal democracy, and his influence has been a disaster for American and global political life.

So, for the reader who seeks to be both critical and sympathetic and to find a middle road between the Straussians and the anti-Straussians, this leaves the question: who is Leo Strauss, and in what context are we to understand his writings?

Ironically, one of the challenges in answering this is that, in contrast to many contemporary thinkers, Strauss appears to write simply and straightforwardly. He largely shuns technical language, finding it abstract and unphilosophical – and so, at the level of sentences or even paragraphs, his writing can appear to need no introduction. The last few books he wrote may seem to be nothing more than uninspiring summaries of the texts on which they claim to be commentaries. It is certainly true that, when Strauss wants to, he can write with great clarity and beauty. The challenge in reading him is to keep track of the subtle and continual shifts and changes that come to light as he moves from one thought to the next. Things quickly become complicated as we start trying to put together the various things Strauss says.

Three further things in Strauss's writing lead to even greater complexity. First, as we have already remarked, at the heart of his thinking Strauss emphasizes the irresolvable, problematic character of existence. This means that tensions and oppositions are themselves essential to Strauss's thought. Even among his students there is wide disagreement about how Strauss resolves, characterizes, or even formulates these tensions. For example, the contrast or tension between reason and revelation is fundamental to Strauss's thought, but Strauss's readers differ in what they see him doing with the reason–revelation "problem." There are atheistic, secularist Straussians and there are faith-based Straussians: both groups find a ground for their position in Strauss's writings. Another example of this fundamental disagreement is Strauss's assessment of the importance of ordinary civic or political morality. Some take Strauss to be a firm defender of such morals; others take the opposite view, that Strauss is in fact contemptuous of ordinary moral understanding. In general, I will not try to resolve these debates, but will suggest a formulation that seems best to cohere with what seem to be Strauss's other thoughts. Staying with the problems more than any solution was in fact a central characteristic Strauss himself discerned in philosophy, which he saw to be the love or pursuit, rather than the actual possession, of wisdom.

The second major challenge to introducing Strauss's thought is that the vast majority of his writings consists of commentaries on other writings, mostly works from the history of political thought in the western intellectual tradition (inclusive of the Jewish and Islamic Middle Ages), from the ancient Greeks to the twentieth century. In his commentaries he often assumed the voice of the author of the writing under discussion, or of one of the characters in a dialogue. Strauss only occasionally wrote in his own voice, and never provided a complete or comprehensive account or analysis of his philosophical claims. This, of course, increases the challenge of sorting out what Strauss's thought is in its own terms. This indirect form of "communication through commentary" is not an accidental feature of Strauss's thought; it belongs to his core claim about how philosophy arises from opinion, and how philosophy functions in the context of opinion.

The third great issue for the reader of Strauss is that Strauss claimed as one of his most important discoveries a tradition of "esoteric" writing in the western philosophical tradition, from the ancient Greeks through to the eighteenth century. He argued that many philosophers hid their teaching under an "exoteric" or outer form. This raises the obvious question: does Strauss himself also practice this art? We will discuss Strauss's understanding of exoteric/esoteric teachings at length in chapter 3 – but at this point, it is important at least to recognize the complication it presents. In claiming to understand Strauss, the reader must acknowledge that Strauss himself might have – or perhaps should be presumed to have – a secret or "esoteric" teaching. This obviously disrupts the normal assumption that authors mean what they say, and so complicates the task of discerning what Strauss might mean.

These challenges to understanding and explaining Strauss's thought have convinced me that a somewhat unusual approach is needed for a book such as this one that is trying to introduce Strauss's thought in a balanced way, both sympathetically and critically. Because there is so much controversy about what Strauss's position is, I have chosen to quote from him much more than is normal in an introductory book. Also, because his published writing is often complex and circuitous, I have made much use of his letters, unpublished writings, and lectures, where he is often clearer and more direct about his views. The huge advantage such an approach affords is that Strauss is a very good writer. His sentences are usually clear and, when he wants to, he can be wonderfully evocative and compelling. We will be trying to use Strauss to help us understand Strauss.

So while things can get complicated in trying to get at what Strauss's thought consists in, and there is a large and vexed secondary literature, we will seek to find our way to the center of his thought by focusing upon the question that was for him at the center of human existence: what is the best or right life? Strauss's work was a continuous response to this question.

The first thing is to provide an outline of Strauss's life, and then to describe briefly some of the basic themes and claims of his thought as it seeks to think the question of the best life.

Who is Leo Strauss?

Leo Strauss was born in 1899 into an observant Jewish family in Germany. Even before attending university, he converted to "simple, straightforward political Zionism" (JPCM 460), and was involved in the Zionist movement during his twenties. Strauss studied philosophy at the University of Marburg and the University of Hamburg. While a student, he served as an assistant to Edmund Husserl, the founder of the school of phenomenology. Strauss attended some classes and seminars of Martin Heidegger, whom Strauss considered to be the greatest thinker of his generation. After completing a doctorate at the University of Hamburg under Ernst Cassirer in 1921, Strauss became a researcher at the Academy for the Science of Judaism in Berlin, focusing on the history of Jewish philosophy, including work on Moses Mendelssohn, Spinoza, and Maimonides. His first book, *Spinoza's Critique of Religion*, was published in 1930. At about this time, Strauss had what he described later as a "change of orientation" that opened up for him the possibility of a recovery of pre-modern rationalism. He later stated that the first expression of his "change of orientation" was to be found in his 1932 review of a book by Carl Schmitt, the important legal theorist who joined the Nazi Party shortly afterward. When the Nazis came to power in 1933, Strauss was in France on a Rockefeller research fellowship. The following year, he moved to England to work on Thomas Hobbes. In 1937, he went to the United States, eventually securing a permanent position at the New School for Social Research in New York City. In 1949, Strauss began two decades of teaching in the Department of Political Science at the University of Chicago. He retired and was named Professor Emeritus at the University of Chicago in 1968, but continued teaching and giving guest lectures at Claremont Men's College and then at St. John's College in Annapolis, Maryland, until his death in 1973.

Themes in Strauss's Thought

What matters most about Leo Strauss's life is not primarily his deeds but his thoughts. There are two basic ways we could approach Strauss's importance as a "key contemporary thinker": one would be chronological, and the second thematic. This book will do a bit of both, but it is primarily thematically structured. This is not an intellectual biography, but in chapters 1 and 2, I will consider Strauss's intellectual development in the context of the Weimar Republic, and especially the significance and meaning of what he calls his "change of orientation." We will also follow him to the United States, where he taught for over thirty years and published the books that established him as one of the leading figures in political philosophy and the history of political philosophy in the mid-twentieth century. We will conclude the book by looking at his influence especially upon American conservative thought and American politics.

While there is a general biographical trajectory through the course of the book, its more basic structure is thematic – and, in order to explore these themes across the range of Strauss's thought, we will often look at writings from different decades in his life. The primary justification for this is that, once Strauss underwent his "change of orientation" sometime around 1930, his thought retained a basic stability of outlook. This is not to deny some important developments and even corrections within his thought, and certainly we will note them when they arise. Nonetheless, the essence of Strauss's philosophical orientation and vision remained remarkably consistent.

Let me turn, then, to the themes that will organize this book and help orient us in making sense of Strauss's thought. This list is by no means exhaustive, but I want to suggest that these five themes do form something like the most fundamental aspects of Strauss's thinking:

1. the return to natural right and the recovery of classical rationalism;
2. the theological-political problem;
3. the recovery of the exoteric/esoteric distinction;
4. classical political philosophy; and
5. the critique of modern political philosophy.

The first three themes will form our first three chapters, and we will explore the development of Strauss's thought in the context of the Weimar Republic in Germany, and in his first few years of exile from Germany in France, England, and the United States. Chapters 4 and 5 will consider the two crucial components of his mature thought, which find expression particularly in work Strauss published while he was at the University of Chicago, and, above all, in his most comprehensive book, *Natural Right and History* (1953).

But it is important to remember that the key earlier themes remain active right through his work: Strauss himself explicitly states that the theological-political problem was *the* theme of his investigations throughout his scholarly career. In chapter 6, we will consider Strauss's legacy and specifically his influence on American politics.

It is a basic claim of this book that Strauss's work as a whole cannot be understood or properly assessed except by seeing it as a response to the crisis of politics, thought, and culture that belonged to the Weimar Republic. Strauss's intellectual project clearly emerged from this context, and understood that crisis as indicative of a deeper and more fundamental crisis in western civilization: the crisis of the West, or nihilism. Our first three chapters will be an effort to understand and explain Strauss's standpoint as a response to the crisis of nihilism. Of course, many of the most significant thinkers of the twentieth century were engaged in responding to similar circumstances. We need to see Strauss's as one such response, but an importantly distinct and compelling one.

Before considering these themes, it will be useful briefly to introduce three thinkers who are especially important in understanding and locating Strauss's position. Friedrich Nietzsche, Edmund Husserl, and Martin Heidegger were crucial figures in articulating the intellectual world in which Strauss came to his own standpoint.

Friedrich Nietzsche (1844–1900), while he lived in the nineteenth century, only came to cultural and intellectual prominence in the first decades of the twentieth century and was, by Strauss's own account, the dominating intellectual presence of the Weimar Republic (1918–33), where Strauss came to intellectual maturity. Nietzsche is famous for his account of European civilization as having been subject to the claim "God is dead." Nietzsche provided the most radical consideration of the implications of this insight into modern culture: the death of God implied the loss not only of religious belief but of the whole framework of morality and science that depended on the claim of an otherworldly foundation. Nietzsche therefore saw his own time as one that was experiencing nihilism. In the face of the abysmal experience of the death of God, Nietzsche saw as illusionary and unsustainable the claims that the end of religion issued in a new egalitarian humanism and new scientific understanding of the world. Nietzsche proposed an alternative way to live in the face of nihilism through three "teachings": the world as "will to power"; the proclamation of the *Übermensch*, the "Overman"; and the doctrine of the Eternal Return of the

Same. Nietzsche explores these thoughts in a number of works, but especially central is *Thus Spoke Zarathustra*. As we shall see, Strauss understood himself as trying to face the demands of Nietzsche's thought.

Edmund Husserl (1859–1938) was important to Strauss in pointing to a way of philosophizing that might allow for a standpoint that could escape Nietzsche's devastating critique of the western tradition of philosophy as implicated in the nihilism western culture found itself possessed by. Husserl developed "phenomenology" as a way to engage in a philosophic reflection on the experienced world that avoids the kind of causal or metaphysical approaches to philosophy that dominated western philosophy, and were especially at work in modern philosophy's turn to questions of knowledge of the external world. Husserl's phenomenology sought to pre-empt the turn to this kind of knowledge by engaging in a philosophy of the description of things as they appeared to the self, bracketing, or excluding, questions of causality or metaphysics. Strauss was deeply impressed by Husserl and took up his turn to the "natural understanding" – the way things appear to us naturally – as a beginning point for a philosophy that might point a way out of the nihilism of the age.

Martin Heidegger (1889–1976) was an assistant to Husserl and developed and radicalized Husserl's standpoint. Strauss encountered Heidegger as a young academic in the circle of Husserl and was deeply impressed by the power of Heidegger's philosophical inquiry both as a philosopher and as an interpreter of classical philosophy. Heidegger recognized that Husserl's phenomenology could be transformed by situating its inquiry in time and history: the self or ego that engages in phenomenological description could and should be seen not as a timeless, situationless being, but as one necessarily confronting a finite, historical situation in which time fundamentally informs that finitude. Heidegger is the intellectual source of existentialism. He agrees with Nietzsche that the modern era is one of nihilism. He finds in his radicalized phenomenology a way both to understand and confront this historical situation more deeply, and to seek to find a way of thinking that might open a stance beyond nihilism. Heidegger's most important book, *Being and Time*, was published in 1927. In 1933, he joined the Nazi Party. In many ways Heidegger's mentor, Husserl came to be deeply disturbed by, and felt betrayed by, the radical tendencies of his student's thinking. Husserl sought in his own last writings to contest Heidegger's claim that his work drew out the proper impli-cation of Husserl's own phenomenology.

Having briefly outlined the standpoints of these three major figures in Strauss's intellectual background, we can turn to sketch five key themes in Strauss's own thought.

The Return to Natural Right

As a young man, Strauss was deeply struck by Nietzsche's charac-terization of the contemporary western world as an age of nihilism. Strauss accepted Nietzsche's account of the self-destruction of reason that produced nihilism as a loss of all moral meaning. The modern world seemed incapable of discerning truth, above all moral and political truth. Strauss's "change of orientation" in the early 1930s was a movement away from Nietzsche made possible by Strauss's recognizing that it was only modern rationalism that was in trouble; pre-modern rationalism could be recovered in order to develop a standpoint without the nihilistic implications of modernity. Further, what pre-modern rationalism allowed was a return to "nature" as a standpoint or standard that would allow the recovery of moral content and moral meaning. Hence the recovery of what Strauss calls "natural right" – Strauss's way of translating the ancient Greek phrase *physei dikaion*, or "what is just or right by nature." If there could be the recovery of a standard of right or justice based upon nature and so independent of history – including the history of modernity – then the apparent victory of modern philosophy over ancient philosophy needed to be reconsidered.

For Strauss, the most developed form of the modern project that ended in nihilism was "historicism," the belief that all human thought and meaning is historically determined and historically limited. Historicism meant that nothing could be said to be simply true or good because, from a historicist perspective, truth and goodness were historically relative. The promise of the recovery of "natural right" was the promise of the recovery of a standard that was not historically relative, but true or good by nature. For Strauss, natural right is what emerges when the power of historicism recedes as it recognizes its nihilistic character. The great benefit of returning to ancient Greek philosophy, above all as shown in the figure of Socrates, is the remarkable fact that there could be the discovery of natural right as an object of philosophical inquiry. It was this insight that was made available to Strauss in his "change of orientation," and was to determine the standpoint of his subsequent thinking.

The Theological-Political Problem

To understand the significance and source of Strauss's change of orientation and recovery of natural right, we must place it in the larger context of Strauss's intellectual concerns. Strauss's own description of this larger context is the "theological-political problem." One way to view this problem is to see it in personal terms reflecting the predicament Strauss found himself in as a Jew who could no longer adhere to the orthodox faith in which he had been raised, but who equally could not identify himself with the larger German culture in which he found himself. Strauss experienced this as an antinomy between modern thought – ultimately Nietzschean atheism – and orthodoxy. The way out of this predicament was, for Strauss, in the return to pre-modern rationalism. Strauss first came to this discovery not in Plato or Socrates, but in medieval Jewish and Islamic thought, above all in the figure of Moses Maimonides (1138–1204).

In Maimonides, Strauss found a particular way of framing and understanding the theological-political problem. The term "theological-political" Strauss borrowed from the title of a book by the seventeenth-century Jewish philosopher Spinoza. Strauss understood the phrase to refer to the need of philosophy to establish itself and to defend its freedom from the forms of authority that belong to religion as well as to political power. In this book, we will look at these two tensions in turn. In chapter 2, we will focus on the tension between philosophy and religion, the tension between "Athens" and "Jerusalem." Strauss argues that the biblical revelation, specifically Judaism, presents the most radical challenge to philosophy and its claims to determine the question of the best way to live on the basis of natural reason alone. For Strauss, the question of "the best life" is the orienting question of human life, and so the contest between reason and revelation is the most basic human question. Strauss's interest in this debate is not simply to secure the claims of reason against any competitor, but more fundamentally to see in the debate itself a shift in the meaning of philosophy. For Strauss, the standpoints of reason and revelation are mutually irrefutable. But recognizing and engaging this "problem" for Strauss gives birth to a deepening understanding of what philosophy is and demonstrates its inherent limits, showing that its very context is constructed of fundamental and permanent problems.

The Exoteric/Esoteric Distinction

One of Strauss's fundamental and recurring arguments is that philosophy, as the life given to questioning in the pursuit of wisdom, is inherently opposed to the nature of the "city" (or, more generally, of society) as a way of life founded upon opinion and above all upon belief in the justice of the laws of the city. In order that philosophers would not be persecuted nor the city be harmed, according to Strauss, philosophers began to conceal their true teaching behind an outer or "exoteric" teaching that would, at least on the surface, suggest that philosophy supported the ways of the city. In other words, the tension between philosophy and the city gave birth to an art of writing for philosophy: the art of esoteric writing.

The exoteric/esoteric distinction can appear to be a plausible claim that philosophers, facing potential persecution, have not always been open about their thoughts, and so interpreters must "read between the lines." At one level, Strauss is certainly saying this. Importantly, however, he connects this historical point to the deeper claim that underlying what appears to be an occasional strategy is a fundamental opposition between philosophy and the city.

Here we can see that the exoteric/esoteric distinction is also a manifestation of another crucial aspect of Strauss's thought: "political philosophy." For Strauss, political philosophy is not primarily a branch or field of philosophy; rather, it is a way in which, or an awareness with which, philosophy is practiced. Political philosophy is philosophy aware of its political context and beginning point. Strauss argues that classical political philosophy is especially self-aware in this regard. It is characteristic of modern political philosophy to practice esoteric writing in the service of seeking to change the world and so eventually to bring about a modern world in which a free, enlightened people can live without the need for such devices. Strauss's judgment, arising from his sense of nihilism, is that this modern project has failed. It is only in classical political philosophy, which is aware of the irreducible difference between philosophy and the city, and which practices esoteric writing in the service of that difference, that we can find a stable standpoint and so escape a nihilistic result.

Classical Political Philosophy

A great deal of Strauss's standpoint rests on his understanding of classical political philosophy, and many of his writings can be seen as contributions to his recovery of classical political philosophy. Strauss articulates this recovery through the interpretation of classical texts, above all texts that have as their focus the figure of Socrates, with whom Strauss associates the origin of political philosophy. The texts central to this for him are the dialogues of Plato, as well as dialogues by Xenophon, Aristophanes' play *The Clouds*, and some comments by Aristotle. However, it would be fair to say that Strauss's consideration of classical political philosophy extends to more than these works: he includes not only other works of classical philosophy and classical literature, but beyond that (and in a more complicated sense) the work of the great Jewish and Islamic philosophers, above all Alfarabi (872–950) and Maimonides, whom Strauss understands to be continuing in the practice of classical political philosophy. Still, the central and defining figure in Strauss's account of classical political philosophy is the Socrates of Plato's dialogues.

Strauss's recovery of classical political philosophy is, as we have seen, a response to the crisis of modernity: nihilism. Further, in Strauss's view, historicism – with what he sees as its moral relativism and moral nihilism – represents the most extreme manifestation of that crisis. For Strauss, what classical political philosophy does is to give access to a reality untouched by history: nature. But the "nature" Strauss finds in classical political philosophy is not a metaphysical account of nature. The traditional reading of Plato and Aristotle and other ancient philosophers finds that Plato's and Aristotle's standpoints bring to light a metaphysical realm of ideas or forms that underlie and cause all reality; this accords with what Nietzsche and Heidegger find. Strauss, following his esoteric reading of texts, argues that this surface or exoteric account is not the true standpoint of classical political philosophy. For the careful reader, argues Strauss, the true teaching of classical philosophy, and above all that of Plato, shows itself to be focused on philosophy as ceaseless questioning, rather than on a metaphysical solution to those questions. What Plato teaches esoterically is Socrates' "knowledge of ignorance," philosophy as the life dedicated to the quest or pursuit of knowledge, rather than to its possession in and by metaphysical knowledge. For Strauss, this is crucial if classical political philosophy is not going to be subject to the critiques of Nietzsche and Heidegger, who argue that the metaphysics of Plato and Aristotle in fact leads to modern nihilism.

For Strauss, the possibility of an ahistorical, non-metaphysical political philosophy rests upon recovering the Socratic beginning, seeing philosophy as arising from the philosopher entering into the *agora*, the space of public opinion, to begin a process of questioning and dialectic that seeks to uncover the abiding reality – nature – that public opinion points to. What this means is a turning to what people say, to their speeches, and not trying to seek an underlying causality that treats what is said in a reductionist way. In doing this, the fullness of humanity can be recovered: the "high" is not seen from the perspective of the "low." Classical political philosophy's turn to speeches can be seen as the beginning necessary to avoid the outcome of moral nihilism that belongs to modernity. Strauss's whole work of scholarship is, then, a sustained effort to recover this way of doing philosophy, as the thing most needful in the face of the crisis of the West.

The Critique of Modernity

The final theme we will explore is Strauss's explanation of the history that has led to what he sees as the modern crisis. The first thing to understand is that history is, for Strauss, fundamentally a history of ideas. The modern world, or "modern project" as he sometimes calls it, is not primarily a result of social, economic, or other historical causes; it is primarily the work of changes in thought, and above all the work of changes in political philosophy. The most fundamental change was a shift in the meaning of political philosophy in the sixteenth and seventeenth centuries so that it was no longer seen to be a life in pursuit of theoretical knowledge, but became dedicated instead to the alteration of political reality. For the modern, knowledge became no longer the knowledge of what is, but of *how to change* what is. In short, political philosophy became dedicated to effecting historical change. More specifically for Strauss, in the modern project historical change was aimed at constructing a world dedicated to fulfilling human needs and purposes.

Strauss came to see the modern project as consisting of three stages or waves that bring out a progressively deeper radicalism. We will have a chance to explore this development in detail in chapter 5. But at this stage, the general point to see is that, according to Strauss, modernity began with a break from the pre-modern made by political philosophy, and came to a kind of conclusion in the crisis of the moral nihilism and relativism of twentieth-century life. For Strauss, this places us, as inhabitants of a modern or postmodern world, in a terrible dilemma. We have lost our capacity to orient ourselves morally and politically. We cannot simply turn back to an earlier moment in modernity; its history has shown that modernity generates its own undoing. Even if we find a way to recover the standpoint of natural right through a study of classical political philosophy, for Strauss it is hard to say how that can and should guide us in a world that is no longer classical. As Strauss stated, "only we living today can find a solution to the problems of today" (CM 11).

Strauss argues that, rather than a "solution," what emerges from the insight that fundamental problems are irresolvable is a way of living with the problems: the recognition that moderation and practical wisdom are the proper standards of political life. Nature can function as a kind of guiding star in terms of natural right, but it does not provide an ideological map. For Strauss, one of the marks of the modern project is its tendency to become ideological, to move toward a fixed determination of the workings of the world. In Strauss's mind such ideologies tend toward reductionism. At the heart of Strauss's political philosophy is an effort to liberate thinking from reductionist or ideological accounts of politics and of the human more generally. For him, it is only when reductionist tendencies are resisted that the fundamental problems can emerge – and that political philosophy will be able to become, as Strauss called it, "first philosophy" (CM 20).

The Thesis of this Book

Beyond trying to introduce readers to the often-challenging thought of Leo Strauss, this book does have a thesis about that thought as a whole. Strauss always called himself a "scholar" and not a "philosopher." This was not simply due to modesty on his part; it is actually central to his basic claim. If Strauss is simply recovering a pre-existing standpoint – that of classical political philosophy

– his basic work is scholarly recovery. But the claim of this book is that Strauss is doing more than "scholarly recovery": he is a key contemporary thinker precisely because his work is philosophically original. He is not simply recovering the thought of Plato, as he presents himself to be doing; nor is he simply occupying an already-established contemporary standpoint, whether it is that of Nietzsche or Heidegger, as some critics of Strauss have alleged. Strauss developed a distinctive contemporary position – and it is this distinctive position that we will be trying to uncover as we go through Strauss's thought.

However, precisely because he is more original than he allows, Strauss's claims to recovery are more open to question than he allows. The focus of this introduction to Strauss will be not primarily on his interpretations of specific texts, but on his own thought. That thought was undoubtedly worked out in and through his readings of ancient and modern political philosophy, but it was not determined by those texts. Our effort will be to see Strauss as himself a key contemporary thinker.

1

Recovering Natural Right in the Weimar Republic

Leo Strauss's intellectual formation took place during the Weimar Republic. The Weimar Republic (1919–33) is the name given to the republic formed following the collapse of the German Reich after the First World War. Under the leadership of Otto von Bismarck in the nineteenth century, the Reich had unified Germany and defeated both the Austro-Hungarian Empire and France. In contrast to Bismarck's Reich, however, as Leo Strauss noted, "The Weimar Republic was weak. It had a single moment of strength, if not of greatness: its strong reaction to the murder of the Jewish Minister of Foreign Affairs, Walther Rathenau, in 1922. On the whole it presented the sorry spectacle of justice without a sword or of justice unable to use the sword" (JPCM 137). It is evident from Strauss's early writings and correspondence that he shared with many of his contemporaries a deep sense of dissatisfaction with the Weimar Republic. The world of the Weimar Republic was remarkable: vibrant, but also strife-ridden, haunted by a lingering sense of illegitimacy and decadence. It has been the subject of innumerable historical studies, novels, plays, and films, and was the seedbed of many of the most significant intellectual and cultural movements of the twentieth century. Experimental art and culture emerged during the Weimar years in a plethora of forms that sought "the new" in radical extremes. The Weimar Republic was Germany's first liberal democracy, but it was not born out of victory, accomplishment, or liberation. Instead it came into being as if it were an imposition foisted upon a defeated Germany by the triumphant liberal democracies of Britain, France, and the United States, which themselves deeply compromised the potential of this new democratic regime by the punitive terms of the Treaty of Versailles. The very name "Weimar Republic" paid testimony to modern liberal developments within German culture, as Strauss noted: "By linking itself to Weimar the German liberal democracy proclaimed its moderate, non-radical character: its resolve to keep a balance between the dedication to the principles of 1789 and the dedication to the highest German tradition" (JPCM 137). However, over the course of just a few years, it became clear that the Weimar Republic was incapable of mediating and moderating the radical tendencies that came to life within it. In opposition to it and its connection with both the Enlightenment and the longer history of modern European thought and culture, there was everywhere a desire for radicality and new beginnings. Politically this took the form of a weakening of the liberal "center," and the turn to destabilizing or revolutionary extremes on both the left and right. On one side, philosophically, the Weimar Republic saw the emergence of a revival and reconstruction of Marxism in groups such as the Frankfurt School. On the other side, "conservative" or right-wing forms emerged that had an existentialist character that called for religious, cultural, or philosophical recovery of the pre-modern, often mixed with an authoritarian ultra-modern or postmodern political vision. Names such as Oswald Spengler, Carl Schmitt, Ernst Jünger, and above all Martin Heidegger can be connected to the latter tendency. The overarching philosophical and literary presence informing the Weimar Republic, however, was undoubtedly Friedrich Nietzsche.

Nietzsche and the Weimar Republic

In 1941, in a public lecture entitled "German Nihilism," Strauss told his American audience: "Of all German philosophers, and indeed of *all* philosophers, none exercised a greater influence on post-war Germany, none was more responsible for the emergence of German nihilism, than was Nietzsche" (GN 372). For many in Strauss's New York audience, National Socialism was the obvious embodiment of "German nihilism." Strauss acknowledged that this was true, but argued that the roots of German nihilism were deeper still, and that they preceded the existence of the Nazi Party. In that lecture, Strauss defined nihilism as "the rejection of the principles of civilization as such" (GN 364). For him, civilization is "the conscious culture of reason" (GN 366), above all the cultivation of science (or more generally philosophy) and morals "and both united" (GN 365). For Strauss and many of his contemporaries, there was a powerful impetus toward nihilism in their experience of the inadequacy of modern forms, especially as these were realized in the Weimar Republic.

Strauss makes this point powerfully in a section of this lecture that is worth considering at some length. He writes: "No one could be satisfied with the post-war world. German liberal democracy of all descriptions seemed to many people to be absolutely unable to cope with the difficulties with which Germany was confronted. This created a profound prejudice, or confirmed a profound prejudice already in existence, against liberal democracy as such" (GN 359). Strauss does not see nihilism as arising simply from the weakness of the liberal democracy of the Weimar Republic; rather, it emerges from the reaction of the new generation of young Germans to the Marxist or socialist solution to this situation:

> The older ones in our midst still remember the time when certain people asserted that the conflicts inherent in the present situation would necessarily lead to a revolution, accompanying or following another World War – a rising of the proletariat and of the proletarianized strata of society which would usher in the withering away of the State, the classless society, the abolition of all exploitation and injustice, the era of final peace. It was this prospect at least as much as the desperate present, which led to nihilism. (GN 359–60)

Strauss describes a reaction in this younger generation in a way that is clearly inspired by Nietzsche's account of modern egalitarianism leading to the era of the "last man":

> The prospect of a pacified planet, without rulers and ruled, of a planetary society devoted to production and consumption only, to the production and consumption of spiritual as well as material merchandise, was positively horrifying to quite a few very intelligent and very decent, if very young, Germans. They did not object to that prospect because they were worrying about their own economic and social position; for certainly in that respect they had no longer anything to lose. Nor did they object to it for religious reasons; for, as one of their spokesmen (E. Jünger) said, they *knew* that they were the sons and grandsons and great-grandsons of godless men. What they hated, was the very prospect of a world in which everyone would be happy and satisfied, in which everyone would have his little pleasure by day and his little pleasure by night, a world in which no great

heart could beat and no great soul could breathe, a world without
real, unmetaphoric, sacrifice, i.e. a world without blood, sweat, and
tears. What to the communists appeared to be the fulfilment of *the*
dream of mankind, appeared to those young Germans as the greatest
debasement of humanity, as the coming of the end of humanity, as
the arrival of the latest man. (GN 360)

But, as Strauss brings out here, this negation of a secular, egalitarian, consumerist humanism was accompanied for these young
Germans by no alternative positive vision:

> They did not really know, and thus they were unable to express in
> a tolerably clear language, what they desired to put in the place of
> the present world and its allegedly necessary future or sequel: the
> only thing of which they were absolutely certain was that the present
> world and all the potentialities of the present world as such, must be
> destroyed in order to prevent the otherwise necessary coming of the
> communist final order: literally anything, the *nothing*, the chaos, the
> jungle, the Wild West, the Hobbian state of nature, seemed to them
> infinitely better than the communist-anarchist-pacifist future. Their
> Yes was inarticulate – they were unable to say more than: No! This
> No proved however sufficient as *the* preface to action, to the action
> of destruction. This is the phenomenon which occurs to me first
> whenever I hear the expression German nihilism. (GN 360)

A curious feature of this lecture, given in New York City in the
middle of the Second World War, is that Strauss shows sympathy
for the "very young Germans" who were drawn not into National
Socialism, but into this deeper, earlier form of German nihilism.
Though Strauss does not specifically say it, it is reasonable to
assume that he himself felt the attraction of this German nihilism.
This is evident particularly in his relation to the thought of Friedrich
Nietzsche, a relationship that has been the source of great scholarly
controversy.

In a letter written in June of 1935 to his friend Karl Löwith,
Strauss confessed: "I can only say that Nietzsche so dominated
and bewitched me between my 22nd and 30th years that I literally
believed everything that I understood of him" (LC 183). Nietzsche's
declarations that "God is dead" and that the West had entered an
age of nihilism were not widely taken up during his own lifetime
– but at the beginning of the twentieth century, and especially in
the wake of the First World War, Nietzsche's account appeared
inescapable, not only for the young Leo Strauss, but for his whole

generation. The sense that the West had entered into a "crisis," an "age of decline," "a loss of meaning," or "the devaluation of the highest values" was compelling (CT 41, GN 370, LI 132). For Strauss's generation, then, the task of thinking was how to understand this state of affairs, and how to escape or get beyond this moment of darkening. By the time of this letter, Strauss could say that he *had been* a "Nietzschean" (LC 182). One might take this to mean that Strauss had simply repudiated Nietzsche in favor of the ancients and the cause of traditional morality. But this would be to misunderstand Strauss's relation to Nietzsche, for it also had a positive aspect, as Strauss's letter to Löwith goes on to establish.

Strauss explains his complex relation to Nietzsche as he responds to Löwith's newly published book, *Nietzsche's Philosophy of the Eternal Recurrence of the Same*: "My doubt concerns a tendency of your critique, which, I believe, does not do justice to Nietzsche. I begin with your splendid formulation which touches the heart of the question and which for me is spoken straight from the soul: repeating antiquity at the peak of modernity" (LC 183). Strauss makes it clear here that he identifies himself with Nietzsche's project of "repeating antiquity at the peak of modernity." What he argues, however, is that Nietzsche fails to complete that project: "I believe that essential difficulties of Nietzsche's teaching are created by its polemical character, and immediately disappear when one distinguishes between polemical approach and the teaching itself" (LC 183). Such a criticism might appear to distinguish Strauss from Nietzsche in a merely external manner: Strauss is declaring himself a Nietzschean who simply uses a different, less polemical, mode of presentation. Indeed, a number of Strauss scholars have read him this way, and argue that Strauss is essentially a secret Nietzschean. But this is to misunderstand what Strauss means by "polemical": even in his first book, *Spinoza's Critique of Religion*, Strauss speaks of polemic as having a substantive effect on the content and approach of thought. Specifically, he sees that enlightened modernity – the stance of Spinoza and Hobbes – is crucially determined by a polemical relation to revealed religion, and above all to Christianity. When Strauss later argues for Machiavelli as the originator of modernity, he will continue to see a "polemical" stance – "anti-theological ire" (WIPP 44) – as crucially determining the shape of modernity. For Strauss, Nietzsche's "teaching" remains trapped in the modernity he intended to escape. Strauss writes to Löwith:

I think that you do not take seriously enough those intentions of Nietzsche which point beyond Nietzsche's teaching. You do not enter into these enough. For it is not sufficient simply to stop where Nietzsche is no longer right; rather one must ask whether or not Nietzsche himself became untrue to his intention to repeat antiquity, and did so as a result of his confinement within modern presuppositions or in polemic against these. (LC 184)

Strauss is arguing that his own position fulfills Nietzsche's intentions by fully achieving a repeating of "antiquity at the peak of modernity." In a paper delivered a few years earlier to a Zionist organization, "Religious Situation of the Present" (1930), Strauss makes the same basic point:

> The tradition has been shaken to its *roots* by Nietzsche. It has altogether forfeited its self-evidence. We stand in the world completely without authority, completely without orientation. Only now has the question [how should one live] regained its full sharpness. We *can* again pose it. We have the possibility of posing it in full seriousness ... We really must begin *entirely* from the beginning.
>
>   We *can* begin entirely from the beginning: we lack any polemical passions against the tradition (we have, after all, nothing from where we could be polemical); and at the same time, the tradition has become completely estranged from us, completely questionable. (RLS 234–5)

What Strauss is indicating here is that, in his insight into the nihilistic character of the contemporary age, Nietzsche had – at the very height of modernity – in fact opened the way for a return to the ancients. Where Nietzsche had failed to realize his intentions, Strauss would endeavor to succeed. In this sense, then, Strauss's call for a return to classical thought is not simply a reactionary move backward: it is also an *outcome* of modernity (SKC 48). In his letter to Löwith, Strauss makes a crucial distinction about what "repeating antiquity at the peak of modernity" means: "From this results first of all the following dualism: a) a modern *approach* to antiquity chiefly based on an immanent critique of modernity, b) the ancient teaching itself" (LC 183). It is important to understand this distinction if one is not only to get clear about what Strauss is saying to Löwith but at the same time to see what he is doing in establishing his own standpoint in the Weimar intellectual milieu. Strauss understands all of modern thought as being caught up in "immanent critique" or, as he puts it, in a "polemical approach." We will look at this dynamic in much greater detail in chapter 5, but Strauss's essential claim is that in a polemical critique the critic becomes "inscribed" in (is immanent to) the object of critique. Strauss sees modernity as caught up in just such a relationship to revelation generally (and medieval Christianity specifically), and he sees each stage, or what he will later call each "wave," of modernity caught up in a similar dynamic. In being so caught, far from escaping the object of its criticism, the critique (in this case Nietzsche's critique) in fact deepens and exacerbates it. For Strauss, the greatness of Nietzsche is that, in his insight into the nihilism of his age, he seeks to get beyond that nihilism by recovering (in Löwith's phrase) "antiquity at the peak of modernity." But, in Strauss's view, because Nietzsche remains polemically engaged with nihilism and its sources, he fails. In this sense, Strauss sees a kind of tragic shape to Nietzsche's intellectual project: precisely by trying to get free of nihilism, Nietzsche comes to exemplify it. In Strauss's view, Nietzsche can both show the way to escape modernity and at the same time be caught in it, and thus rightly be found "responsible for the emergence of German nihilism" (GN 372). Nietzsche's thought, then, functions both as a model for Strauss and as that standpoint of which he is most deeply critical. But on what basis should Strauss think that he can escape the fate of Nietzsche himself, who failed to escape from the grip of nihilism because of the polemical impulse to get beyond nihilism? In order to see the answer to this we need to say a little bit more about Nietzsche.

What underlies Nietzsche's analysis of nihilism is a sense that nihilism is not simply the character of a certain moment, the nineteenth- or twentieth-century experience of the "death of God." The death of God is not just a metaphor for the decline of religious belief and practice at a particular time. Nietzsche sees that the whole of the western tradition is implicated in it. All metaphysical claims, all sense of a truth beyond appearance, are at stake. So, for Nietzsche, the death of God is not simply the arrival of modern humanist secularity. In fact, Nietzsche sees that secularity is still entrapped in the ascetic ideal or metaphysical tradition it seeks to repudiate. For Nietzsche, modern Enlightenment principles of freedom, rationality, and human happiness implicitly depend upon the Christianity they came to oppose. The death of modern humanistic culture, modern secular morality, and modern scientific knowing are all unmoored from any ground through the death of God or the devaluation of the highest values. Hence the death of God is not the emergence of a secular humanity, but rather the awareness that this modern liberation and accomplishment are empty. Atheistic, or this-worldly, Enlightenment hope for a free, prosperous humanity liberated from otherworldly fear or aspiration, for Nietzsche, proves itself to be ungrounded, and in fact leads to nothing but nihilism itself.

Strauss himself made this point in a 1940 lecture:

> The new atheism is opposed not only to the belief in a personal God and to pantheism, but equally to the *morality* of the Bible, to the belief in progress, in human brotherhood and equality, in the dignity of man as man, in short to all moral standards which, as it believed, lose their meaning once they are separated from their religious basis. (LI 130)

Nihilism does not simply mean "the death of God"; nihilism is rooted in, and is the final manifestation of, all the life-denying, otherworldly constructions born, Nietzsche argues, of a *ressentiment* toward life. Thus any getting beyond nihilism involves also getting before, or prior to, the sources of nihilism – finding a reality, a life forgotten or turned away from, but that has been always present. Nietzsche calls this principle "the will to power" and "the eternal return of the same." For Nietzsche, nihilism is born of the twin *ressentiments* of (1) Socratic rationalism, which turns from the Dionysian world of tragedy or endless becoming, and (2) the Hebraic turn from nature and worldliness to the one God and his moral law. A similar account of contemporary nihilism as exposing a forgotten principle or way of life recurs in many thinkers, into our own time.[1] In Heidegger, for example, nihilism is seen as a "forgetting of Being," with a recovery occurring by a turn to the Pre-Socratic thinkers and poets of Being who can allow us to recover from this forgetting. So we can place Strauss's own position into the pattern indicated by Nietzsche, that getting beyond nihilism involves at the same time a return to antiquity in order to encounter a reality of which nihilism is the denial.

There is a further feature of this common pattern found in many accounts of nihilism: the critic of nihilism discovers in previous critics both a valuable and insightful critique of nihilism and its sources and, at the same time (because of a polemical opposition to nihilism), a failure to be liberated from the object of the critique.

---

[1] For a small sample: neo-Thomists (such as Jacques Maritain and Étienne Gilson), Karl Löwith, George Grant, John Milbank, Alasdair MacIntyre, and Eric Voegelin.

In Heidegger, Nietzsche will be found to be the last metaphysician – not in spite of, but because of, his critique of metaphysics. In this sense, the criticism Strauss makes to Löwith about Nietzsche's polemical stance preventing his recovery of antiquity (and so being free of nihilism) belongs to this pattern. But what Strauss is claiming for himself is that he has liberated himself from this cycle of seeking and yet failing to get beyond nihilism, because he sees his own response as free of polemic.

Strauss's Relation to Heidegger

To better assess Strauss's claim that he is able to realize a non-polemical recovery of ancient thought and thus get beyond nihilism, we need to develop more fully our discussion of his relationship to his intellectual context. Specifically, we need to consider Strauss's relation to Martin Heidegger, whom Strauss first encountered in 1922 when Heidegger was "one of the unknown young men in Husserl's entourage" (JPCM 461). Strauss later said of Heidegger that he "surpasses in speculative intelligence all his contemporaries and is at the same time intellectually the counterpart to what Hitler was politically" (JPCM 450). Strauss had begun his own university studies at the University of Marburg, close to Kirchhain, the town in which he had grown up. At that time the "Marburg School" of philosophy had been under the influence of Hermann Cohen, the great Jewish neo-Kantian. When Strauss arrived in Marburg, Cohen had recently died, but his brand of neo-Kantianism was still dominant. Neo-Kantianism was, as the name suggests, a standpoint that sought to revive the idealism of Immanuel Kant in order to ground and give rational justification for scientific and moral thought, in opposition to the materialism and naturalism of much of mid-nineteenth-century philosophy. As such, it was part of the wider revival of neo-idealism that dominated European universities at the end of the nineteenth and beginning of the twentieth centuries. Strauss spoke of himself at this time as "a doubting and dubious adherent of the Marburg school of neo-Kantianism" (SPPP 31). Important to the young Strauss was Max Weber, the most impressive contemporary product of German neo-Kantianism, both a founder of sociology and a father of the Weimar Republic. Strauss would write his doctoral dissertation on Friedrich Heinrich Jacobi under the supervision of Ernst Cassirer, Cohen's most important student.

But by the time he encountered Heidegger, Strauss had already moved away from his attachment to neo-Kantianism through a developing interest in phenomenology, the philosophical approach established by Edmund Husserl. Strauss became Husserl's assistant for a year, and this is when he became deeply impressed by Heidegger, who, according to Strauss, "radicalized Husserl's critique of the school of Marburg and turned it against Husserl" (JPCM 461). The essence of Husserl's critique was recalled by Strauss in this way:

> Husserl explained to me ... the characteristic of his own work in about these terms: "the Marburg school begins with the roof, while I begin with the foundation." This meant that for the school of Marburg the sole task of the fundamental part of philosophy was the theory of scientific experience, the analysis of scientific thought. Husserl however had realized more profoundly than anybody else that the scientific understanding of the world, far from being the perfection of our natural understanding, is derivative from the latter in such a way as to make us oblivious of the very foundations of the scientific understanding: all philosophic understanding must start from our common understanding of the world, from our understanding of the world as sensibly perceived prior to all theorizing. (SPPP 31)

But, Strauss goes on to argue, Heidegger crucially modified Husserl's beginning point in the natural understanding: "Heidegger went much further than Husserl in the same direction: the primary theme is not the object of perception but the full thing as experienced as part of the individual human context, the individual world to which it belongs." For Heidegger this human context is necessarily historical, so, as Strauss notes, "This implies that one can no longer speak of our 'natural' understanding of the world; every understanding of the world is 'historical'" (SPPP 31).

What Husserl gave to Heidegger and Strauss was a more fundamental or natural starting point in phenomenology. Strauss, like Heidegger, saw in Husserl's reformulation of philosophy from out of a "natural understanding" a way to begin philosophy that could escape the sources of nihilism identified by Nietzsche and others.[2]

---

[2] See Strauss's comments in "The Living Issues of German Postwar Philosophy," where he speaks of a deeper movement of "thinkers who in relative secrecy discovered, or rediscovered, a basis more in accordance with the nature of things than that underlying the preceding period had been." He speaks of "that deeper movement being practically identical with the development of phenomenology." (LI 117)

But before we consider how Strauss builds on Husserl, let us first follow Heidegger's own radicalization of Husserl. As a point of contrast, it will help us better to understand Strauss's position.

As Strauss recalled, Heidegger's radicalization had to do with bringing out the essentially historical or temporal character of Husserl's natural consciousness. Over the course of the mid-1920s, Heidegger developed his radical, historicist phenomenology that found its significant formulation in *Being and Time* (1927). A number of commentators on Strauss have pointed to deep and important connections between the thought of Strauss and that of Heidegger. As was the case with his relation to Nietzsche, Strauss has both a positive and negative connection to Heidegger. On one side, Heidegger will function as a foil for Strauss: Heidegger is the greatest proponent of "radical historicism," the standpoint Strauss identifies in *Natural Right and History* as that which most deeply obscures the recognition of classical natural right that he seeks to recover. In this way, for Strauss, Heidegger's thought can be identified with the most radical articulation of nihilism that is "the crisis of our time" (CT 41). Strauss is also critical of Heidegger in other ways, perhaps most obviously in the way he links Heidegger's thought to his decision to join the Nazi Party in 1933.

So far, this seems to present Heidegger as Strauss's most powerful opponent. But Strauss also writes of "the possibility which Heidegger had opened without intending it: the possibility of a genuine return to classical philosophy, to the philosophy of Aristotle and of Plato, a return with open eyes and in full clarity about the infinite difficulties which it entails" (JPCM 450). Strauss's colleague and lifelong friend, Jacob Klein, pointed out that "by uprooting and not simply rejecting the tradition of philosophy" Heidegger "made it possible for the first time after many centuries – one hesitates to say how many – to see the roots of the tradition as they are and thus perhaps to know, what so many merely believe, that those roots are the only natural and healthy roots" (JPCM 450).

So, as he did in his account of Nietzsche, Strauss sees in Heidegger a figure who points beyond his own teaching to a recovery of ancient thought. Strauss, who attended some of Heidegger's lectures on Aristotle's *Metaphysics* in the early 1920s, developed this point in 1940: "And this was perhaps the most profound impression which the younger generation experienced in Germany during the period in question: under the guidance of Heidegger, people came to see that Aristotle and Plato had *not* been understood" (LI 134). The parallel between Strauss's thought and Heidegger's, based on their common beginning from Husserl, must be seen as more than simply a turn to the ancients. Strauss will build into that return aspects of Heidegger's critique of nihilism, above all the effort to establish a form of philosophical thinking free of traditional metaphysics. The inspiration of Husserl's return to "natural understanding" that Strauss shares with Heidegger will be crucial in this endeavor. But first, in order better to understand what is distinctive in Strauss's approach, it is important to see exactly what characterizes Strauss's own analysis of nihilism and the standpoint that is free of it.

Strauss's Account of Nihilism

The most obvious point of distinction between Strauss and both Nietzsche and Heidegger is that Strauss sees nihilism as primarily moral nihilism, concerned with the question "how do I live?" or "what is the right or best life?" For Nietzsche and Heidegger, on the other hand, moral nihilism is only an aspect of a more fundamental metaphysical or ontological nihilism. This is perhaps clearer in Heidegger – but even for Nietzsche, the devaluation of the highest values is a loss not simply of moral meaning, but of all meaning. It is a crisis of the will as the source of all meaning. For Nietzsche and for Heidegger, nihilism or the death of God is most fundamentally a metaphysical or ontological event. It involves the loss of meaning through the collapse of the metaphysical or ontological structures, including religious forms, that came to be in the West. Heidegger and Nietzsche agree that the basic source of those metaphysical structures lay in the founding figures of western metaphysics: Socrates and Plato. As Nietzsche famously describes it in *The Gay Science*, the experience of nihilism in the nineteenth century – the death of God – involves the wiping away of the horizon created by those metaphysical structures. Nihilism arises as the result of the modern outcome of those traditional structures: modern rationalism, moralism, and science. For Heidegger, this is captured by the term "technology."

In seeing nihilism as primarily moral, Strauss provides a distinctive analysis. The crisis of the West is a moral and political one, more fundamentally than it is an ontological or metaphysical one. In other words, the crisis is not primarily a crisis of the meaning of life; it is a crisis, rather, about what is the best life to live. It is very important to see that what Strauss is not concerned with is moral decay or the decline of conventional morality; rather, Strauss understands moral nihilism as the loss of moral orientation per se. Under the conditions of modern nihilism, there is an incapacity to raise the question of the Good or the right way of life at all. Strauss recognizes the role "technology" has played in this moral crisis but, unlike Heidegger, Strauss sees technology as a subordinate and contributing factor. The fundamental loss at work in nihilism is not the forgetfulness of Being, as Heidegger somewhat mysteriously puts it, but the "oblivion of eternity," as Strauss (perhaps equally mysteriously) describes the crisis of our time (WIPP 55). What is lost sight of for Strauss is "nature," and more specifically "natural right." We will consider what natural right means for Strauss in greater detail in chapter 4, but as a beginning it is enough to understand that natural right signifies standards of human living established in or by nature, and so beyond the changes effected by history. "Natural right" is Strauss's translation of the ancient Greek phrase *physei dikaion* or "what is by nature right or just" (SPPP 138). According to Strauss, what produces the oblivion of natural right is the modern project, which takes historicism as its most developed form. In this way, we can see that the place occupied by technology in Heidegger is occupied in Strauss by historicism.

Positivism and Historicism

In many of his mature American writings, Strauss begins with a discussion of positivism and historicism, to help his reader recognize and understand the crisis of the West as a crisis in moral and political understanding. Such a discussion provides something of a reiteration of Strauss's own intellectual formation, moving from the neo-Kantianism that informed Max Weber's positivism through the historicism Strauss discovered in Nietzsche and above all in Heidegger. To better grasp that movement in Strauss, it will be helpful to outline briefly his account of the standpoints of positivism and historicism. Together they constitute "relativism," which is Strauss's formulation for the larger cultural phenomenon of the loss of any sense of grounding or standards for moral determinations. Moral "relativism" is another way to speak of moral nihilism for Strauss. According to him, the fundamental character of the contemporary that makes it nihilistic is the pervasiveness of positivism and historicism, which together occlude the possibility of morality and of the right way of life.

Positivism is a nineteenth- and twentieth-century movement

that seeks to release humanity from the chains of religion and metaphysics by claiming that science is the sole source of truth. For Strauss, the term is especially connected to the effort to create objective or value-free social sciences. In Strauss's world, this is most fully realized in the thought of Max Weber (1864–1920), the greatest social scientist in Germany at the beginning of the twentieth century, a figure who impressed Strauss in his first years at university. Weber claimed that, in order to be a science, a social science needed to be "value free." Weber's understanding of sociology, including its claims to be a value-free science, was crucially indebted to neo-Kantianism, the dominant philosophy in the German universities at the time. Positivism claimed that truth, the realm of facts, was the domain of the sciences. Other human standpoints might well claim truths – moral truths, religious truths, aesthetic truths – but these could not be recognized as "objective" or factual claims, because they were determined by values that were primarily subjective and therefore without a factual or objective basis. While social sciences are characterized by their study of such values, they seek to conduct their study or science in a value-free way. The only basis of "values" lay in human choice or decision. An individual may hold a certain set of values to be true; what the social scientist investigated, however, was not the validity of the value claim itself but rather how the value in question functioned in the causality of social life and social forms. In other words, a social science considers values relative to the causes because of which those values are chosen. Positivism presupposed and taught relativism. What Strauss admired in Weber was the intellectual honesty with which Weber faced the fact/value distinction, the distinction by which values were found to be without truth. For Weber, that means that, no matter how personally significant or "ultimate" it might be to an individual or a society, a "value" has no cognitive validity. Strauss argued that there was clearly a certain kind of nihilism at work in this reduction of moral claims to mere "values," but, for Weber, one could still find a "vocation" in upholding the standpoint of science itself.

Strauss was particularly interested in the political implications of positivism. Value relativism appears to be supportive of a liberalism of tolerance since no value system could claim a special status over any other. A liberal regime such as the Weimar Republic would be the regime that could mediate disputes among "equal" value systems, allowing their co-existence in a liberal society. Both value-free social science and liberalism seem to occupy a value-free standpoint. But, according to Strauss, an apparent compatibility between value-free social science and liberal tolerance is just that, merely apparent. As Strauss brings out in a number of writings, Weber recognized that our most fundamental values – including liberal values – have no basis beyond a pure willing of them. In Weber's positivist universe, as Strauss enjoyed pointing out, there is no reason to prefer civilization to cannibalism (NRH 3).

For Strauss, positivism was in the end only a kind of shallow nihilism. More profound, and seemingly destructive of all claims to moral standards or principles, was historicism, above all the radical historicism of Nietzsche and Heidegger. Strauss saw that in historicism, the apparent capacity to distinguish scientific facts from subjective values is altogether undermined. For him, historicism reveals science not to be "objective" as it claimed to be, independent of subjective human purposes. Nietzsche sees science, rather, as merely one among many perspectives that have arisen in history and will be dissolved back into history. He makes a critique of science as but another form of the will to truth, begun by Socrates and Plato. So, science belongs to the history of metaphysics. Nietzsche argues that not simply Christianity or religion or secularized moral values are being devalued by the death of God, but so also is science and its claims to a status independent of valuing or willing. As Strauss put it, "Positivism necessarily transforms itself into historicism" (WIPP 25). Historicism is the claim that all knowledge and all human belief is historically relative. It is the most complete and consistent form of relativism.

In *Natural Right and History*, Strauss says that for historicists "all human thought is historical and hence unable ever to grasp anything eternal" (NRH 12). It is important to understand that here Strauss is using the term "eternal" not in a specifically theological sense, but in a contrastive sense, to refer to that which is beyond or not subject to history. Both nature and God are in this sense "eternal." Strauss puts it this way:

> The view that truth is eternal and that there are eternal standards, was contradicted by historical consciousness, i.e. by the opinion that all "truths" and standards are necessarily relative to a given historical situation, and that, consequently, a mature philosophy can raise no higher claim than that to express the spirit of the period to which it belongs. (LI 132)

Strauss uses Plato's image of the cave from the *Republic* to capture his point: every society, every city, is a cave with its own "values," or ways, or opinions for determining what is right; but Plato argues that philosophy can allow an ascent from this cave to a realm of "nature" by which knowledge of what is right by nature can be discovered. According to Strauss, historical consciousness or historicism precludes any such possibility.

Strauss will also distinguish the historicism that arises in the nineteenth century in Hegel or "the historical school" from the later development he calls "radical historicism." What distinguishes this radical historicism, for Strauss, is that it historicizes not simply the content of human thinking or human culture, but the very being of the human. He sees that this more radical historicism begins with Nietzsche's insight into the significance of the death of God, and is completed by Heidegger's account of human being as inherently temporal. The term Heidegger uses to capture this more radical form of historicism is "historicity," spoken of as a dimension of human existence. Strauss will also speak more generally of the rise of "historical consciousness" as an aspect of human being that Nietzsche and other historicists see to be a new and privileged form of awareness.

So, for Strauss, the most radical and comprehensive form of nihilism is historicism, and above all that form of historicism being thought in the philosophies of Nietzsche and Heidegger. For Strauss, this means that Nietzsche and Heidegger have failed to grasp properly the nihilism of their era or its roots. It also means that, far from escaping the power of nihilism, Nietzsche and Heidegger have only exacerbated it. A number of scholars of Strauss's work see his position as essentially identical to that of Nietzsche or Heidegger, or both. Certainly it is true that, in a general way, Strauss agrees with Nietzsche and Heidegger about the nihilistic crisis of the contemporary, and with their recognition of the need to recover a principle that always has been, but has been forgotten or turned away from, whose recovery allows us to get free of nihilism. Strauss was clearly deeply influenced and inspired by both Nietzsche and Heidegger and can be seen as taking up many elements of their thought. But – and this is an absolutely central point – Strauss significantly disagrees with the diagnoses offered by Nietzsche and Heidegger and, more fundamentally, seeks a different account of the recovered principle or reality. For Strauss, the recovered reality is not will to power (Nietzsche), or Being (Heidegger): it is nature or "natural right." Natural right is primarily, or at least in the first instance, a moral principle, a principle that speaks to the question: how is one to live?

One further point of contrast arises in Strauss, relative to Nietzsche's and Heidegger's accounts of nihilism. For Nietzsche and Heidegger there is a return to a forgotten principle and also, in the contemporary moment of recovery, a transformation of it, effected by the long history of nihilism. So, what for Nietzsche comes after the death of God, or for Heidegger after the end of metaphysics, is that what is recovered is necessarily also new or different. Such a transformed recovery is a necessary implication of the historicism of both these positions. For this very reason, the standpoint that Strauss attains in his recovery of "nature," in his recovery of ancient thought, cannot be new; it is a return to the eternal, to what is precisely beyond historical change.

For Strauss, then, what is beyond nihilism is a discovery and not a new project, or will, or destiny. There are a number of important implications that belong to this thought. One of those implications underlines and gives new meaning to Strauss's comments to Löwith in 1935 that Nietzsche's failure to return to the ancients arose from his polemics; that is, the polemical stance of Nietzsche is implicated in an entrapment of thought by history. For Strauss, the polemical relationship to nihilism and its sources, such as he attributes to Nietzsche, is a willful relationship that seeks to effect a change in history, to negate or overcome nihilism. As will become clearer shortly, Strauss sees this polemical stance at work not only in Nietzsche, but in the modern project as a whole. In Strauss's connection between polemicism and historical change, historicism is shown to be not just the final phase of the modern project, but its underlying truth. However, before we can understand this better, we need to see more clearly what Strauss thinks modernity is establishing itself against. We need to understand what Strauss discovered in the thought of Socrates and Plato that for him provided a remedy for modern nihilism.

The Recovery of Natural Right

As we have seen, Strauss traces the origins of the moral-political project that was undergoing nihilistic crisis in the nineteenth and twentieth centuries not to ancient Greece, but to early modern Europe, and to the thought of Hobbes and (as Strauss later came to judge) Machiavelli. Thus, for Strauss, it is not the whole western tradition that is in nihilistic crisis; what is in crisis is what Strauss calls the "modern project." He argues that the remedy for this crisis is to be found in the thought of Socrates and Plato, who for Nietzsche and Heidegger were the very source of nihilism, not its overcoming. As we have already seen, Strauss described himself as being a "Nietzschean" (and therefore a historicist) between the ages of twenty-two and thirty. In the preface he wrote for the 1965 English translation of his first book, *Spinoza's Critique of Religion* (1930), Strauss says that, in its time, the book was "based on the premise, sanctioned by powerful prejudice, that a return to pre-modern philosophy is impossible" (SCR 31). In the period following that book's publication, however, Strauss's thought underwent a "change of orientation" that suggested to him that "it would be unwise to say farewell to reason" (SCR 31). Strauss "began therefore to wonder whether the self-destruction of reason was not the inevitable outcome of modern rationalism as distinguished from pre-modern rationalism, especially Jewish-medieval rationalism and its classical (Aristotelian and Platonic) foundation" (SCR 31). Strauss's "change of orientation" is about his coming to see a position that allows for the recovery of the pre-modern. Ultimately, for Strauss, this is the possibility of a return to ancient, and most decisively Platonic, political philosophy. The details of this "reorientation," as it has come to be called in Strauss scholarship, are a complex matter. However, it is important to see that Strauss's reorientation is not simply a flight from, or break from, Nietzsche; instead, as his letter to Löwith indicates, it is rather about discerning in Nietzsche and modern thought more generally an abiding (if forgotten) relation to a nature that Strauss thought was only recoverable in and through classical rationality.

Strauss tells us in his own account of his development that his "change of orientation ... found its first expression, not entirely by accident" in his critique of Carl Schmitt's 1932 book, *The Concept of the Political* (SCR 31). Schmitt was a brilliant legal scholar who reflected on the legal, constitutional, and conceptual weaknesses of the Weimar Republic and liberalism as these were experienced by the young Germans Strauss wrote about in his "German Nihilism" lecture. Schmitt was impressed by Strauss's review, but shortly after supporting Strauss's scholarly career, Schmitt joined the Nazi Party. It is not possible to go into the details of this intellectual relationship here, but it is notable that it is in his review of Schmitt's book that Strauss announces his "change of orientation." Strauss is sympathetic to much of what is at work in Schmitt's critique of liberalism and its moral and political vacuity. Against the desire of liberalism for consensus and humanistic culture, Schmitt contrasts the inescapable requirement of what he calls "the concept of the political" and the need of "the political" (the state) for "decision," above all between friend and enemy. Schmitt turned to Hobbes's state of nature as a way to clarify and bring to light the inherently finite, conflicted, and irreducibly political character of human interaction. But Strauss argues that Schmitt's use of Hobbes's account of the state of nature to recover the political in fact fails to escape from the liberal "horizon" Schmitt is criticizing. Strauss ends by arguing that "the critique introduced by Schmitt against liberalism can therefore be completed only if one succeeds in gaining a horizon beyond liberalism" (CP 107). That is, right within this review, Strauss indicates how one might get beyond the horizon of liberalism by recovering a different account of nature than is found in Hobbes and continued in Schmitt's critique of liberalism and the liberal account of culture. This different account of nature is the pre-modern or classical account that Strauss comes to in his "change of orientation."

In his review of Schmitt, Strauss points out two characterizations of nature, one ancient, the other modern. In the ancient account, nature is conceived as an "exemplary order" (what Strauss later calls "natural right"); in the modern, nature is "a disorder to be eliminated" (CP 88–9). Relative to these two accounts of nature are contrasting stances: "cultivating nature" (the ancient stance) or "conquering nature" (the modern stance). Strauss's change of orientation arose from his realization that nature as "exemplary order" could be recovered even at the height of modernity. The possibility of such a recovery depended upon recovering a pre-modern rationalism not subject to the self-destruction that Strauss agreed with Nietzsche and Heidegger was the fate of modern reason experienced in nihilism. Trying to understand Strauss's account of this recovery will be the work of chapter 4, but first, to help us understand how Strauss might conceive this turn to an ancient account of nature as a response to German nihilism, we need to see a little of what he is discerning here.

For Strauss, the "nature" that is the object of Socratic or Platonic philosophy is not specifically external nature conceived as a non-human external reality that is the subject matter of our natural sciences. For Strauss, such an account of nature places a modern limitation upon nature: nature (*physis* for the ancient Greeks) is, rather, all beings – but perhaps especially, or most centrally, human being. Strauss argues that, until philosophy arose, humans were unaware of nature per se or did not think about nature, at least not in a developed way. For Strauss, philosophy is the awareness of nature, above all in contrast to convention or art (what humans make). According to Strauss, prior to the discovery of nature, there were various "ways," or forms of life, or cultures as we might now say. The humans who lived according to these ways did not fundamentally question them. In *Natural Right and History*, Strauss provides an account of the emergence of philosophy as the questioning that arises when the plurality of ways raises the concern of what way is best or right by nature. Nature thus emerges as a reality for philosophy and as its proper object, according to Strauss. We will explore this account of philosophy in some detail in chapter 4. But for our purposes at this point, we can note that what "nature," or natural right, means more specifically for Strauss in the 1930s is that there is a right or justice that serves as a standard beyond both convention and history. That there is such a thing as "natural right" is a possibility rendered almost unthinkable by historicism and the assumptions underlying modernity.

On the face of it, it would seem to be a requirement of nature, understood as abiding beyond all convention and history, that it be necessarily accessible, at least in principle, to humans everywhere and always, and so to us today. The laws of nature that modern science investigates appear to have exactly this character; so why not natural right? If there is a right or justice that is by nature and not convention or an outcome of history, it should be always present for us. But Strauss argues that, according to Plato and ancient philosophy generally, precisely because it is investigated by and through human things, the study of natural right is not directly available to all humans in their immediate self-understanding. Strauss invokes Plato's image of the cave to capture our entrapment in *doxa*, in opinion, which functions as images on the wall of our cave, our city that operates within its ways or conventions. As Strauss puts it: "The natural difficulties of philosophizing have their classical depiction in Plato's allegory of the cave" (RLS 248). Plato points to philosophy as the means by which those able to can ascend from this cave into the light, into truth or wisdom. This ascent is made through the speeches, the *logoi*, of Greek citizens. These pre-philosophic speeches are double-sided or ambiguous: on the one side, they are in part merely conventional, representing the "way" of this people; on the other side, they reflect or point to the philosophic, to nature and natural right. Later, in "What Is Political

Philosophy?" – an essay published in 1957 that summarizes much of his position – Strauss articulates clearly what is specifically valuable about the approach undertaken by classical political philosophy:

> Classical political philosophy is non-traditional, because it belongs to the fertile moment when all political traditions were shaken, and there was not yet in existence a tradition of political philosophy. In all later epochs, the philosophers' study of political things was mediated by a tradition of political philosophy which acted like a screen between the philosopher and political things, regardless of whether the individual philosopher cherished or rejected that tradition. From this it follows that the classical philosophers see the political things with a freshness and directness which have never been equalled. They look at political things in the perspective of the enlightened citizen or statesman. (WIPP 27)

In his third book, *The Political Philosophy of Hobbes* (1936), Strauss develops this natural or Platonic approach to philosophy in some detail, in contrast to Hobbes's modern approach. He notes that what Plato establishes is an approach that begins from the "speeches" of ordinary citizens and then engages in a dialectic, a questioning of those speeches, in order to bring to light the essences implicit in them. Strauss sees that in this way the Platonic approach establishes "standards," a term he uses frequently in the 1930s:

> Speech alone, and not the always equivocal deeds, originally reveals to man the standard by which he can order his actions and test himself, take his bearings in life and nature, in a way completely undistorted and, in principle, independent of the possibility of reali-zation. This is the reason for Plato's "escape" into speech, and for the theory thereby given of the transcendence of ideas; only by means of speech does man know of the transcendence of virtue. (PPH 144–5)

Strauss sees that these "ideas" found in the speeches of citizens indicate the natural standards that give content and determination to human life. But he is equally clear that these standards are not metaphysical or cosmological. Plato "turns away from things, not to speech in itself, but to speech in its contradictoriness, as he opposes to 'physiology' not an 'ontology' but dialectic" (PPH 145). Or, as Strauss explains, "Plato does not without further ado oppose to materialist-mechanistic physics a spiritualist-teleological physics, but keeps to what can be understood without any far-fetched 'tragic' apparatus, to what the 'Athenians' *say*" (PPH 143).

What this means is that the nature or standards that Plato discerns are not metaphysical entities, but ideas that arise in and for philosophical dialectic. This is the crucial role of "reason" in Strauss's recovery of the ancients. It is reason alone that can discern these ideas, not a self-sufficient or merely metaphysical or speculative reason, but a reason or reasoning that begins with, and remains in contact with, the "speeches," the opinions, of ordinary citizens. This is the way that nature, as Strauss conceives it, is brought to light. So, for Strauss, nature is functioning in two connected but distinguishable ways: (1) as the standards that can be known by philosophical reflection, by dialectic, as arising from what a thing is, its essence, and so are binding upon it; and (2) as the opinions of ordinary citizens who have a "natural understanding" that is both open, and yet inadequate, to these "ideas" or essences.

Relative to this last point – the beginning of dialectic in the natural understanding – Strauss is certainly indebted to Husserl. Strauss spoke clearly of this debt in a 1943 letter to Eric Voegelin: "Husserl has seen with incomparable clarity that the restoration of philosophy or science – because he denies that that which today passes as science is genuine science – presupposes the restoration of the Platonic-Aristotelian level of questioning" (FPP 17). Strauss accepts Heidegger's critique of Husserl to the extent that Strauss too abandons what he terms Husserl's "egology," or transcendental consciousness, in the name of a turn to life. But crucially for Strauss, this turn is not, as it is for Heidegger, to *pragmata* (things done) and to time as the horizon of Being. Rather, for Strauss the turn is to speeches (*logoi*) and moral and political life as the specifically natural human form of awareness and openness. Strauss describes Plato's (and Socrates') turn to human things and human speeches in a 1946 letter: "Plato 'flees,' as is well known, from these 'things' (*pragamata*) into the *logoi*, because the *pragmata* give no answer *directly*, but are mute riddles" (LCM 112). For Strauss, the properly human form of openness to what is, to the "whole," is in speeches and not in practical making, as it is for Heidegger. Crucial for Strauss is that Plato thereby places rationality as the core human capacity for such openness. We will look at this in more detail in chapter 4.

As we have seen, Strauss argues that, by staying within the hold of historicism and historicity, Heidegger fails to liberate himself from modernity. Strauss finds in Plato the way to return to a properly natural standpoint that fulfills Husserl's intentions. He makes this point in a letter from 1932 that is a part of his wonderfully interesting correspondence with Gerhard Krüger, a contemporary and student of Heidegger who shared a number of intellectual interests with Strauss:

> You see a contradiction in the fact that I believe in a *"natural"* basis *and* view antiquity to be the standard. I am inclined to assume – until there is evidence to the contrary – that antiquity (more precisely: Socrates-Plato) is the standard *precisely because* it philosophized *naturally* i.e. originally inquired into the order that is *natural* for human beings. The fact that this possibility was opened up in Greece and only there – that is a matter of indifference as long as it remains the case that Socrates-Plato's question and answer are the natural question and the natural answer: *in* philosophizing, Socrates is *already* no longer Greek, but instead a human being ... In this sense, philosophy has *always* been and has remained unhistorical. That we *today* cannot get by without history is a fact external to philosophy. (SKC 39)

This quotation helps us see why for Strauss, Socrates and his appearances in Plato, and to a lesser extent in Xenophon, hold such a special place. In his turning to human things, to the opinions of the city (the cave), Socrates is the founder of "political philosophy" and so brings to light the classical conception of natural right. Recovering the natural questioning of Socrates is the means by which we can recover access to the natural basis for addressing the most fundamental question: how one ought to live.

Whether it is accurate to call Strauss's approach to Plato and to classical philosophy in general "phenomenological" is a tricky matter. It is potentially confusing because of the ways Strauss departs from both Husserl and Heidegger, and more broadly from existentialism (FPP 63). However, it is clear that Strauss identifies Socrates' and Plato's approach to philosophy with what can be broadly spoken of as a Husserlian or phenomenological approach that seeks to avoid a metaphysical or cosmological stand-point and so conforms to Nietzsche's and Heidegger's critiques of metaphysics. Strauss made this point in 1940:

> It had been an implication of phenomenology to distinguish between the *scientific* view of [the] world (the view, elaborated by *modern* science) and the *natural* view of the world, the idea being that that natural view is prior to, and the basis of, the scientific view: the scientific view of the world emerges out of the natural view by virtue of a specific modification of approach. Now it became clear that that basic

view, the starting point of the view elaborated by modern science, more precisely: that the world as it is present for, and experienced by, that natural view, had been the subject of Plato's and Aristotle's analyses. Plato and Aristotle appeared to have discussed adequately what had *not* been discussed by the founders of modern philosophy, nor by their successors. (LI 136)

For Strauss, this bringing together of a (broadly speaking) phenomenological approach with Platonic philosophy is precisely what Nietzsche, Husserl and Heidegger's *Destruktion* or de-sedimentation of the tradition accomplishes. It reveals the "healthy roots" of that tradition. Nihilism brings to light this non-metaphysical approach. But it can equally be said that what Husserl calls for, what each of these figures calls for, is still informed by the contemporary – and so the approach crucially predetermines the Socrates or Plato or Aristotle that such an approach can bring to light. Later, in what one of Strauss's students called his "golden sentence" (Benardete, "Leo Strauss' *The City and Man*," 1), Strauss captured his phenomenological approach: "The problem inherent in the surface of things, and only in the surface of things, is the heart of things" (TM 13). In Strauss's view, this is the character of ancient, and above all Socratic-Platonic, philosophizing. It is the standpoint that allows a non-metaphysical nature and natural right to emerge through the dialectical questioning of, and through the "surface" displayed in, speeches. For Strauss, the recovery of this standpoint is the only true escape from nihilism or historicism: it allows the eternal, a nature beyond all historical happening, to appear. It is our release from historical consciousness. It is the standpoint directed by our most natural question: how one ought to live.

It is precisely our incapacity to answer this question that for Strauss is the mark of modern nihilism. In a 1932 lecture, Strauss explained:

> We, too, are still natural beings. That we are still natural shows itself in the fact that we, confronted with the ignorance of what is right, escape into the *question* concerning what is right – escape from the unnaturalness of our situation. The *need* to know, and therefore the questioning, is the best guarantee that we are still natural beings, humans – but that we *are not capable of* questioning is the clear symptom of our being threatened in our humanity in a way that humans have never been threatened. (RLS 245)

While we are still natural beings we dwell in an unnatural situation;

Strauss's striking image for this in the 1930s was that we live no longer in Plato's cave, but in a cave beneath that cave: "The natural difficulties of philosophizing have their classical depiction in Plato's allegory of the cave. The historical difficulty may be illustrated by saying: there *now* exists another cave *beneath* the Platonic cave" (RLS 248). The simplest way to describe this deeper cave is "historicism" (SKC 48). Strauss will speak of this cave as our "historical consciousness" that prevents our discerning, or even beginning to discern, nature and the standards present in nature: natural right.

The Second Cave

In the early 1930s, Strauss frequently used the image of a second cave, a cave below the cave that Plato describes, to capture the situation of modern humanity. As we have seen, he identified this second cave with historical consciousness, the belief that human beings are inherently historical. For Strauss, the terrible irony here is that this new consciousness is not a gain, but a *loss* of awareness. For him, the "modern project" is inherently oriented to historical change, to a negating of the pre-modern world and its account of nature. As such, modernity can never be overcome through historicism. He sees modernity and historicism not (though they often present themselves this way) as liberations from tradition, but, because of the negative or polemical connection to tradition, as an ever-deeper enmeshing in tradition:

> But we cannot answer immediately as we are; for we know that we are deeply entangled in a tradition; we are yet much further down than Plato's cave dwellers. We must raise ourselves to the origin of the tradition, to the level of *natural ignorance*. If we wanted to concern ourselves with the present situation, we would be doing nothing other than the cave dwellers who describe the interior of their cave. (RLS 235)

Strauss is aware that all our tendencies are to try to get beyond the past into some new liberating moment, but for him such moments of "progress," of release and escape, even in the hands of Nietzsche or Heidegger, in fact further and deepen the hold of history and historical consciousness upon us. It is vital to see the logic at work here. Strauss sees that the basis of modernity is precisely the moment of negation, the moment of saying "No" to what is – and that is, above all, nature. We will explore this further in chapter 5, but it is vital to see here that even an act of "negating" the second cave would only deepen its hold, because such negation, engaging in such a "polemical approach," is the very being of this cave (PL 135–6). In the 1930s Strauss's whole work in uncovering the nature of modernity is to bring to light its negative character.

One way in which Strauss captures the dilemma or paradox of historical consciousness – that it is both a seemingly new consciousness and at the same time a loss of awareness – is to focus on "depth" or "inwardness." This recognition of "depth" is there in his image of the second, *deeper* cave (SKC 52–4). Historical consciousness appears to bring to light a new dimension of human existence. But for Strauss the "depth" of modernity is illusory: it is a purely human and unnatural construct. He grants a greater "depth" to all modern thinkers, but in so doing argues that this depth is paid for by a loss of radicality or originality: modern thinkers have lost access to their roots, to the origin.

Strauss's claim is that the source of the modern "depth" lies in the negative beginning of the modern project in its relation to ancient accounts of nature, and even more in its relation to revelation. Even before his "change of orientation," Strauss had already argued in *Spinoza's Critique of Religion* that modern thought was tied to revelation by its very opposition to it. Depth, inwardness, and (more broadly) modern self-consciousness arise in and from this negative stance. This claim has clear parallels with Nietzsche's account of the origins of nihilism. Even more interesting is that, in a series of letters to Gerhard Krüger, Strauss establishes the source of this "depth" in Christianity: "The problem of the 'second cave' is the problem of historicism. The 'substantive and historical core' of historicism is, *as you correctly state*, 'Christ's factual domination/ dominion over post-classical humanity.' What follows for the one who does *not* believe, who thus denies the right, i.e. the divine right, of this domination?" (SKC 52). Strauss traces the human negation that constitutes history to the theological negation or domination inherent in the Christian claim to transformational revelation. For Strauss, then, the second cave is essentially constituted in and by Christian revelation.

This leads to the very difficult question about the extent to which Strauss understands modernity as a form of secularized Christianity: we will see in chapter 5 that this is a complicated matter. For the time being, what needs to be seen is that Strauss understands modernity to be entangled in revelation, above all the

Christian revelation, precisely in and by its effort to *historically* – that is, actively and effectively – displace that very religion. Modern depth, inwardness, and self-consciousness arise from this negating modern project. From this point of view, "historical consciousness" is not just a certain development in modernity, it is the inner claim and form of modernity itself (PPH 57–8, 105–6). So Strauss fully acknowledges Heidegger's "depth," but he sees it premised on an unnatural and unradical delusion (SKC 48).

The way out of nihilism, then, is not to look to a new historical moment, or even to a "fate" or "destining" beyond all human doing, such as Heidegger begins to look for. Rather, for Strauss, the way beyond nihilism is to allow, and to follow to its end, the self-destruction of historical consciousness:

> Under the presupposition of historical consciousness, the question concerning the right life compels us to ask the question concerning the intellectual situation of the present. Since *this* question cannot be answered, then the question concerning the right life seems no longer answerable. Should it be answerable, this would be possible only by *calling historical consciousness into question*. But is this not a fantastic undertaking? *How* may historical consciousness be called into question? By recognizing basically this: historical consciousness is itself historically conditioned, therefore itself destined to give way to another consciousness. There is a world, that is, a real, historical world beyond historical consciousness. That this possibility exists *in principle* no one will dispute. But, it will be said, this world is the barbarism that awaits us no matter what; historical consciousness will go away if humanity unlearns what it has learned arduously enough over the past centuries; the renunciation of historical consciousness is identical with the relapse into a stage of lesser reflection. (RLS 245)

Rather than fleeing it, Strauss embraces this moment of lesser reflection: it is what a return to the ancients makes possible, a return to the natural standpoint: "We become again, what we cannot be before, *natural* philosophers, i.e. philosophers who approach the natural, the basic and original question of philosophy in a natural, an adequate way" (LI 133). But, as Strauss recognizes in the Krüger correspondence, the attaining of such a "naive" standpoint is not naively available (SKC 53–4). A new, higher reflection is called for, precisely to allow for an escape from the second cave of historical consciousness. Strauss described this challenge in a footnote in his second book, *Philosophy and Law* (1935), where he suggests that such a higher reflection is available only if the Enlightenment critique of the tradition is radicalized, as it was by Nietzsche, into a critique of the principles of the tradition (both the Greek and the Biblical), so that an original understanding of these principles again becomes possible. To that end and only to that end is the "historicizing" of philosophy justified and necessary: only the history of philosophy makes possible the ascent from the second, "unnatural" cave, into which we have fallen less because of the tradition itself than because of the tradition of polemics against the tradition, into that first, "natural" cave which Plato's image depicts, to emerge from which into the light is the original meaning of philosophizing. (PL 136)

Strauss is here outlining his own project: the historical recovery of the radical and natural standpoint discovered in the original meaning of philosophizing. He detected in the thought of Nietzsche the intention of such a recovery: "the recovery of antiquity at the peak of modernity." Strauss saw in Nietzsche the beginnings of an awareness of the overcoming of historical consciousness. Yet Nietzsche remained ensnared in that very consciousness through his continuing attachment – his polemical attachment – to will, to overcoming, to the future, to history. Strauss believes that in his "unpolemical" recovery of nature and of natural right, through the return to antiquity, he can point to a standpoint beyond nihilism, because that standpoint – nature – is beyond history itself. He can fulfill Nietzsche's intentions by being liberated from Nietzsche's teaching. In 1940, Strauss spoke of Nietzsche's intentions in these terms:

If I understand him correctly, his deepest concern was with philosophy, and not with politics ("philosophy and State are incompatible"); and that philosophy, in order to be really philosophy, and not some sort of dogmatism, is the sake of *natural* men, of men capable and willing to live "under the sky," of men who do not need the shelter of the cave, of *any* cave. Such a cave, such an artificial protection against the *elementary* problems, he descried, not only in the pre-modern tradition (of providence), but likewise in the modern tradition. It was against "history," against the belief that "history" can decide any question, that progress can ever make superfluous the discussion of the primary questions, against the belief that history, that indeed any human things, are the elementary subject of philosophy, that he reasserted hypothetically the doctrine of eternal return: to drive home that the elementary, the natural subject of philosophy still is, and always will be, as it had been for the Greeks: the *kosmos*, the world. (LI 137–8)

Strauss's "change of orientation" occurred through his recognizing that a recovery of classical political philosophy made possible a return to nature. Here Nietzsche's "intention," as Strauss described it to Löwith in 1935, could be effected, free of polemics, historicism, and nihilism. But to understand the full meaning of that change of orientation, it needs to be placed in the wider context of Strauss's life, and of the theme that primarily defined that life: the theological-political problem.

2

The Theological-Political Problem

Reflecting on his intellectual life, in 1964 Strauss wrote that "the theological-political problem has remained *the* theme of my investigations" (JPCM 453). In this chapter, we will have a chance to place the "change of orientation" that occurred in Strauss's investigations, and his recovery of natural right and pre-modern philosophy generally, in the wider context of this theme. While it can be said that the recovery of natural right is only an aspect of the theological-political problem, Strauss's "change of orientation" fundamentally alters and determines the wider theme, and so our understanding of it should help us make sense of "*the* theme" of Strauss's investigations. Then we will be able to see how Strauss's change of orientation both arises from and reorients the theological-political problem.

What, in fact, does Strauss mean by "the theological-political problem"? The phrase comes from the title of a work by Baruch Spinoza (1632–77), the *Tractatus Theologico-Politicus* or *Theological-Political Treatise*, which was the subject of Strauss's first book. The subtitle of Spinoza's treatise reads: "By means of which it is shown not only that Freedom of Philosophising can be allowed in Preserving Piety and the Peace of the Republic: but also that it is not possible for such Freedom to be upheld except when accompanied by the Peace of the Republic and Piety Themselves" (Spinoza, *Theological-Political Treatise*, 387).While Strauss may have doubted that this claim in fact represents the actual argument of Spinoza's book, still it points us to the basic sense of Strauss's phrase: the theological-political problem is the problem of establishing philosophy in the context of the claims of both religion and politics. For Strauss, religion and politics are in the first instance forms of authority: they determine the way of life of a society; philosophy, by contrast, is that way of life that fundamentally questions authority. Hence the theological-political problem is born.

As we will see more fully in chapter 5, Strauss argues that, through a fusion of philosophy and politics, modernity seeks to realize a solution to that problem by dissolving the authority of religion and establishing a humanity free in the world. We have seen that for Strauss this "modern project" (the modern solution to the theological-political problem) fails, resulting in the crisis of our time, the age of nihilism. Strauss sees that this crisis opens up the possibility of a return to a pre-modern standpoint that recognizes the irresolvable tension between philosophy and religion and politics. As Strauss's borrowed term "theological-political" suggests, there cannot be a simple separation of religion from politics – and this is central to Strauss's position. For him, religion and politics together form the total context of the "way of life" of any society.

Strauss's closest and lifelong friend, Jacob Klein, said of Strauss: "Now, while Mr. Strauss and I were studying we had many, I should say, endless conversations about many things. His primary interests were two questions: one, the question of God; and two, the question of politics" (JPCM 458). These "primary interests" that Klein identifies were by no means simply arbitrary, but arose from the conditions of Strauss's existence as a young Jew in Weimar Germany. While this may be true of the origin of these interests, however, it would be a betrayal of Strauss's standpoint to reduce his interest simply to those conditions. Strauss raised these concerns to philosophical reflection by recognizing that, for philosophy, the challenge of religion is determinative of philosophy. As part of the theological-political problem, the confrontation of philosophy with religion forms a crucial aspect of what Strauss means by the phrase "political philosophy." Political philosophy, for Strauss, is philosophy as aware of its context (both political and religious). This is so significant for the whole character of philosophy that Strauss says: "in its original form political philosophy broadly understood is the core of philosophy or rather 'the first philosophy'" (CM 20). Strauss gives the phrase "political philosophy" an unusual meaning: it is not primarily a field of philosophy, it is a *way of doing* philosophy, and as such is also a determination of philosophy. Political philosophy in this sense is philosophy informed by the theological-political problem. The recovery of philosophy in this sense is at the heart of Strauss's intellectual project, and will be our focus in this and the following chapter. We shall focus on the theological-political problem in its political dimension primarily in the next chapter; in this chapter we will consider particularly the relation of philosophy to religion.

Perhaps one of the simplest expressions of the tension between philosophy and religion is captured in Strauss's formulation: "No alternative is more fundamental than the alternative: human guidance or divine guidance. *Tertium non datur* [A third alternative is not given]" (RR 149). Strauss develops this thought in *Natural Right and History*:

> The fundamental question, therefore, is whether men can acquire that knowledge of the good without which they cannot guide their lives individually or collectively by the unaided efforts of their natural powers, or whether they are dependent for that knowledge on divine revelation. No alternative is more fundamental than this: human guidance or divine guidance. The first possibility is charac-teristic of philosophy or science in the original sense of the term, the second is presented in the Bible. The dilemma cannot be evaded by any harmonization or synthesis. (NRH 74)

So, at least in its religious dimension, the theological-political problem can be understood to be the problem of guidance in relation to the question we have already seen is central to Strauss: how one is to live one's life. As we shall come to see, the irresolvable distinction between philosophy and religion – which cannot be synthesized – is an utterly vital claim for Strauss. The obscuring of this distinction, above all as played out in modernity's relation to revelation, was for Strauss the source of his "theologico-political predicament" as a young man.

Strauss's Theologico-Political Predicament

In 1965, Leo Strauss described himself during his early years as "a young Jew born and raised in Germany who found himself in the grips of the theologico-political predicament" (JPCM 137). Leora Batnitzky has suggested that Strauss's use of the term "predic-ament" in this context instead of "problem" is meant to capture the personal circumstances that first drew Strauss into the more reflective stance of a "problem" (Batnitzky, "Leo Strauss and the

Theologico-Political Predicament," 41–2). Strauss encountered the theological-political problem in the "predicament" of being a Jew born into an orthodox family in modernizing Germany. Strauss notes that his education in the *Gymnasium* (German high school) began the process by which he could no longer be held by his orthodox upbringing. He charmingly describes the process of what must have been a disturbing transition:

> In the *Gymnasium* I became exposed to the message of German humanism. Furtively I read Schopenhauer and Nietzsche. When I was sixteen and we read the *Laches* in school, I formed the plan, or the wish, to spend my life reading Plato and breeding rabbits while earning my livelihood as a rural postmaster. Without being aware of it, I had moved rather far away from my Jewish home, without any rebellion. When I was seventeen, I was converted to Zionism – to simple, straightforward political Zionism. (JPCM 460)

As Strauss's account implies, his exposure to German humanism, while secularizing him, did not have the effect of converting him to identifying himself as a German. Rather he identified himself with a secular, political Jewish identity. Strauss was always clear that he was "Jew, and *not* German" (SKC 22). In the days before the Weimar Republic, such a stance made perfect sense: Strauss no longer found it possible to be a believing Jew, but neither could he belong to the German nation, whose culture and even philosophy he always saw as inherently German, in the same way that he found universalism or humanism inherent in Greek philosophy (JPCM 140).

With the advent of liberal democracy in the form of the Weimar Republic, it might appear that Strauss's "theologico-political predicament" could, at least in principle, be resolved. By distinguishing a public sphere, indifferent to or tolerant of religious belief or non-belief, from a private sphere that permits the adherence to any religious or secular view, liberalism seems to allow the predicament to disappear. One can be fully a citizen of the republic, and a Jew or Christian or atheist in private. This was the route of a certain form of Jewish assimilation: one could be assimilated to the general public life, and yet retain one's Jewish identity (or not, as the case might be). But Strauss did not find in liberalism a full or complete resolution of his predicament or problem, but rather just a reconfiguration of it:

> To realize that the Jewish problem is insoluble means never to forget the truth proclaimed by Zionism regarding the limitations of

liberalism. Liberalism stands and falls by the distinction between state and society or by the recognition of a private sphere, protected by the law but impervious to the law, with the understanding that, above all, religion as particular religion belongs to the private sphere. As certainly as the liberal state will not "discriminate" against its Jewish citizens, as certainly is it constitutionally unable and even unwilling to prevent "discrimination" against Jews on the part of individuals or groups. To recognize a private sphere in the sense indicated means to permit private "discrimination," to protect it, and thus in fact to foster it. The liberal state cannot provide a solution to the Jewish problem, for such a solution would require the legal prohibition against every kind of "discrimination," i.e., the abolition of the private sphere, the denial of the difference between state and society, the destruction of the liberal state. (JPCM 143–4)

During the 1920s, and throughout his own twenties, as well as being a "Nietzschean" Strauss was a political Zionist. But he was by no means a straightforward Zionist. He was continually raising fundamental problems not only with forms of Zionism or Jewish existence that he did not take up, but also with his own political Zionism. In this, Strauss in no way saw himself as betraying his Jewish roots. Being Jewish was for him revelatory not simply of the "Jewish problem" – as the status of Jews in Germany and Europe more broadly was referred to – but of the whole human condition, if experienced and viewed honestly and with probity. Reflecting later on his life as a Jew in the Weimar Republic, Strauss writes:

Finite, relative problems can be solved; infinite, absolute problems cannot be solved. In other words, human beings will never create a society which is free from contradictions. From every point of view it looks as if the Jewish people were the chosen people, at least in the sense that the Jewish problem is the most manifest symbol of the human problem insofar as it is a social or political problem. (JPCM 143)

This insight, the revelatory character of the "Jewish problem" for all humanity, is at the very center of both Strauss's life and his thought. It will fundamentally inform not only his alienation from modernity, with its drive to "solve" problems, but also his understanding of what characterizes the nature disclosed by ancient philosophy. He will, for example, come to understand Plato's ideas as "fundamental and permanent problems" (WIPP 39). When he described the theological-political problem as "*the* theme of my investigations," Strauss provided a formula that captures the fundamentally problematic character of human, and not just Jewish, reality.

In the first instance, however, Strauss's concern was with the problematic character of Jewish – and more specifically German Jewish – existence. Not only did Strauss see assimilation to a German liberal democracy as an impossible betrayal of his existence as a Jew, but also over the course of the 1920s he came to see that all forms of Zionism were inherently problematic. He saw that even his political Zionism was simply another form of assimilation in which the Jewish nation, the Jewish people, would be like all other people in governing and ruling themselves, a nation among nations and not a people apart, chosen by God. In fact, to a widely dispersed people seeking simply their own land and self-government, political Zionism might not mean a return to Israel: a land anywhere could serve just as well as a sphere for autonomy. Thus Strauss came to see that the abstractness of political Zionism caused it to give way to "cultural Zionism" – the standpoint that argues for Zionism as the preservation and self-realization of what belongs to a specifically Jewish culture or Jewish spirit (*Geist*). However excellent the products of Jewish "culture," for Strauss, Jewish culture (and hence Jewish cultural Zionism) has an internal contradiction. Judaism, and therefore Jewish "culture," is inherently constituted not by human agency but by divine agency. It is God who chooses the Jewish people and reveals His Law to them. Strauss argued: "When cultural Zionism understands itself, it turns into religious Zionism. But when religious Zionism understands itself, it is in the first place Jewish faith and only secondarily Zionism. It must regard as blasphemous the notion of a human solution to the Jewish problem" (JPCM 143). So, finally, religious Zionism returns one to orthodoxy as the only truly Jewish standpoint: it is the Jewish standpoint that has not tried to attain a synthesis or compromise with modernity – which is, as Strauss argued, inherently constituted by its (negative) relation to Christianity. Only orthodoxy is not a betrayal or corruption of Judaism.

As a young Jew and scholar, Strauss came to experience something that fundamentally informed his whole intellectual career: the refusal of all claims to synthesize or blend distinct standpoints or distinct ways of life. Strauss's tendency as a young Zionist was to radicalize and emphasize differences to the point of complete opposition. But his whole intellectual standpoint is in fact constituted by a set of oppositions that he argues are incapable of synthesis or resolution. Every synthesis, for Strauss, is either a dishonest and unstable amalgam or the implicit domination of one standpoint by another. There are no true syntheses: fundamental problems are not capable of fundamental solutions.

So Strauss found himself in the extraordinary position of upholding as the only truly valid Jewish position an orthodoxy that he himself could not, in his lack of belief, inhabit.[1] At the same time, living in a modern liberal Germany in which he could also not find a home, Strauss upheld as a purely political position an explicitly atheistic political Zionism (EW 124–37). The perfect vehicle for Strauss's exploration of this theological-political predicament is his first book, *Spinoza's Critique of Religion*, in which he played out a debate between Spinoza and orthodoxy. Spinoza's claim to ground a scientific, humanistic, irreligious, liberal modernity was put in debate with the claims of orthodox belief in an omnipotent, creative God who has revealed Himself in the Bible to His chosen people. Through much of the late 1920s and early 1930s, Strauss wrote his book on Spinoza as part of his employment with the Akademie für die Wissenschaft des Judentums (Academy for the Science of Judaism). His goal in this book was to contest the belief that religion (and especially religious orthodoxy) had been defeated, as Spinoza claims, by the rise of modern rationality and particularly modern science, including modern biblical science. A Nietzschean tinge can be detected in Strauss's account here: when Strauss turns to Spinoza, his effort is to show that Spinoza betrays what Nietzsche called a "will to truth." For Strauss, Spinoza's critique of religion does not arise out of its professed rationality; rather, Spinoza's moral impulse to "disprove" the God of religious piety, whether Jewish or Christian, is what in fact generates his rationality.

Strauss's object in *Spinoza's Critique of Religion* is threefold:

1. to expose the failure of Spinoza's claim to have disproved or rationally undermined the claims of orthodoxy;
2. equally, to expose the incapacity of orthodoxy to dispose of or disprove the claims of modern rationality; and so
3. to show each to be a "stance" or standpoint relative to the other.

---

[1] It is important, as Strauss makes clear, not to confuse this orthodoxy with neo-orthodoxy, that standpoint developed most notably by Franz Rosenzweig, to whom Strauss's first book was dedicated, and who was a personal acquaintance. Strauss evidently admired Rosenzweig, but found in what was "new" in his orthodoxy a collusion with modernity that in fact rendered it exactly unorthodox.

Strauss argues that the actual historical undermining of religious orthodoxy in modern European culture was accomplished not theoretically but practically, first through the practical success of modern science, then (more importantly) through the practical success of modern rhetoric: namely, the Enlightenment tactic of mocking religious orthodoxy. As he put it: "Hence the antagonism between Spinoza and Judaism, between unbelief and belief, is ultimately not theoretical, but moral" (JPCM 171).

By 1928, with the completion of *Spinoza's Critique of Religion*, Strauss had established a radical, irresolvable opposition between modern rationality and religious orthodoxy, to which logic he later returned in his striking "Introduction" to *Philosophy and Law* (1935). There Strauss explained his "change of orientation," his recovery of pre-modern rationalism, by rehearsing the logic that led to it: namely, that it was for him a way to get beyond the insoluble conflict between orthodoxy and modernity.

Strauss begins *Philosophy and Law* by reminding the reader that the most basic form of this conflict is the alternative "orthodoxy or Enlightenment." He first defends the centrality and inescapability of this opposition in the face of various modern efforts to moderate or synthesize its terms. Strauss then goes on to effect his critique or radicalization of Enlightenment thought in essentially the Nietzschean terms he came to in his Spinoza book. Strauss noted that this analysis issued "in the discovery of the radical 'historicity' of man and his world as the definitive overcoming of the idea of an eternal nature, an eternal truth" and this discovery "finally understands modern natural science as one historically contingent form of 'world-construction' among others" (PL 33). This brings to light Strauss's claim that modernity is not primarily a victory of reason, but a work of will:

> Hence, if modern natural science cannot justify the modern ideal, and if there is nonetheless unmistakably a relation between the modern ideal and modern natural science, one sees oneself compelled to ask whether it is not, on the contrary, the modern ideal that is in truth the basis of modern natural science, and thus whether it is not precisely a new belief rather than the new knowledge that justifies the Enlightenment. (PL 34)

This statement issues in a pages-long paragraph by which Strauss establishes that the apparent victory of Enlightenment is in truth the victory of a new kind of atheism, the atheism of "probity." While

Strauss does not name this standpoint, its broadly Nietzschean character seems undeniable:

> This new fortitude, being the willingness to look man's forsakenness in its face, being the courage to welcome the terrible truth, being toughness against the inclination of man to deceive himself about his situation, is probity. It is this probity, "intellectual probity," that bids us reject all attempts to "mediate" between the Enlightenment and orthodoxy – both those of the moderate Enlightenment and especially those of the post-Enlightenment synthesis – not only as inadequate, but also and especially as without probity; it forces the alternative "Enlightenment or orthodoxy" and, since it believes it finds the deepest unprobity in the principles of the tradition itself, it bids us to renounce the very word "God." (PL 37)

This Nietzschean atheism of probity that Strauss outlines knows itself to be a radical, post-biblical atheism that is at the same time entangled in revelation, even in and because of its defiance of it. As Strauss puts it, "it accepts the thesis, the negation of the Enlightenment, on the basis of a way of thinking which became possible only through the Bible" (PL 37).

What this final standpoint, this atheism of probity, brings to light is the true conflict: "Thus at last the 'truth' of the alternative 'orthodoxy or Enlightenment' is revealed as the alternative 'orthodoxy or atheism'" (PL 38). But then, in a moment of striking openness, Strauss writes:

> The situation thus formed, the present situation, appears to be insoluble for the Jew who cannot be orthodox and who must consider purely political Zionism, the only 'solution of the Jewish problem' possible on the basis of atheism, as a resolution that is indeed highly honorable but not, in earnest and in the long run, adequate. (PL 38)

This was precisely Strauss's own intellectual dilemma in 1928 when he completed *Spinoza's Critique of Religion*. Yet here, he goes on to say that "this situation not only appears insoluble but actually is so, as long as one clings to the modern premises" (PL 38). Here we can see that what distinguishes Strauss's work in the early 1930s is his transformation of the theological-political problem from its earlier form, in which revelation and reason are antagonistically opposed, to his discovery and recovery of pre-modern rationality, thus reflecting his "change of orientation." As we shall see, Strauss's reorientation does not provide a standpoint that synthesizes or resolves the opposition found in his Spinoza book, but it allows it to be recast. The way Strauss expresses it in a footnote to *Philosophy and Law* is to call for a "theologico-political treatise," but one that, in order to get beyond modernity, "must take exactly the opposite direction from the theological-political treatises of the seventeenth century, especially those of Hobbes and Spinoza" (PL 138). This proposal could be understood as a description of Strauss's scholarly project as a whole.

The Discovery of Pre-Modern Rationality and Revelation

In chapter 1 we discussed Strauss's reorientation in terms of a recovery of classical rationality and, above all, a recovery of nature as this appears in Socratic-Platonic philosophy. However, this is not where Strauss began his reorientation. His turn was more indirect; it was through his work as a scholar of medieval Jewish and Islamic thought – crucially informed, of course, by ancient philosophy – that Strauss began to see a way forward. The details are not entirely clear,[2] but it appears that sometime in 1929 or 1930, while Strauss was struggling with the thought of Moses Maimonides, he had a defining moment that opened his mind to the possibilities of pre-modern rationality:

> One day, when reading in a Latin translation Avicenna's treatise *On the Division of the Sciences*, I came across this sentence (I quote from memory): the standard work on prophecy and revelation is Plato's *Laws*. Then I began to begin to understand Maimonides's prophetology and eventually, as I believe, the whole *Guide of the Perplexed*. (JPCM 463)

It is by no means obvious how this quotation from Avicenna should open up Strauss's reorientation and point to the recovery of classical natural right. However, the significance of the statement becomes clearer when put in the context of Strauss's intellectual predicament, the insoluble opposition between orthodoxy and the post-biblical atheism of probity that he outlined in the Introduction to *Philosophy and Law*. Through his encounter with Heidegger, Strauss had already come to see the possibility of a non-traditional

---

[2] See Heinrich Meier, "How Strauss Became Strauss," in RLS 13–32.

reading of ancient texts; as he explained, "under the guidance of Heidegger, people came to see that Aristotle and Plato had *not* been understood" (LI 134). What continued to hold Strauss captive was a "powerful prejudice, that a return to premodern philosophy is impossible" (JPCM 173). The basis of this prejudice was that, to him, the historical and human significance of biblical revelation at work in both orthodoxy and modern atheism suggested such a return to be impossible. As "atheism of probity" recognized, the advent of revelation, especially through its effects in stimulating modernity, had transformed human life too deeply for any complete return to the ancients. What Avicenna's remark suggests to Strauss is that such a prejudice is questionable: for Avicenna, even in the face of revelation, Plato's *Laws* is still the classic work on prophecy. Plato remains as directly true in the post-revelatory context of Islam or Judaism as he was for the ancient Greeks.

Further, the Avicenna text points to Plato's *Laws* – his political philosophy – as the context within which to understand prophetology. What this suggests is that revelation and the vehicle of that revelation, the prophet, fall not within metaphysics, but within political philosophy. This connection proved deeply illuminating for Strauss in his understanding of Maimonides, and of Jewish and Islamic medieval thought generally. As he put it in his introduction to *Philosophy and Law*, "we shall attempt in what follows to point out the leading idea of the medieval Enlightenment that has become lost to the modern Enlightenment and its heirs, and through an understanding of which many modern certainties and doubts lose their force: the idea of Law" (PL 39). In contrast to Christianity, which makes belief the principal requirement of revelation, for Judaism and also for Islam the primary revelation is Law, and the primary form of adherence is obedience or submission to that Law. Strauss finds in medieval Judaism an account of religion and revelation free of modern inwardness and the spiritualizing tendencies that for him mar modern Jewish philosophy. This allows an account of Judaism free of modernity, free of what Strauss elsewhere speaks of as "the second cave."

The key to articulating this standpoint in Strauss is through examining Maimonides's account of prophetology. It is, of course, perfectly reasonable to wonder how sorting through the details of medieval Jewish thought about prophetology is going to help us understand Leo Strauss as a key contemporary thinker. But Strauss's work on Maimonides helps bring to light the core issue for Strauss – his continuing confrontation with historicism. Strauss's reorientation rests on his capacity to discover a standpoint in which the confrontation of philosophy and religion can get beyond these modern terms of engagement. Strauss had seen that at the heart of modernity is the claim that there can be real historical change to what it is to be human. He had seen that the basis of this claim lay in the interaction of biblical revelation and history. Revelation is the original claim to a possibility of human transformation. This is straightforwardly obvious in the case of Christianity, whose revelation involves the transforming of the divine–human relationship. Is this true of the religions of the Law? If revelation is primarily political and legal, and not an alteration of the human condition through the revelation of previously undisclosed knowledge, then it might be possible to retain (in its original sense) philosophy that has for its object nature (knowable to the ancients) and revelation that has for its object the ordering of believers under the best or revealed Law. As a revelation of belief, Christianity called upon philosophy to be what Thomas Aquinas called a "handmaiden" to Sacred Doctrine, and required a transformation of philosophy or a synthesis between reason and revelation. Revelation understood in Jewish and Islamic thought as revelation of the Law requires no such alteration to the classical account of the relationship between philosophy and religion. As we will see, there are important questions to ask about how Jewish or Islamic revelation affects the more general relationship between philosophy and religion, but the preservation of the basic distinction between philosophy as theoretical and religion as belonging to the city, to law, is for Strauss crucial to the continuation of political philosophy in its original sense into the medieval period. The work of distinguishing and then practically coordinating theory and practice was, according to Strauss's account of Maimonides, the mission of the prophet.

Strauss was already a considerable scholar of Maimonides and medieval Jewish thought when he wrote *Spinoza's Critique of Religion*, completed in 1928. But the Maimonides Strauss presents there is fairly conventional, a believing Jew who reconciles philosophy and revelation (SCR 165). In the early 1930s, however, Strauss recasts this scholarship and starts reading Maimonides in the light of the hint offered by Avicenna, which he finds confirmed by investigating the great tenth-century Islamic philosopher Alfarabi. Alfarabi had a powerful influence on Maimonides, and Strauss makes use of Alfarabi's explicit account of philosophy, and especially of political philosophy and prophetology, to interpret Maimonides.

Scholars have spoken of a "Farabian turn" in Strauss's reading of Maimonides (Tanguay, *Leo Strauss: An Intellectual Biography*, 79–98). The effect of this turn is to reduce the theological or theoretical character of revelation, so that in revelation there are no metaphysical truths unknowable by reason. Strauss discovers in both Alfarabi and Maimonides that revelation is primarily the revelation of Law and so is fundamentally "political."

The crucial agent of revelation is the prophet. Over the course of the 1930s, Strauss comes to align Maimonides's teaching on the prophet with Alfarabi's account, in which "the prophet" corresponds to the Platonic account of the philosopher-king as outlined in Plato's *Republic*. But there is a crucial difference. For Socrates in the *Republic*, it is a matter of hope or chance that the best regime, the rule of the philosopher-king, might be realized on earth: for Judaism or Islam, this hope has been made actual through the prophet.

In the early 1930s, and even in *Philosophy and Law* (1935), Strauss still maintains a distinction between the teaching of Maimonides and that of Alfarabi. At this point, Strauss argues that for Alfarabi revelation teaches nothing that cannot be known by philosophy as an activity of natural reason. For Alfarabi, the prophet is distinguished from the philosopher not in cognitive ability but in powers of imagination. These powers allow both communication of truth in images and the exercise of a political legislative function. In *Philosophy and Law*, Strauss argues that Maimonides distinguished Moses as the highest prophet because Moses is given by revelation access to a truth that exceeds reason (PL 107–9). In the late 1930s, however, Strauss moves away from seeing in Maimonides's account of the prophet a "higher" theoretical knowledge. This is the "Farabian turn": Strauss sees now that, as for Alfarabi, in Maimonides revelation has become the revelation of Law, not of any theoretical truth inaccessible to natural reason. For Strauss, then, the central form of thought – "first philosophy" – in Maimonides was not metaphysics, but political philosophy. What this crucially means is that, for Strauss, Maimonides is living and thinking the theological-political problem in its most developed form.

This change in Strauss's account of Maimonides is amplified by his discovery of the exoteric/esoteric distinction, which we will discuss fully in chapter 3. By 1938, when Strauss is settling in the United States, he writes to his close friend Jacob Klein:

> If I let this bomb blow in a few years (should I live that long), a huge battle will flare up. [Nahum] Glatzer … said to me that for Judaism

Maimonides is more important than the Bible – thus if one deprives
Judaism of Maimonides, one deprives it of its root ... Thus, it will
yield the interesting result that a merely historical observation – the
observation that Maimonides was absolutely not a Jew in his belief –
is of extremely timely significance: the incompatibility in principle of
philosophy and Judaism ... will be demonstrated *ad oculos* [visibly].
(Bernstein, *Leo Strauss on the Borders of Judaism, Philosophy, and
History*, 34)

Strauss certainly allows that Maimonides appears (and has
frequently been interpreted) to teach not only the reconciliation
of reason and revelation, but that revelation completes reason by
providing access to truths unknown to reason alone (such as the
creation of the world). The "Farabian turn" and Strauss's new sense
of esoteric writing allow him to conclude that, for Maimonides and
Alfarabi, philosophy remains unaffected by revelation. According
to Strauss, a philosopher such as Maimonides practices the art of
esoteric writing – that is, conceals a true more radical teaching
under an exoteric appearance of conformity to orthodox belief. The
exoteric/esoteric distinction is crucial in protecting both the beliefs
(necessary for Law) and the questioning of those beliefs (necessary
for philosophy). For Strauss, this takes us into the world of what
he calls "political philosophy." As "political," as Law, religion in its
relation to philosophy is part of Strauss's understanding of political
philosophy. Maimonides is for Strauss the political philosopher
who masterfully appears to support and sustain Jewish piety by
publicly reconciling the beliefs necessary to Judaism with the
claims of philosophy. But in fact, hiddenly, as Strauss later states in
the introduction to *Persecution and the Art of Writing*: "Jews of the
philosophic competence of [Yehuda] Halevi and Maimonides took
it for granted that being a Jew and being a philosopher are mutually
exclusive" (PAW 19).

The Opposition Between Reason and Revelation:
Athens and Jerusalem

For Strauss, then, on what does the exclusivity of philosophy and
revelation rest? Crucially, it does not rest primarily on the differences or indeed oppositions between philosophy and revelation
in terms of their content. More fundamentally, they are opposed
as ways of life. The real opposition is not a question of whether

philosophy is able to rationally refute the claims of religion, or of religion rejecting the claims of reason. Rather, the opposition rests in two inherently incompatible ways of life: Strauss sees not philosophy, but *philosophizing*, as a way of life – and not revelation, but *loving obedience*, as a way of life.

Strauss's writings on Maimonides, especially through his "Farabian turn" in the late 1930s and early 1940s, mark the stages by which the theological-political problem becomes rearticulated in his work in its "theological" dimension as the opposition between Athens and Jerusalem, the ways of philosophy and revelation. The problem of the relationship between religion and philosophy was, of course, already a concern in the ancient city. As Strauss notes, Athens and Jerusalem share the question of "divine law" (JPCM 107, 112–13). In fact, the two have much in common at the level of morality – most importantly, the high place of justice in both (JPCM 106–7). But for Strauss there is a crucial difference here: "The common ground between the Bible and Greek philosophy is the problem of divine law. They solve that problem in a diametrically opposed manner" (JPCM 107). According to Strauss, divine law is at first the "ancestral" by which the specific "ways" of a people are grounded in their gods, their divinized ancestors. The "problem of divine law" arises because there is a plurality of such "ways." Athens and Jerusalem "solve" this problem in opposed ways: Athens seeks a "nature" discoverable by philosophy as prior to the many laws or "ways." But, for Strauss, the importance of Jerusalem is that Jewish revelation is also a response to this plurality:

> the author or authors of the Bible were aware of the problem of the variety of the divine laws. In other words, they realized ... what are the absolutely necessary conditions if one particular law should be *the* divine law. How has one to conceive of the whole if one particular, and therefore contingent, law of one particular, contingent tribe is to be *the* divine law? The answer is: it must be a personal God; the first cause must be God; He must be omnipotent, not controlled and not controllable. But to be knowable means to be controllable, and therefore He must not be knowable in the strict sense of the term. (JPCM 114)

The Jewish revelation (and the other Abrahamic religions in its wake) radicalizes the standpoint of divine law in three ways (RR 166–7):

1. God is the one omnipotent God, creator of heaven and earth, whose ways are completely unknowable;
2. this God communicates by revelation and so directly and beyond the poetic forms that belong to mythology; and
3. what God reveals is Law that is directly binding through full obedience and provides a comprehensive way of life.

We need to see why this form of divine law, the Law of Judaism, will pose such a challenge to philosophy, to Athens.

Strauss points to a fundamental point of contact between Athens and Jerusalem that also indicates their existential divergence. He writes, "is there a notion, a word that points to the highest that the Bible on the one hand and the greatest works of the Greeks claim to convey? There is such a word: wisdom" (JPCM 379). But it is at this high point that Strauss sees that the fundamental distinction – and indeed opposition – between Athens and Jerusalem emerges: "According to the Bible, the beginning of wisdom is fear of the Lord; according to the Greek philosophers, the beginning of wisdom is wonder. We are thus compelled from the very beginning to make a choice, to take a stand" (JPCM 379–80). Strauss frames this opposition between Athens and Jerusalem as a distinction between chosen standpoints. In "Progress or Return" (1952), an earlier formulation of the same basic problematic, he writes: "we have this radical opposition: the Bible refuses to be integrated into a philosophical framework, just as philosophy refuses to be integrated into a biblical framework" (JPCM 121). Earlier in the same lecture, Strauss puts it this way:

> No one can be both a philosopher and a theologian, or, for that matter, a third which is beyond the conflict between philosophy and theology, or a synthesis of both. But every one of us can be and ought to be either the one or the other, the philosopher open to the challenge of theology, or the theologian open to the challenge of philosophy. (JPCM 117)

In a manner reminiscent of some remarks of Nietzsche in the Preface to *Beyond Good and Evil*, Strauss argues the irresolvable tension between Athens and Jerusalem is the source, the "two roots," of the vitality of western civilization. So for Strauss, the "radical opposition" between the two is the ground for a confidence in the continuing vitality of the West (JPCM 105).

But why are these distinct "cities" in such opposition? Why can they not be reconciled or synthesized or even brought together, according to Strauss? It is because he frames them as "ways of life," and so one cannot, with integrity live both at the same time:

> But a closer study shows that what happened and has been happening in the West for many centuries, is not a harmonization but an attempt at harmonization. These attempts at harmonization were doomed to failure for the following reason: each of these two roots of the Western world sets forth one thing as the one thing needful, and the one thing needful proclaimed by the Bible is incompatible, as it is understood by the Bible, with the one thing needful proclaimed by Greek philosophy, as it is understood by Greek philosophy. To put it very simply and therefore somewhat crudely, the one thing needful according to Greek philosophy is the life of autonomous understanding. The one thing needful as spoken by the Bible is the life of obedient love. The harmonizations and synthesizations are possible because Greek philosophy can *use* obedient love in a subservient function, and the Bible can *use* philosophy as a handmaid; but what is so used in each case rebels against such use, and therefore the conflict is really a radical one. (JPCM 104)

One could call this opposition of differing accounts of "the one thing needful" an existential opposition, much like the opposed forms of life that Kierkegaard explores in *Either/Or*.

It is useful here to recall the beginnings of Strauss's being in the "grip of the theologico-political predicament." Strauss began by seeking to liberate himself from the dominance of modern rationality. He found that modern rationality and its inner self-destruction was inherently implicated by not simply its opposition but its antagonism to religion, to Jerusalem. For Strauss, Jerusalem is not simply another opposed "way of life" to which one can be open; it is rather (especially in the form of Christianity) that form that modern rationality must be opposed to in order for modernity to establish itself; modernity, against its own deepest intentions, becomes inscribed by what it opposes. In a way, then, modern rationality represents a combined opposition to both Athens and Jerusalem (JPCM 399). It is the standpoint produced through the negation of both ancient nature and biblical revelation. The opposition between Athens and Jerusalem functions not only to distinguish Athenian pre-modern philosophy from modern rationality insofar as it is a rationality free of Christian admixture; equally, it points to a Judaism free from synthesis and inwardness – a Judaism of the Law.

Strauss's fullest or most developed account of the theological-political problem, then, is in terms of the opposition between Athens and Jerusalem. But there are some obvious perplexities about this opposition. As we saw in chapter 1, central to Strauss's project is the discovery and recovery of an ahistorical nature and natural right, a nature that appears to philosophy as a set of fundamental problems that, as permanent or eternal, belong to human nature. But clearly biblical revelation is not coeval with man; more specifically, the actual confrontation between Athens and Jerusalem is a historical event that only occurs at some point in the Hellenistic period. If Jerusalem is a historically contingent event, how is it that the opposition of Jerusalem and Athens can be a permanent, fundamental problem?

Strauss is by no means blind to this issue. In fact, the basic problem of the relation of nature to historical contingency is central to his standpoint. Strauss's way to think about the question of historical contingency is to see all historical developments (Judaism, modernity, philosophy itself) as realizing potentialities built into the nature of things, and above all, human things. Even so, there is a significant ambivalence or tension in Strauss's argument that we need to explore. In the case of the advent of revelation, he argues (and he sees Alfarabi, Avicenna, and Maimonides preceding him in this) that in principle Plato had already anticipated the prophet and his revelatory work, which is fundamentally political (JPCM 115; PL 122–33). From one side, then, this means that the event of biblical revelation, or at least its confrontation with philosophy, adds nothing transformative to what belongs to the nature of things exposed by classical philosophical thought. On the other hand, it does effect a change in the conditions of philosophy: philosophy now needs to address itself to the revelation of Law and the actuality of the philosopher-king in history in the form of the prophet. For Strauss, this context then both deepens and weakens philosophy: it changes the relation of philosophy to its political or legal context, and yet also dissolves (or at least moderates) the ancient pursuit of the best regime insofar as it is actual in and through revealed Law (PL 132–3).

As we have seen, what distinguished for Strauss the peculiar rationality of the biblical account from all merely mythological or ancestral accounts is that it breaks from the worldly or finite nature of mythology. Biblical revelation as post-mythological distinguishes Jerusalem as a powerful challenge to Athens, in contrast to the mythological religion that belonged to ancient Greece. What this observation suggests is that the Athens/Jerusalem distinction is a special form of the philosophy/religion distinction. For Strauss, the philosophy/religion distinction connects to another fundamental dichotomy, that of the exoteric/esoteric. Strauss identifies the esoteric in Plato with his philosophic teaching engaged in radical questioning (including questioning of the public religious life of the city), and the exoteric teaching as that which upholds religion by presenting a mutually supportive relation between philosophy and the religious public opinion that sustains the life of the city. But what, then, does this mean for biblical (above all Jewish) revelation? How can Jerusalem be a genuine, irreducible alternative to philosophy if it is merely exoteric, merely a form of opinion held within the horizon of the city? Equally, if biblical revelation is crucially post-mythological and not subordinate to philosophy, how is its appearance not a world-changing event such as to alter the structure of the "permanent problems," and so alter and deepen both history and the nature of humanity (SKC 53)?

Are there, then, events in history that are of such an order as to alter nature, alter the structure of the permanent problems? Is the advent of Jerusalem one such event? Strauss's most fundamental claim is that history takes place within nature, which itself remains unaffected. But the emergence of Jerusalem, like the emergence of modernity, is a real historical change. As we shall see when we look more closely at Strauss's account of modernity in chapter 5, there are real effects for human life and thought in the coming-to-be of the modern world. So also for the advent of Jerusalem, both in itself (the coming-to-be of Judaism) and for philosophy in the explicit emergence of the divide between Athens and Jerusalem. In both cases, ancient philosophy had already anticipated such possibilities. On a number of occasions, Strauss argues that there is nothing basic to modernity that was not in principle already present, or at least available, to ancient thought (OT 178). This is also true in the case of Jerusalem, and above all in the role of the prophet: Plato's *Laws* are, according to Avicenna, already the standard for (and therefore anticipate) the prophet of revelation. Of course, this is also why the "Farabian turn" in Strauss's thought is so crucial: the actual advent of the prophet does not make available a knowledge that would either transform philosophy or alter what is theoretically knowable. This is why the basic claims (as Strauss understands them) of Judaism and Islam as revelations of Law – and not, as with Christianity, of a new truth to be believed – do not alter the fundamental terms of the theological-political problem, and so philosophy is preserved as the thinking or questioning of an enduring, permanent nature.

At the level of nature and of philosophy as the quest to know nature, no change in history can be effective or transformative. But Jerusalem and modernity are real historical changes, so they change the conditions under which nature is known. There is, then, an ambiguity about the status of Jerusalem – the extent to which it falls within the natural order known to Athens, and the extent to which it exceeds what could be encountered in Athens. In one sense, the high point for Strauss is Plato or Socrates, the originators of political philosophy. From this perspective, medieval philosophy is less original and less radical in its formulations, for revelation weakens such questions as the pursuit of the best regime, insofar as revelation has in fact met this object (PL 132). On the other hand, for Strauss, Maimonides can emerge as the high point in encountering the fundamental character of the theological-political problem, and in thinking through the dichotomy between Athens and Jerusalem. Strauss sees that Maimonides must face philosophically the challenge of religion in its most developed form. From this perspective, Maimonides points not to the "solution" of the theological-political problem, but to the most comprehensive way to live that problem.

As we are coming to see, for Strauss, political philosophy is not primarily a field of philosophy but a way of engaging in philosophy as a whole, through a consciousness or awareness of the necessary political location of philosophy. This awareness he names as the "theological-political problem." The development of Jerusalem, like the development of modernity, is for Strauss the realization of certain possibilities internal to the "theological-political problem." As such, both Jerusalem and modernity in certain ways endanger philosophy in its original Socratic-Platonic vocation, as aspects of that questioning take on historical determination. However, as determinations, they also bring to light more explicit confrontations by which political philosophy can deepen its self-awareness as political philosophy. In this sense, precisely because Jerusalem functions as an alternative and challenge to Athens, it strengthens philosophy in its own task of questioning.

Philosophy Defined by its Opposition to Religion

It is important to clarify the challenge that revelation poses for reason in Strauss's thought, for he rehearses the debate between reason and revelation a number of times and in a variety of contexts in his work. Even though Strauss is clearly an inhabitant of Athens, he seems to need to return to the challenge of Jerusalem. In the debates Strauss sets up between reason and religion, he often frames the issue as a matter of rational refutation: does reason refute revelation? Or does revelation refute reason? At this level, the claim of reason is to establish itself against revelation by demonstrating that revelation cannot maintain its standpoint. Reason argues against revelation on the basis of the autonomy of reason, or on the basis of reason's knowledge of nature, or reason's knowledge of history, or reason's knowledge of God. In these terms – largely the terms of modern rationality – Strauss argues that reason succeeds at one level: it is able to refute the claims of revelation as claims of knowledge. But reason fails on another level: it cannot refute the claims of revelation as claims of belief, especially belief in an omnipotent God beyond nature and humanity who reveals Himself in Scripture. Reason can refute revelation on the terms or assumptions of reason, but not on the terms or assumptions of revelation. Revelation mirrors this condition: revelation cannot refute reason on reason's terms. In this way, reason cannot prove its premises; it can only assert or will them – and the same is true of belief. As a result, we have a standoff, which (Strauss is delighted to point out) means that revelation wins, because it never claimed to ground itself in reason, but only in belief:

> Philosophy, the life devoted to the quest for evident knowledge available to man as man, would itself rest on an unevident, arbitrary, or blind decision. This would merely confirm the thesis of faith, that there is no possibility of consistency, of a consistent and thoroughly sincere life, without belief in revelation. The mere fact that philosophy and revelation cannot refute each other would constitute the refutation of philosophy by revelation. (NRH 75)

It would seem that Strauss here is undermining his own way of life, the life devoted to philosophy. Some commentators quite reasonably find Strauss's claim that faith refutes reason unsustainable, and so look for a refutation of this refutation. It is not obvious that Strauss provides such a comprehensive refutation: how can Strauss, who is clearly on the side of Athens, declare Jerusalem victorious?

Strauss's Own Relation to Athens and Jerusalem

Most commentators (at least most sympathetic commentators) see the centrality of the theological-political problem in Strauss and explicate it in largely similar terms. Nonetheless, widely different readings of Strauss's own relation to the theological-political problem are possible. For some, the problem is resolved on the side of Athens, by philosophy disproving or reducing revelation to an exoteric political teaching. For others, Jerusalem is presented as fully valid, indeed the foundational standpoint to which Athens must be seen as equal or even secondary. Finally, for many other commentators, the problem remains a problem, to be lived in various ways. Strauss's various formulations of it over his intellectual career can lead to differing ways of seeing the problem as either an "existential" opposition or a voluntaristic one requiring a decision. Others try to resolve it by finding religion and philosophy each to reside in different aspects of the soul, differing forms of *eros*. There is a textual basis in Strauss for all these different ways of formulating both the tension of the theological-political problem and how any specific individual is to live this tension.

But in Strauss himself, one thing is clear: he was not, and was not able to be, orthodox in his beliefs. Indeed, in his correspondence he described himself as unbelieving and in fact an atheist (SKC 17, 57). In his career and writing, he evidently aligned himself with "Athens" as a way of life, in terms of the "one thing needful." But if this much is reasonably clear, what does it mean for the debate between Athens and Jerusalem?

In order to get some sense of the status of Strauss as a citizen of "Athens" as a way of life, it is important to recall that he began his scholarly career by criticizing the moderns, such as Spinoza, for claiming to have disproved the standpoint of revelation, insofar as revelation was by and of an omnipotent, unknowable God who could not be reduced to the reality available to scientific demonstration. For Strauss, modernity's atheism was implicated in its antagonism toward the God it denies by its need to refute revealed religion in order to establish itself. This means two things for Athens. First, it cannot be atheistic in the modern sense of claiming to have disproved or rationally refuted the standpoint of Jerusalem:

"A philosophy which believes that it can refute the possibility of revelation – and a philosophy which does not believe that: *this* is the real meaning of la querelle des anciens et des modernes [the quarrel of the ancients and the moderns]" (RR 177). According to Strauss, for Athens and for the Socratic political philosopher, atheism can be at best an "opinion," a "solution" to the theological-political problem that the philosopher may incline to but which is less fundamental than the problem itself. Second, the stance of ancient philosophy in relation to its own activity, its self-awareness as political philosophy, will therefore not be the same as that of modern philosophy. As we shall explore at greater length in chapter 5, modern political philosophy for Strauss rests upon an inherently negative or willful posture. Ancient political philosophy arises as a way of life of questioning, and so of "not knowing," moved by an *eros*, an inclination within the soul, to seek to know.

In sorting out what Strauss is saying in any given text about the theological-political problem, it is thus important to take note of the context: is the context modernity, or is it the pre-modern? For him, the theological-political problem is lived differently in different contexts. As a number of scholars have noted, it is in the context of modern philosophy that Strauss presents the debate between Athens and Jerusalem as reducing to a debate between opposed beliefs: modern rationality or biblical revelation. In this debate, it is as if each is ultimately grounded in an assertion of will, producing an initial stalemate, which (as we noted above) nonetheless resounds to the victory of religion, because religion does not claim to be grounded in knowledge, but precisely in belief. Is faith's capacity to defeat reason, then, only true in its opposition to modern reason?

This failure of reason to establish itself as self-grounded is the failure of modern or systematic or metaphysical reason. But for Strauss, philosophy – specifically Socratic political philosophy, which is given to questioning – is not vulnerable to this defeat. It accepts the irrefutability of religion and does not seek to enter into a contest with it, on its terms. The Socratic standpoint (the knowledge of one's ignorance) remains with a merely human quest for a merely human wisdom (PAW 105). From this standpoint, what the philosopher seeks is not proof that philosophy is the right way of life, but rather that the philosophical way of life is evidently the best way of life:

> the question of utmost urgency, the question which does not permit
> suspense, is the question of how one should live. Now, this question

is settled for Socrates by the fact that he is a philosopher. As a philosopher, he knows that we are ignorant of the most important things. The ignorance, the evident fact of this ignorance, evidently proves that quest for knowledge of the most important things is the most important thing for us. (RCPR 259)

According to Strauss, it is the evidence of ignorance and the knowledge of ignorance that establish philosophy as the evidently best life.

From the standpoint of Socratic ignorance, then, philosophy escapes the trap of the debate between philosophy and religion by not seeking to claim a standpoint from which to refute religion. It will live with the problem of reason and revelation as a problem and not seek its resolution, but as a way of life be committed to philosophy.

How can such a modest wisdom not be defeated by the claims of religion? Here Strauss points to a critique of these claims not by refutation, but by explanation, and specifically by a genealogical explanation of religion.

The Genealogy of Religion

One way of framing the effect and character of a genealogy of religion in Strauss is through a distinction found in Strauss's account of Yehuda Halevi's *Kuzari*, a medieval Jewish text, between human wisdom and divine wisdom (PAW 95–141, JPCM 121). We noted earlier that Strauss distinguished the wisdom of Athens that begins in wonder from the wisdom of Jerusalem that begins in the fear of the Lord (JPCM 379–80). As Strauss understands it, philosophy stays at the level of human wisdom, or even only strives for human wisdom. Human reason cannot refute divine reason in terms of divine reason, or even in terms of the revelation of that divine reason. But human reason can *explain* the claims of divine reason as merely human claims.

Heinrich Meier, one of the most important Strauss scholars, argues that Strauss's refutation of religion occurs in a set of notes for "Reason and Revelation," an unpublished talk he gave in 1948. But, as Michael Zuckert has correctly pointed out, the genealogical account of religion Strauss outlines there does not rise to the level of a refutation; rather, it is an explanation of religion from the perspective of an account of the human soul, or an account of human nature and its requirements from the perspective of philosophy as human wisdom (Zuckert, "Straussians," 267–9). In the notes for "Reason and Revelation," Strauss's genealogical critique of religion has eleven stages, but it can be boiled down to a basic dynamic (RR 166–7). Strauss is arguing that religion is the standpoint that gives authority to the "ways," the laws of a society. Religion is, in this sense, fundamentally political. The dynamic of religion – most fully realized with the emergence of biblical revelation – is the dynamic of obedient belief. In the Abrahamic religions, this is radicalized so that obedient belief is both absolute and completely comprehensive. As a human historical reality, religion can then be genealogically explained, as Strauss notes: "The task of the philosopher is to understand how the original (mythical) idea of the *theos nomos* [divine law] is modified by the radical understanding of the moral implication and thus transformed into the idea of revelation" (RR 165).

Strauss's use of a genealogical account of religion does not appear only in these unpublished notes, but is common in Strauss's writings, especially (as we will see in chapter 4) in his account of the emergence of philosophy in *Natural Right and History*. I am here following Heinrich Meier in implicitly referring to Nietzsche by using the term "genealogy" to describe what Strauss is doing in his account of the genesis of religion. The Nietzschean sense of genealogy involves the explanation of a human dimension – of morality, in the case of Nietzsche's famous book *The Genealogy of Morals* – arising out of human needs or requirements that precede that dimension. For Strauss, religion arises out of the need for authority in adherence to the "ways" of a people. A series of intensifications of this underlying requirement brings about the revelation of the Bible. Strauss is perfectly aware that no religion would describe itself in such terms. But for him, it is the standpoint of religion on its own terms, the claim of divine wisdom, that reason cannot refute.

What the genealogy of religion does for the philosophical life is to explain religion within the terms of human wisdom. So, from within the sphere of the philosophic life, it is able to dissolve any claim of religion (the life of belief) to be the best way of life. Once again, we find in Strauss that the way to escape the self-destruction of reason foisted on those who seek a more philosophically determinative standpoint is through the limitation of philosophy to the standpoint of a non-metaphysical questioning grounded in natural experience. For Strauss, the theological-political problem is the means by which philosophy comes to know itself *as* political philosophy.

What is Missing from Strauss's Account

Strauss expends a great deal of effort in establishing the irrefutability of religion. He presents this opposition as, simply, the way things are: Athens and Jerusalem are irreconcilable. For Strauss, this is more an existential assertion than an argument: for him, they are simply two irreconcilable ways of life. He declares all reconciliations or syntheses as failures. Large swaths of theology and religious practice are seemingly dismissed without real investigation.

Perhaps the most important historical lacuna is created by Strauss's dismissal of Neoplatonism. While less widely known today, Neoplatonism, begun by Plotinus (204/5–270), was a way of reading Plato, initially in a pagan religious context, as a way of life that was both philosophic and religious. All of the Abrahamic religions in the medieval period were deeply influenced by Neoplatonism, philosophically and theologically. On the face of it, both Maimonides and Alfarabi appear to be followers and adapters of Neoplatonism. In his accounts of Maimonides and Alfarabi, Strauss explicitly rejects the role and place of Neoplatonism in their thought (FP 362). In order to preserve the opposition of Athens and Jerusalem in these thinkers, however, Strauss excludes a standpoint that has deep synthesizing and reconciling principles. While there are a number of scholars of medieval Islamic and Jewish thought who have welcomed and endorsed Strauss's approach to Maimonides and Alfarabi, there are many who resist his reading. As we shall see, Strauss's capacity to sustain his account of medieval Jewish and Islamic thought requires his use of the exoteric/esoteric distinction that we will explore in chapter 3. This is equally true of Strauss's account of Plato: those aspects of Plato that were used by the Neoplatonists to establish their positions in Plato's writings tend to be read by Strauss as external or exoteric to the true teaching of Plato, above all to Plato's account of the ideas. The elimination of an ascent to a properly metaphysical realm (which appears warranted by much in Plato and Aristotle) is a vital prerequisite for Strauss in maintaining the distinction of Athens and Jerusalem as irreconcilable. For Neoplatonism, while philosophy and religion have different beginning points – which Strauss also argues – this does not preclude a recognition of a reconciliation and completion that is brought about from each side.

Strauss's claims about the mutual exclusion of Athens and Jerusalem are central to his account of philosophy. First, the distinction between Athens and Jerusalem points to the false requirement of modernity, which is to establish a philosophic stand-point capable of refuting or defeating Jerusalem, or, more broadly, defeating the claims of religion. For Strauss, the modern project's impossible claim leads to its undoing in the self-destruction of modern reason that culminates in nihilism. Second, according to Strauss pre-modern philosophy is also crucially limited by the irrefutability of religion. A fundamental character of ancient philosophy, especially of Socratic-Platonic philosophy, is that it remains with the primacy of the fundamental problems or questions. The fundamental irrefutability of religion predetermines an incapacity of philosophy to attain completeness or a systematic stance that might dominate its object, nature, by rising above it in thought. Not only is the object of philosophy – nature or the whole – inherently mysterious, rendering any claim to knowledge questionable, but so also is philosophy itself. The theological-political problem throws philosophy back upon itself, making it aware of its own question-ability by the inextinguishable challenge of religion.

Strauss as Jewish Thinker

A whole field of Strauss scholarship has been dedicated to under-standing Strauss as a specifically Jewish thinker, but we have only been able to touch upon this subject here. He has been seen by scholars as helping to articulate a distinctively Jewish approach to modernity, and as contributing to questions of how Judaism or Jewish thought can be sustained in the contemporary context. While there have been several books and articles connecting and comparing Strauss to other contemporary Jewish thinkers, such as Emmanuel Levinas, Emil Fackenheim, Martin Buber, and Gershom Scholem, there is an obvious tension in regarding Strauss as a Jewish thinker in the religious sense. What Strauss said of Maimonides – "he was absolutely not a Jew in his belief" – must surely be said of Strauss himself. While Strauss's "atheism" and adherence to Athens sought to honor and not to destroy Jerusalem, in his thinking he could only speak of the vision of Jerusalem as a "delusion," if a noble one (JPCM 328). While Strauss contributed extensively to the scholarship of the history of Jewish philosophy, and wrote occasional pieces that interpret Jewish Scripture (above all accounts of Genesis), it is not primarily in such undertakings that Strauss commends himself as a Jewish thinker. Rather, it is in his articulation of the theological-political problem. This articulation intends to be of universal significance, yet in Strauss arises from a specifically Jewish understanding and experience of history. Strauss shared in the deep suffering of his generation of European Jews but refused Heinrich Heine's claim that: "Judaism is not a religion but a misfortune" (JPCM 313). Rather, Strauss always and consistently saw Judaism as a blessing. Indeed, he saw the suffering and the blessing in Judaism as interconnected. From the beginning, this was for Strauss the guide to his thinking:

> Finite, relative problems can be solved; infinite, absolute problems cannot be solved. In other words, human beings will never create a society which is free from contradictions. From every point of view it looks as if the Jewish people were the chosen people, at least in the sense that the Jewish problem is the most manifest symbol of the human problem insofar as it is a social or political problem. (JPCM 143)

It was not given to Strauss to live his "Judaism" as a matter of faith and practice, but rather as a citizen of Athens, as adhering to his understanding of Socratic philosophy as a stance of questioning and abiding amid the permanent problems. Strauss lived the "Jewish problem" as the human problem. From this standpoint, above all the standpoint that recognizes the relation of Athens and Jerusalem, Strauss's thought functions as a purgative in contemporary Jewish thinking, refusing all seemingly attractive syntheses with not only modernity but Athens as well. From Strauss's position, no contemporary Jewish thinker is spared: Hermann Cohen, Martin Buber, Franz Rosenzweig, Emil Fackenheim, and others are all found wanting by Strauss – not by the standards of Athens, but by the standards of Jerusalem.

A positive "Jewish philosophy" does not seem to be possible on Strauss's terms, but his thought has proved a bracing tonic for many who seek to discover how Judaism is to think itself in the contemporary context. Strauss argues that any such reflection must begin with two fundamental tensions or oppositions: that between the modern and the pre-modern, and that between Athens and Jerusalem. More generally, all such reflections must face the theological-political problem.

3

Esoteric Writing and Political Philosophy

For many readers of Strauss, the most significant of his accomplishments was his recovery of the pervasive, but evidently hidden, art of what he called "esoteric writing." From the late 1930s on, Strauss argued in a number of places that there was a "forgotten kind of writing" – namely, a writing that operated on two levels: the first is a text's exoteric or surface meaning, and the second its esoteric or hidden, secret teaching. Strauss argued that many writers – ancient, medieval, and modern – made use of the art of esoteric writing to convey two meanings at the same time. One meaning would apparently conform to, or at least be more acceptable to, the social context of a writer – while, at the same time, by various devices (such as contradictions, obvious errors, hints, and indications) pointing to an alternative, more radical, and less acceptable teaching. The claim that writers do not always say what they mean or believe – and even say what they do not believe – is certainly not a new idea. In fact, Strauss argued that there are many writers prior to 1800 who openly state that they or other authors are doing precisely that.

Certainly, many historians of thought and culture have recognized instances in which authors did not fully disclose their complete view of something. This is perhaps especially true of many early modern thinkers, who were often accused by contemporaries of being secret atheists, or materialists, or one of the many other positions contrary to the requirements of Christian orthodoxy. Scholars have concurred with this notion of "hidden meaning" in various individual instances, sometimes even seeing it as a stance shared among certain philosophers, especially in the eighteenth century. But Strauss is not pointing to this recognized incidental or occasional use of "esotericism." Rather, he is speaking of a pervasive and fairly systematic use of it, a practice or art that is centuries old, and in which the most philosophically gifted participated.

According to Strauss, this practice lasted from the world of ancient Greece until approximately 1800. That it ended around 1800 is significant, for Strauss argues that the contemporary age is heir to more than a century of forgetting, or even denial, of the esoteric art. As a result, modern scholars have systematically failed to grasp the deeper, intended teaching of the texts. What has been the fundamental source of this blindness, according to Strauss, has been the pervasive acceptance of historicism. What historicism does is place every thinker and every philosopher within their time and their social order and argue that their thought is bound by the limits of this order and is fundamentally a product of it. This means that contemporary scholars will tend to align the thoughts of thinkers with the things that they say that are most in conformity with their historical context: the modern scholar grasps only the exoteric teaching, and thus merely assimilates the thinker to this teaching.

Now, it must be said that historicism does not logically exclude esotericism: in fact, one of Strauss's greatest intellectual companions, Alexandre Kojève – whom we will consider in greater detail in chapter 4 – was himself a historicist who at the same time accepted Strauss's account of esoteric writing.[1] Nonetheless, it is Strauss's argument that generally modern scholars are not only blind to esoteric meaning but deeply resistant to his claims about esotericism, because their historicism requires their reduction of thinkers to their historical context. Esotericism promises the capacity to escape from that historical context – and, for Strauss, the basis of this escape lies most deeply in the presence of a nature that is beyond the movement of history. To be blind to esotericism can thus appear to be a blindness to the very freedom of human thought, and therefore to assume that humans are bound to the "cave" of their particular time and place in history.

Before we turn to the reasons or causes for the art of esoteric writing, we need to understand more clearly what Strauss means by it. The terms "esoteric" or "exoteric/esoteric distinction" can have (and historically have had) a variety of meanings. Strauss

---

[1] See Alexandre Kojève, "The Emperor Julian and His Art of Writing," in Joseph Cropsey, *Ancients and Moderns: Essays on the Tradition of Political Philosophy in Honor of Leo Strauss* (Basic Books, 1964), pp. 95–113.

wants above all to distinguish his use from the sense in which these terms have been seen to refer to religious and mystical experience or language. The kind of esoteric writing Strauss wants to uncover is fully rational and philosophic. Even here, however, there can be grounds for confusion. An ancient philosopher such as Aristotle uses the phrase "exoteric writings," but seems to be referring to philosophical texts designed for popular consumption, while "esoteric" would, by contrast, be seen to refer to the more technical or strictly philosophic text that belongs within the school. So while there may be important differences between these two kinds of texts, there is for Aristotle no sense of a "secret" teaching. Similarly, in the period Strauss identifies as being *after* the era of esoteric writing, Hegel explicitly critiques the notion of an esoteric philosophy as being a hidden or secret teaching, while arguing that philosophy itself, because of its difficulty and speculative, dialectical character, is inherently esoteric. This is not the sense of esotericism Strauss intends.

Another form of esotericism that Strauss needs to exclude from his account is the esotericism that belongs to Neoplatonism, and indeed other forms of Hellenistic and Roman Platonism and spirituality. Neoplatonism saw itself as both a school of philosophy and a way of life, at once rational and spiritual, deriving from the inner teaching of Plato's dialogues. The Neoplatonist would engage in an ascent, at once philosophical and religious, to an esoteric knowledge that language could convey only inadequately and imperfectly. The development of Hellenistic Platonism culminating in Neoplatonism produces a tradition or set of traditions of philosophy that is taken up in the Jewish, Islamic, and Christian Middle Ages. This kind of Platonism lasts more than a millennium, and, while inherently esoteric, does not represent what Strauss understands by "the art of esoteric writing." In fact, Strauss's initial recovery of esoteric writing involved declaring that the obvious presence of Neoplatonism in medieval Jewish and Islamic writers such as Alfarabi and Maimonides was itself a form of exotericism.

Things are evidently complicated here. One implication of this complexity is that when Maimonides or Alfarabi indicates an esoteric level to his writings, it could be understood in one of two ways: either as an aspect internal to Neoplatonic philosophy, or as indicating a "secret" teaching in denial of Neoplatonic philosophy. It is crucial to Strauss's approach that he is able to affirm the second claim. One of the things Strauss's understanding of esotericism does is to allow him to discover in Plato and figures within the

Platonic tradition a teaching – a form of philosophy – that is non-metaphysical: for Strauss, both metaphysical and mystical forms of Platonism have built upon a teaching of Plato that is merely exoteric. This is clearly crucial to Strauss's project: his recovery of Platonic philosophy, and the nature and natural right he finds present in it, is possible only because it is not the Platonism that belongs to the long tradition of Platonic metaphysics and spirituality. That is the exoteric Platonism that for Strauss is the object of Nietzsche's and Heidegger's entirely justified critiques. And for Strauss, these critiques – just like the entire Neoplatonic tradition – turn out to have entirely missed the true teaching of Plato.

In a number of his commentaries on philosophical texts, Strauss gives various accounts of the rationale for esoteric writing and how the scholar might discern it, but he also addresses this question directly in three thematic accounts: "Exoteric Teaching" (written in 1939); "Persecution and the Art of Writing" (published in 1941); and "On a Forgotten Kind of Writing" (published in 1954). The first of these essays was not published during Strauss's lifetime, and the third is a defense of the second from various criticisms that were made when that essay was republished as the title essay of a 1952 collection. At the same time as he was writing "Exoteric Teaching," Strauss also wrote "The Spirit of Sparta, or the Taste of Xenophon" (published in 1939), which functioned as a test case for how to read an esoteric writing (Meier, *Leo Strauss and the Theological-Political Problem*, 23n32). In these early writings, Strauss is clearly articulating a scholarly program for the recovery of a lost world of philosophical reflection. According to Laurence Lampert, Strauss discovered the world of esoteric writing only in the late 1930s (Lampert, "Strauss's Recovery of Esotericism," 63–92). Lampert makes this claim based on a fascinating set of remarks found in Strauss's correspondence with Jacob Klein from this time. Other scholars argue that Strauss was already discerning esoteric teachings at much earlier stages in his intellectual development. Strauss mentions esoteric or hidden arguments in a number of texts from the early and mid-1930s. Further, even before his reorientation of the early 1930s Strauss's interpretive tendency was to radicalize standpoints, undermining more moderate, balanced, or synthetic claims found in philosophical texts, and seeking to bring to light a more radical standpoint or tendency at work in the thinker. This can be seen even in Strauss's first book, *Spinoza's Critique of Religion* (1930). Strauss's introduction to *Philosophy and Law*, as we saw in the previous chapter, shows the same drive to radicalize opposites, this time turning the opposition between Enlightenment and orthodoxy into the opposition between atheism and orthodoxy (PL 38).

In "Persecution and the Art of Writing," Strauss makes an interesting claim that seems to reflect on the point just made, and may help to establish a biographical basis for his discovery of esoteric writing:

> we sometimes observe a conflict between a traditional, superficial and doxographic interpretation of some great writer of the past, and a more intelligent, deeper and monographic interpretation. They are equally exact, so far as both are borne out by explicit statements of the writer concerned. Only a few people at present, however, consider the possibility that the traditional interpretation may reflect the exoteric teaching of the author, whereas the monographic interpretation stops halfway between the exoteric and esoteric teaching of the author. (PAW 31)

The way that the exoteric/esoteric distinction both serves, and arises from, Strauss's own tendency to drive standpoints to radical opposition suggests that there is more at work in the distinction than simply the recovery of a certain historical rhetorical practice.

Strauss's point of entry into the practice of reading an esoteric text in "Persecution and the Art of Writing" is there in the title of the paper: writers hide their thoughts because they fear persecution. Initially in the essay, Strauss argues that our blindness to this phenomenon is not in the first instance due to historicism; rather, it is a result of the prevailing liberalism of the previous century or more. This article was written during wartime, and in it Strauss suggests that the contemporary rise of non-liberal regimes is providing a direct experience of what might motivate writers to hide their thoughts. That writers have engaged in hiding their views under oppressive regimes is evidently difficult to deny, and even Strauss's critics have been, to varying degrees, happy to recognize the existence of such practices. But it is important to realize at the same time that the claim that esotericism arises from the avoidance of persecution is really for Strauss only an empirically plausible entry point: as his argument develops, he seeks to connect the rediscovery of esoteric writing to a set of more substantive claims.

In 2014, Arthur Melzer published *Philosophy Between the Lines: The Lost History of Esoteric Writing*, a defense of and scholarly justification for Strauss's claims about the practice of esoteric writing. This book, together with Melzer's extensive online appendix "A Chronological

Compilation of Testimonial Evidence for Esotericism," has been greeted by many as providing the crucial missing evidence to support Strauss's argument. One of the most useful aspects of Melzer's book is that it extracts from Strauss's scholarship four basic types of esotericism (sometimes with further sub-categories):

1. defensive (esotericism defending the writer from persecution);
2. protective (esotericism acting to protect society from the effects of the hidden teaching);
3. pedagogical (esotericism acting as a device to draw in and educate potential philosophers); and
4. political (esotericism functioning rhetorically to produce political results).

In Melzer's classification, the final form (political esotericism) belongs especially – and in an importantly distinctive way – to modern thought (Melzer, *Philosophy Between the Lines*, 125–284).

For Strauss himself, the more basic ground of the exoteric/esoteric divide is the deeper source of both of Melzer's first two types, the defensive and protective aspects. Strauss argues that esotericism rests on a "natural" distinction between "philosophy" and "the city," and that the philosopher must preserve this difference for the benefit of both sides:

> In studying certain earlier thinkers, I became aware of this way of conceiving the relation between the quest for truth (philosophy or science) and society: Philosophy or science, the highest activity of man, is the attempt to replace opinion about "all things" by knowledge of "all things"; but opinion is the element of society; philosophy or science is therefore the attempt to dissolve the element in which society breathes, and thus it endangers society. (WIPP 221)

As we shall see in greater detail in chapter 4, Strauss argues that every society is "closed": by this he means that it lives within a horizon of beliefs or opinions by which it is able to orient itself, above all, in terms of right and wrong, good and evil. Every society depends upon having an answer to what is the best or right way to live. Without a closed horizon, a city is disoriented in its capacity to act in the world. By contrast to the closed city, philosophy functions by questioning every given horizon of opinion. There is a fundamental contrast, indeed opposition, between the philosopher's way of life and the citizen's way of life. Both philosophy and the city may be good, but they are in practice irreconcilable goods. The opposition between philosophy and the city is the most fundamental ground for esoteric writing, at least the kind Strauss is interested in. For Strauss, esotericism does not arise at its most fundamental level because a particular view (political, religious, or otherwise) is contrary to what constitutes orthodox opinion in any given society. It is true that Strauss's initial approach to esoteric writing was on the basis of the persecution of views that were socially unacceptable; but now the basis of esotericism is the ways of life that are inherently incompatible. So we have moved from seeing esotericism as a device of defense (in that it is able to convey views whose content is unacceptable) to a claim that esotericism rests on the dynamic of the relationship between philosophy and the city. In chapter 2 we saw a similar dynamic at work in Strauss's account of the relationship between the "ways of life" that separate Athens and Jerusalem, or philosophy and revelation. Esotericism exists to keep apart ways of life that are mutually incompatible. Here what is being "defended" by the philosopher is not simply an unorthodox teaching, but a whole way of life destructive of the city. For the city, what is being "protected" is not just its particular orthodox opinions, but the whole social order that is endangered by the very activity necessary to philosophy, the relentless questioning of opinion. Thus, for Strauss, "Esotericism necessarily follows from the original meaning of philosophy, provided that it is assumed that opinion is the element of society" (WIPP 227).

The blindness of liberalism, then, is blindness not simply to the seemingly unnecessary practice of esotericism in a free and tolerant liberal democracy, but to the very problem that generates esotericism. Liberalism believes that there is an inherent harmony between a liberal society and philosophy or science. A historically minded liberal might allow Strauss's point in relation to earlier, illiberal social orders, but would fundamentally maintain that there is no inherent or natural opposition between society and philosophy or science, or enlightenment more generally. Strauss fully recognizes this when speaking of esoteric writing: "One may add that this kind of literature disappeared only at a rather recent date: its disappearance was simultaneous with the disappearance of persecution, just as its reappearance is simultaneous with the reappearance of persecution" (SSTX 535). For Strauss, liberalism – the emergence of a society free of persecution – was a fundamental goal of those philosophers who initiated the modern project: "They believed that suppression of free inquiry, and of publication of the results of free inquiry, was accidental, an outcome of the faulty construction of the body politic, and that the kingdom of general darkness could be replaced by the republic of universal light" (PAW 33).

Of course, Strauss's whole standpoint emerges out of the twentieth-century crisis of modern liberal democracy. For him, what is "unnatural" is the standpoint of liberal democracy and its belief that, in principle, free inquiry and political life are mutually compatible, indeed mutually sustaining. It is important to recognize that it is basic to Strauss's position that there is an inherent instability to liberal democracy, and a forgetting of philosophy in its original sense.

However, the very fact that Strauss writes explicitly or exoterically about the art of esoteric writing is in some tension with the way in which he sees this deeper source of esoteric writing in the opposition between philosophy and the city. As Strauss puts it in "Persecution and the Art of Writing": "The attitude of an earlier type of writers was fundamentally different. They believed that the gulf separating 'the wise' and 'the vulgar' was a basic fact of human nature which could not be influenced by any progress of popular education: philosophy, or science, was essentially a privilege of 'the few'" (PAW 34). Strauss appears to be popularizing esotericism itself by writing openly about what has been hidden. While earlier writers such as Maimonides or Plato do occasionally explicitly indicate a hidden dimension to their writings, they do not provide the kind of scholarly explication characteristic of Strauss's commentaries: this would obviously undermine the art of esoteric writing. So Strauss must depart from esoteric practice to bring that practice to light. To combat liberal, modernist assumptions, Strauss appears to behave like a liberal. This deep ambivalence in Strauss – between his intellectual adherence to the pre-modern and his existence within the modern – will be explored more fully when we turn in chapter 6 to Strauss's relation to American democratic liberalism.

The issue with Strauss's apparent "exotericism about esotericism" is not to suggest that he is simply contradicting himself, but to point to the deeper question at work in the exoteric/esoteric distinction. This can be described as the theological-political problem in its political manifestation, or more simply as the question of political philosophy. In developing his understanding of the exoteric/ esoteric distinction, Strauss is clarifying the meaning of political philosophy as the self-awareness of philosophy itself.

Strauss saw that the earlier pre-liberal thinkers were convinced that the opposition between philosophy and the city was inherently irresolvable. For them, what motivated esoteric writing was not simply the fear of persecution: "It would, however, betray too low a view of the philosophic writers of the past if one assumed that they concealed their thoughts merely for fear of persecution or of violent death. They concealed the truth from the vulgar because they considered the vulgar to be unfit to digest the truth" (SSTX 535). It is very important to see that, in Strauss's thinking, what distinguishes ancient philosophy from the city is not just that it is an activity that dissolves the "horizon" of the city, but also that it relates to its object in a crucially different fashion. Philosophy is theoretical or contemplative. In its original or ancient sense as a life of theoretical inquiry or questioning, philosophy is beyond the practical ends of the city:

> The philosopher's dominating passion is the desire for truth, i.e., for knowledge of the eternal order, or the eternal cause or causes of the whole. As he looks up in search for the eternal order, all human things and all human concerns reveal themselves to him in all clarity as paltry and ephemeral. (OT 198)

Because no city can have such a theoretical detachment from its beliefs and practices, the city is necessarily in tension with philosophy, both as a matter of what each takes to be "true," and as a matter of how each functions as a way of life: the opposition is between the practical life and the contemplative life. The philosopher must protect the city not only from the philosopher's contemplative, questioning way of life, but also from being required to face the fact of the necessarily incomplete, or indeed false, claims in which the city must believe. That is, the philosopher is called upon to defend both the city from philosophy and philosophy from the city, and so must seek to present philosophy as in fact supportive of the city:

> In what then does philosophic politics consist? In satisfying the city that the philosophers are not atheists, that they do not desecrate everything sacred to the city, that they reverence what the city reverences, that they are not subversives, in short that they are not irresponsible adventurers but good citizens and even the best of citizens. (OT 206)

So, according to Strauss, philosophers – or at least ancient philosophers – deceive the city, producing "noble lies" that suggest that there is a reconciliation between the city and philosophy, when by nature there is and can only be conflict. This awareness of the division between philosophy and the city is what for Strauss is the deeper meaning of the term "political philosophy," and connects the discussion of esotericism to the theological-political problem we discussed in chapter 2. While political philosophy is apparently but a branch of philosophy, what Strauss means by "political philosophy" is, in fact, the political presentation of philosophy as a whole. In this way, the apparently rhetorical issue of esoteric writing is not simply rhetorical at all; for Strauss, it leads to an understanding of the crucial transformation of philosophy, the Socratic turn in philosophy that reveals political philosophy as "first philosophy," constitutive of philosophy in its original sense.

Another perspective from which it is clear that Strauss's recovery of esotericism was not simply a question of historical research into a rhetorical device is to see that this recovery belongs to his "Farabian turn" in the 1930s. In those years, Strauss came to see that revelation – at least in the understanding of medieval Islamic and Jewish philosophers like Alfarabi or Maimonides – is not transformative of philosophy or of the whole it seeks to know, but is entirely political in its nature: it is a revelation of Law. In this sense, medieval philosophy is continuous with ancient philosophy, above all Plato's *Laws*. In fact, Strauss's rediscovery of esoteric writing occurred during his study of Alfarabi and Maimonides, and his recovery of it in those writers led to his rediscovery of it in the ancients. But, as we have already seen in chapter 2, this "Farabian turn" was also a development of Strauss's complex relation to the crisis of nihilism and to his recovery of "antiquity at the peak of modernity": that is, it was both a development from, and a critique of, Nietzsche.

For a number of Strauss critics, his recovery of esoteric writing – and above all the premises that underlie it – reveals the influence of Nietzsche upon Strauss. The basic logic of Strauss's distinction between the philosopher and the city and the need for esoteric writing seems to follow a Nietzschean logic (NRH 26). It rests on a claim that the basic form of historical life, which is the city, must be "closed" in contrast to the "open" or zetetic, questioning, character of the philosopher. It is a good question why, for Strauss, the city must be closed. In *Natural Right and History*, Strauss argues that the city needs to be closed to allow for the possibility of higher human activities (NRH 130–2). But as we have seen from Strauss's account of esotericism, the closedness of the city also belongs to the need to preserve opinion, without which the life of the city is incoherent. In *Nietzsche and the Modern Crisis of the Humanities*, Peter Levine argues that Strauss shares with Nietzsche the conviction that there is a phenomenology of identity – the identity of a city or society – premised upon horizon construction in the face of an unlivable or unthinkable "reality": the will to power for Nietzsche, the "fundamental problems" for Strauss. For this phenomenology of identity, the alternatives are the necessary closedness of the city, or a radical departure for those who can move outside the horizon or cave the city depends upon. For Strauss these latter are the philosophers. An alternative to the phenomenology of identity is a phenomenology of practices, which Levine relates to humanism. According to a phenomenology of practices, there cannot be (nor need there be) a standpoint beyond historical life; in this view, positions only develop within history. It is this latter phenomenology that contemporary communitarians like Charles Taylor and Alasdair MacIntyre have developed. From this standpoint, every city is both closed and open: it is subject to ongoing historical change within the formation of its identity. Certainly, there can be more or less "openness" to what is other than the city, but it never takes the absolute distinction of closed or open, opinion or philosophy, that Strauss posits. In this broad sense, Strauss's account of the philosopher and the city upon which his account of esotericism is premised follows a Nietzschean logic. But it is also important to distinguish the position of Strauss from that of Nietzsche within this common approach.

In a number of places, Strauss emphasizes that the difference between the philosopher and the citizen is not simply a relative or marginal distinction: it is not only a difference in ways of life, it is also a difference in rank (R 67). For Strauss, Nietzsche's desire to recover an order of rank in the face of the leveling character of modern egalitarianism is a point of contact in Nietzsche with an ancient account of nature (IPP 97, SPPP 190). The most famous articulation of rank in Nietzsche is found in *Beyond Good and Evil* and in *The Genealogy of Morals*, where he makes the distinction between the strong and the weak, masters and slaves. It can seem very compelling to see this same Nietzschean distinction repeated in Strauss's account of the philosopher, strong enough to face the irresolvable, comfortless fundamental problems of existence, as opposed to the weaker citizen, who needs the noble lies of the city by which civil life and religious meaning can be sustained. Strauss himself makes a remarkable claim about the connection between

Nietzsche's strong "philosophers of the future" and Plato's philosophers, but registers a crucial difference:

> This is not to deny that the philosophers of the future as Nietzsche
> described them remind one much more than Nietzsche himself seems
> to have thought of Plato's philosopher. For while Plato had seen the
> features in question as clearly as Nietzsche, and perhaps more clearly
> than Nietzsche, he had intimated rather than stated his deepest
> insights. But there is one decisive difference between Nietzsche's
> philosophy of the future and Plato's philosophy. Nietzsche's philos-
> opher of the future is an heir to the Bible. He is an heir to that
> deepening of the soul which has been effected by the Biblical belief in
> a God that is holy. The philosopher of the future, as distinct from the
> classical philosopher, will be concerned with the holy. His philoso-
> phizing will be intrinsically religious. (RCPR 40–1)

It is certainly reasonable to see a parallel between Nietzsche's
account of the philosophers of the future, or more generally of those
strong enough to affirm the world as will to power, and Strauss's
philosopher – but it is only a parallel. For Strauss, as this passage
indicates, the philosopher is without the religious inwardness of
the biblical tradition, with its continuing presence in modernity
and its historicism. Strauss discovers in Plato and pre-modern
philosophy generally a standpoint that liberates philosophy from
an involvement with will. Another way to put this is that, for
Strauss, pre-modern philosophy is theoretical: it seeks to *know*
the whole, or nature, rather than to change it. Esoteric writing is a
strategy to preserve and protect both the philosopher and the city
in their natural difference. For Nietzsche, modern nihilism "wipes
away the horizon" so that there can be a free, creative willing in the
context of this horizonless existence (WIPP 54–5). By contrast, for
Strauss, beyond the city there is the horizon of nature – and so the
ascent from the standpoint of the city effected by philosophy brings
with it the emergence of nature. What this means is that in Strauss's
thought the role of the classical philosopher is not primarily to
will or to transform. Because of this, the role of esoteric writing is
primarily to preserve the space for theoretical thinking.

The philosopher, as philosopher, is radically detached from the
city. It is perfectly reasonable to ask why the philosopher, as Strauss
describes him, would write at all. Strauss brings out three ways in
which the philosopher is drawn back into the city through the art
of esoteric writing:

1. the philosopher as human, as a member of the city, even if also detached inwardly, must seek to engage in defensive and protective esotericism for the good of the city and the good of philosophy;
2. the philosopher is drawn into writing because the philosopher also seeks to expose potential philosophers to the possibility of philosophy; and
3. most fundamental and internal to the character of political philosophy as first philosophy is that esoteric writing is the literary realization of the self-awareness of political philosophy attained in and through the theological-political problem.

We have already discussed the first point (which corresponds to Melzer's first two types) as the defensive and protective dimensions of esotericism. But according to Strauss, there is also a pedagogical dimension (Melzer's third type of esotericism). Strauss argues that the philosopher seeks to communicate with potential philosophers to draw such "puppies" (an expression Strauss borrowed from Plato) into the philosophic life through an esotericism that appeals to their thoughtfulness and simultaneously educates their ambition by directing it to the philosophic life and away from practical ends (PAW 36). This is how Strauss sees the work of Plato's *Republic*, in the way it portrays Socrates' education of Glaucon and Adeimantus from political ambitions toward philosophy as the life of highest human aspiration and fulfillment, while exposing the inherent incompleteness and ambiguity of political life. From this perspective, esotericism does seek to act upon the reader. Its great advantage is that it acts differently upon different readers: to the city, it conveys exoterically the reconciliation of philosophy and the city; to the philosopher and potential philosopher (the intelligent, careful reader) it conveys the opposite, esoterically.

Esoteric Writing as Political Philosophy

But before turning to the final type of esoteric teaching that Melzer identifies – the political dimension of esoteric writing that Melzer associates especially with modern political philosophy – we need to explore a little more what is at work in Strauss's account of esoteric writing within the terms of classical political philosophy, above all Socratic political philosophy. This is to explore the somewhat cryptic third point I listed above: esotericism is at its deepest

level not a mere technique but the expression of political philosophy's self-awareness and self-understanding. In fact, esotericism is
political philosophy.

To begin to approach this thought it is best to start externally
by considering the exoteric dimension of classical philosophy.
Specifically, what is the status of the apparently metaphysical
content of ancient philosophical texts, especially those by Plato? On
the face of it, the metaphysical teachings found in Plato's dialogues
or in Aristotle's treatises would appear to be not obviously or simply
conforming to the orthodox beliefs of the "city." In his teaching of
the doctrine of the ideas or of the Good, Plato's Socrates appears
to be abandoning the gods of the city; this seems to be equally the
case with Aristotle's account of God as "thought thinking thought."
For many, including Nietzsche and Heidegger, this teaching of a
metaphysical reality is precisely what is both distinctive of these
founders of metaphysics and fundamental to their thinking. But
Strauss makes clear in a number of places that, for him, these
metaphysical teachings – and, above all the doctrine of ideas in
Plato – are exoteric: the true Platonic teaching is non-metaphysical.
This is not to say that Plato's use of the language of ideas is
simply empty or meaningless, as we shall see. But for Strauss,
the metaphysical account, in its obvious meaning as pointing to
metaphysical causes and principles, is an exoteric teaching.

What, then, is the status of this metaphysical teaching in Strauss's
account? For him, metaphysics functions as that device by which
philosophy reconciles itself, *as* philosophy, to the city. It convinces
the city that philosophy, even while it criticizes the city's literal
beliefs, defends and supports their underlying rationality. In the
same way, Plato purges Greek religion of its mythological contradictions and irrationality, and points to an underlying metaphysical
reality that those myths and religious practices could be said to
figure. According to Strauss, in the exoteric teaching of the *Guide
for the Perplexed* Maimonides provides the most obvious example
of this; while apparently helping the perplexed reader come to see
the philosophical truth found in the allegorical or metaphorical
character of the Bible, and so reconciling philosophy and revelation,
Maimonides hiddenly teaches their irreconcilability, as we noted in
chapter 2. In Strauss's thinking, the philosopher seeks to modify
the beliefs of the city so as to make room for philosophy – and
even to suggest that philosophy is the best support for what is
true and abiding in what is religiously believed. So those who read

and understand Plato and other classical political philosophers as metaphysicians are getting hold of only the exoteric teaching.

What this means is that Strauss has effected a crucial result for his larger philosophic project through his discovery of esoteric writing. Central to Strauss's whole project is the claim that he will discover in the ancients a form of rationality that is beyond Nietzsche's and Heidegger's critique of the tradition as a form of metaphysical thinking that results in nihilism. Nietzsche calls such metaphysics the will to truth and Heidegger calls it "onto-theology." Strauss wishes to discover a kind of circle by which antiquity appears at the peak of modernity, when nihilism brings to light the self-destruction of modernity. In his recovery of antiquity, of classical political philosophy, Strauss builds on the phenomenology of Husserl and Heidegger but purges it of its historicism – of its relation to will, and its being infused with the "depth" of biblical revelation. As we saw in chapter 1, according to Strauss's analysis, only if classical political philosophy has such a character can it in fact provide us with a standpoint free of modernity's nihilism.

At the same time, it is necessary that this "result" already be there in the ancients, in order that it may be rediscovered by a modernity that has come to know its own emptiness. If Socrates and Plato were the founders of metaphysics, as they seem to be and as both Nietzsche and Heidegger understood them to be, then there would be no prior standpoint to "discover," free of metaphysics. Strauss's position would have to emerge as a contemporary standpoint. But Strauss's discovery of the art of reading between the lines has demonstrated that this traditional reading of Plato is all a terrible mistake, a confusion of an exoteric enactment by Plato with Plato's true, intentional teaching, which becomes available only if we follow his hints, indications, and implications.

The claim here is breathtaking: Strauss is saying that what the forgotten art of writing and reading reveals is the truth of a non-metaphysical philosophizing, wonderfully in harmony with the demands of twentieth-century philosophy, and yet there as the inner teaching of the tradition going back to Plato. This inner teaching is what Strauss's discovery now makes available. The unity between the end of the tradition and its beginning is thus effected in and through the art of careful reading. It is of course perfectly reasonable to ask whether this careful reading between the lines is not a projection instead of a discovery by which the texts are made to elicit a standpoint conformable to contemporary philosophic demands.

There are a number of ways in which Strauss's whole approach has certain features in common with what Vincent Descombes has called "the masters of suspicion": Marx, Nietzsche, and Freud, perhaps especially Freud (Descombes, *Modern French Philosophy*, 3). One could readily build up a set of parallels between Freudian psychoanalysis and Straussian careful reading, with this important difference: that the hidden object in Strauss's reading is a conscious construction, whereas in psychoanalytic thought the hidden object is an unconscious construction. The difficulties of directly refuting Strauss's hermeneutic may be compared to the difficulties of refuting psychoanalysis; both point to an object available only to those who practice an art that requires as its premise the prior acceptance of the existence of that object – the hidden text or the unconscious mind. This is by no means to suggest that Strauss's interpretations are, at the level of specific claims, impervious to criticism – they are and have been subject to just such critique. But like psycho-analysis, the standpoint as a whole is wonderfully resistant to such criticisms, tending to view the critiques as themselves forms of resistance by those incapable of a deeper knowledge.

At its deepest level, for Strauss, esoteric reading and esoteric writing belong to the inner character of political philosophy and to the self-awareness that he sees as constitutive of political philosophy. In this sense, esotericism is the realization of political philosophy as constituted through the theological-political problem. We will have the opportunity to consider this in more detail in chapter 4, when we look at Strauss's account of the standpoint of classical political philosophy. What is important to note here, however, is that, for Strauss, the reading of a pre-modern esoteric text – and above all a Platonic dialogue as the highest form of esoteric writing and political philosophy – is to engage with that text "dialectically," as Strauss understands this Platonic term. So for Strauss, Socratic dialectics is inherently self-reflective: this stance is captured by Socratic philosophy as the "knowledge of ignorance." In dialectics there is a reflection of the part and the whole; their difference and their connection. The relation of the city and philosophy is a form of this logic. The city is necessarily partial and significantly closed to the whole: its element is opinion. By contrast, the philosopher lives a life open to the whole. The dialectical moment is to recognize the connection at work even in the distinction. The philosopher's self-knowledge is to know that every philosopher is also a part of the city and so must share in the life of the city. Equally, the city, while closed, is not simply closed; it must also recognize what is above the city. Political philosophy is, then, the self-awareness of the philosopher as not simply thinking dialectically but living and being dialectical. So esoteric writing, as the art by which both the distinction and the relation of philosophy and city are preserved and recognized, is simply the expression of the dialectical character of life itself. Strauss made this point in speaking about Alfarabi's understanding of Plato:

> One must go one step further and say, using the language of an ancient, that *sophia* and *sophrosune*, or philosophy (as quest for the truth about the whole) and self-knowledge (as realization of the need of that truth as well as of the difficulties obstructing its discovery and its communication) cannot be separated from each other. (FP 366)

For Strauss this self-awareness of the dialectical character of both thought and life and of their interconnection is the especial accomplishment of the Platonic dialogue. This awareness is captured in the title of the last book Strauss published: *The Argument and Action of Plato's Laws* (1973). For Strauss, esoteric writing and esoteric reading embody the awareness of this double character to philosophical life: through this self-awareness, political philosophy as the interplay between philosophy and the city necessarily manifests itself in the argument and action of any text. The work of reading between the lines, the art of interpreting an esoteric text, is, then, to be already engaging in the political philosophy of the author of that text. Plato's esotericism is not just an external technique of concealment, but is rather political philosophy already. In this sense, Strauss unites the intention of the author – understanding the philosopher as he understands himself – and the philosophical teaching of the text. Historical recovery and philosophical understanding are in fact one and the same thing. If this were not the case, then the esoteric teaching would be lost on potential philosophers. Strauss claims that what he calls "careful readers" – those who recover the esoteric teaching – are the same as philosophic readers. This is only true, however, if what is philosophic is not simply the hidden teaching, but also the mode and means by which that teaching can be brought to light. In short, esotericism – at least at its highest, and above all at its Platonic height – is not simply a rhetorical device. It is philosophy itself.

All of this is to say that, in the Socratic turn, practice – human things – became theoretical, became internal to philosophy itself. Esotericism is born not accidentally but necessarily with political philosophy. Strauss was fond of speaking of a logographic necessity at work in political philosophy, specifically in Plato's dialogues:

> nothing is accidental in a Platonic dialogue; everything is necessary at the place where it occurs. Everything which would be accidental outside of the dialogue becomes meaningful within the dialogue. In all actual conversations chance plays a considerable role: all Platonic dialogues are radically fictitious. The Platonic dialogue is based on a fundamental falsehood, a beautiful or beautifying falsehood, *viz.* on the denial of chance. (CM 60)

This is what underlies Strauss's claim that in esoteric writers, "mistakes" are fully self-conscious and deliberate: they are the accidental and occasional raised up to the realm of necessity. For Strauss, political philosophy is the awareness of this necessity: it arises from the need of political philosophy to think its context in action. What this means is that esotericism is no longer simply a decoding of a hidden teaching, but is the art of bringing to light a second text, a second argument, that emerges from the interplay of the explicit argument and the action of the text, and is inherently political-philosophical. The "action" is everything extra-argumentative that was in the hands of the writer – settings, dramatic elements, word choices, characters in a dialogue, turns of phrase, silence, audience, and so on. All of this is part of what Strauss called "logographic necessity." The Platonic dialogue is the model of the fullest realization of the interplay of "argument" and "action" in this sense. The interplay of argument and action in a Platonic dialogue is at once the essence of esoteric writing – it is the way it is done – and the perfect embodiment of the central dialectic of political philosophy: the relation of philosophy (the realm of argument) to the city (the realm of action).

We have traced Strauss's account of esotericism through a series of stages. It begins with the entirely plausible and easily demonstrable claim that writers have concealed their thoughts because of a fear of persecution. This claim then becomes significantly broadened and deepened by seeing that, for Strauss, the source of esoteric writing rests not primarily in the content of the secret teaching, but in the ways of life that give rise to that teaching – in philosophy as a life of questioning and in the city as a life based on opinion. Political philosophy consists in specifically questioning that opinion received by authority. With this awareness, esoteric writing becomes the specific manifestation of political philosophy and in fact belongs to it as its own self-expression. The recovery of classical political philosophy that Strauss's thought calls for, then, requires the recovery of the capacity to read esoteric writing. In fact, he sees that to read esoteric writing is to engage, at the level of the history of political philosophy, in what the Platonic philosopher does in relation to the opinions of the city. The rules and practices Strauss calls for in the reading of an esoteric text are the practice of dialectic, but exercised on texts from the history of political philosophy. In spite of their very important differences, for both the dialectical engagement with opinion and the dialectical consideration of texts, Strauss's "golden sentence" applies: "The problem inherent in the surface of things, and only in the surface of things, is the heart of things" (TM 13). For, Strauss writes, "there is no surer protection against the understanding of anything than taking for granted or otherwise despising the obvious and the surface" (TM 13).

We ended chapter 1 by considering Strauss's scholarly program of recovering the standpoint of the Platonic cave and escaping the second cave of historicism through engaging in the scholarly work of a non-historicist historical recovery. What Strauss understands this work to be is now clarified: it is the recovery of the art of reading esoteric writing. Further, as we now see, this is really a transformation of scholarship into philosophy. Strauss made this point in a 1959 lecture, "What Is Liberal Education?":

> We cannot be philosophers, but we can love philosophy; we can try to philosophize. This philosophizing consists at any rate primarily and in a way chiefly in listening to the conversation between the great philosophers or, more generally and more cautiously, between the greatest minds, and therefore in studying the great books ... we must bring about that conversation. The greatest minds utter monologues. We must transform their monologues into a dialogue, their "side by side" into a "together." The greatest minds utter monologues even when they write dialogues. (IPP 317)

Strauss's philosophy is his scholarship. His many commentaries on the history of political philosophy are themselves acts of political philosophy. Strauss notes that Plato did not write dialogues with characters from "among minds of the highest order" (IPP 317). In this sense, the study of the history of political philosophy through the esoteric writings of "men of the highest order" is to engage a philosophical dialogue, a dialectic, at an altogether new level. The scholar has learned to philosophize.

Modern Esoteric Writing

For Strauss, fundamental to all aspects of pre-modern esoteric writing is the irreducible distinction between the standpoint of the philosopher and the standpoint of the city. The protective, defensive, and pedagogical aspects of esoteric writing that Strauss identifies all rest on this claim. But according to Strauss's account, it is precisely the irreducibility or permanence of the distinction between philosophy and the city that is contested by modern political philosophy. As we saw in chapter 1, what distinguishes modern political philosophy is that it seeks to change and overcome nature and the apparently permanent order of nature. Modern political philosophy is modern because it is engaged in what Strauss calls the modern project: namely the transformation of moral and political life and the conquest of nature to serve humanity in its needs and aspirations. With the achievement of this goal of an enlightened, free humanity, there would be no need of esoteric writing: philosophy and the city would be perfectly united. The blindness of liberal modernity to the art of esoteric writing rests, for Strauss, on liberalism's assumption that in good measure it has already attained to the stage of this free society, at least in principle. But for moderns of an earlier age there is still an empirical state of opposition between philosophy and the city. Indeed, the early modern political philosophers strengthen the opposition between the standpoint of philosophy and the city or existing society, but that opposition is now one that the philosopher no longer accepts as natural and irreducible but rather as historically contingent, and so seeks to overcome over time. As Strauss puts it, the modern sees this opposition as "accidental" (PAW 33).

In chapter 5, we will come to see more fully Strauss's account of the logic of modern political philosophy. But here it is important to recognize that, in Strauss's view, because modern political philosophy seeks not simply to understand the world but to change it, the modern political philosopher will make a different, more political use of the art of esoteric writing. Thus the character of political philosophy is fundamentally changing. Insofar as it seeks to unite theory and practice and insofar as it seeks to unite philosophy and the city through a general enlightenment, modern political philosophy is willing to be considerably bolder and less veiled in its subversiveness. It is, then, not accidental that both contemporaries of these early modern political philosophers and the scholars of today are more likely to question the apparently pious statements made by modern philosophers, and to suspect modern political philosophy of a more radical, naturalist, atheistic character. According to Strauss, part of the intention of modern political philosophy is to be subversive of the opinion of traditional belief that supports and sustains the religious and political life of pre-modern Europe. But equally, according to Strauss, completely explicit subversion would result in persecution and suppression by the authorities and thus undermine their efforts.

Many of the modern figures considered by Strauss – figures such as Machiavelli, Hobbes, Spinoza, Locke, and Rousseau – fairly openly presented their thought as in some tension with Christian orthodoxy, but they often did so without being explicitly atheistic, or even non- or anti- Christian. Strauss argues that the deistic or only vaguely Christian positions presented by many early modern philosophers were in fact exoteric. A number of these thinkers were accused of atheism or heterodoxy, but Strauss sees that their apparent "boldness" was strategic: first, it hid a more radical boldness, whose concealment allowed for certain elements in society to support the bold (but still acceptable) public teaching, which they would not or could not have done if the thinker had been more explicit. Second, precisely because of its vagueness, the explicit teaching helped to corrode orthodoxy by making it susceptible to a certain call to "reasonableness," which helped humanize and relativize the religious claims. For Strauss, it was the very success of this new modern political esotericism that led to the rise of liberalism and other forms of modernity, and above all to modern historicism – which in turn led to the contemporary forgetting of esoteric writing.

As we will see in chapter 5, in Strauss's understanding of the modern project as seeking to bring about a society that fulfills the needs and purposes of a free, secular humanity, there can be no reconciliation with either orthodox religion or an ancient account of nature. The hermeneutic task of the scholar of early modern texts is to engage in the art of reading between the lines, this time not to see the distinction between philosophy and the city, but to see their integration as the work of this modern project. Dialectic now serves the task of dissolving all apparent claims in these texts to a reconciliation of older claims with modernity. The power of Strauss's readings of these early modern texts is to reveal this more radical, intentional center of these works. In this we experience the modern world as willed and intended, and not the happenstance of a long and complex historical development. Strauss's art of reading between the lines gives its practitioner not only a sense of discovering a hitherto-unknown depth to these works, but, more significantly, a capacity to grasp and rise above the modern world in its unfolding by having understood its inner intention.

The Art of Reading Esoteric Writings

The rediscovery of esoteric writing is connected in Strauss's thought and his scholarship to fundamental aspects of his thinking. What appears initially as a purely factual historical question – was the art of esoteric writing practiced by many or most philosophers in the past? – takes on a much deeper import when it is given the hermeneutical role it has in Strauss's account of the history of the West. For this very reason, scholars coming from different intellectual standpoints have been resistant to Strauss's claims to scholarly exactitude. There is a whole series of issues that arise in the application of Strauss's technique. Strauss himself admits that the art of reading and deciphering an esoteric text has an inherently subjective or interpretive element, given the nature of its object (GC 6–7). Still, he recommends to the historian (who is subject to "historical exactness") – rather than the philosopher – a set of rules:

> He will then follow such rules as these: Reading between the lines is strictly prohibited in all cases where it would be less exact than not doing so. Only such reading between the lines as starts from an exact consideration of the explicit statements of the author is legitimate. The context in which a statement occurs, and the literary character of the whole work as well as its plan, must be perfectly understood before an interpretation of the statement can reasonably claim to be adequate or even correct. One is not entitled to delete a passage nor to emend its text, before one has fully considered all reasonable possibilities of understanding the passage as it stands – one of these possibilities being that the passage may be ironic. If a master of the art of writing commits such blunders as would shame an intelligent high school boy, it is reasonable to assume that they are intentional, especially if the author discusses, however incidentally, the possibility of intentional blunders in writing. (PAW 30)

Strauss continues to outline some further rules that he sees as properly guiding the historian under the principles of historical exactness in the recovery of esoteric writing. While Strauss presents this work as an act of historical exactitude, evidently subject to reasonable disagreement, as we have seen it is actually a work deeply embedded in a set of philosophical commitments. But this is what makes Strauss's scholarly project so peculiar. The art of esoteric writing is, for Strauss, the result of the gap between the philosopher and the city. It is peculiarly the mark of the philosopher that he is able to detect and decipher this writing. But Strauss has made it a work of scholarly exactitude subject to rules and methods.

Further, in his scholarship Strauss extends this art well beyond the practice of philosophers. In fact, while he attributes it especially to philosophers of the highest rank, he also detects it among much less regularly embraced figures of philosophical acumen such as Xenophon. When Strauss first started writing excitedly to his friend Jacob Klein in the late 1930s about his more self-conscious discovery of esotericism, Strauss found it at work in Hesiod and Herodotus and any number of non-philosophic authors. When he made such discoveries, he described these writings not as history or theogony or whatever genre they appeared to come from, but as philosophy (Lampert, "Strauss's Recovery of Esotericism," 63–76).

What is extraordinary is not only the seeming abandonment of traditional historical methods, but also the seeming transformation of what appears to be traditional into what is a radical disruption of orthodox opinion. Strauss's art of reading between the lines blends together exactitude or probity with radicality. He argues that in their writing such "philosophers" – who now include poets, historians, and religious figures, among others – are in perfect control of their texts, so that every contradiction, hint, or indication can be seen as intended and pointing to an esoteric text. Further, Strauss requires of these philosophic authors that they have as their inner purpose the most radical or "shocking" teaching concerning religious or political matters. While a number of different teachings are uncovered by Strauss, there is also a certain commonality among them, in terms of both the general standpoint that constitutes "philosophy" and its subject matter. Strauss regularly uncovers in texts the absence of any real metaphysical reflection; rather, he tends to focus on the "fundamental problems" as he outlines them himself, especially the problem of the relation of philosophy to the city. Further, the philosophy Strauss uncovers is independent not only of revelation, but of any ascent to, or knowledge of, God. All standpoints that might unite philosophical and theological claims are dissolved in the pursuit of the radical, shocking teaching that the city cannot contain. So while Strauss's readings certainly present themselves as seeking to open up texts beyond the presuppositions of historicism, and as recovering the thought of the author as that author understood it, Strauss's actual readings tend to rediscover his own wider historical-philosophical claims, unveiled in a series of steps and suggestions that lead the reader artfully from the "surface" meaning to the hidden depths.

The Objectivity of Reading Between the Lines

Strauss's claim to scholarly objectivity has been challenged by a number of critics. What these critics find in Strauss's approach is not a model of historical exactitude, but in fact an opportunity for arbitrary or distorting (indeed, systematically distorting) readings.

Certainly, Strauss often begins with contradictions or "mistakes" found in a text. The interpretive difficulty is twofold: (1) explaining the error; and (2) drawing conclusions and implications from the fact of the error. There are, of course, many possible explanations for an error being present in a text – for example, a scribal or printing error, an oversight, or perhaps only an apparent error due to our interpretive or reading assumptions (for instance, a too-literal reading of a text). Even if one decides that such an error or contradiction exists and that it is "intended," it is a further matter to be able to determine how to read that intention. Strauss views such errors, mistakes, or contradictions as invitations to proceed further, and to develop an interpretation from hints or indications. In developing these hints and suggestions, Strauss treats the works of a philosopher as a kind of self-complete whole, which is consciously structured to draw the reader into the deeper teaching, by the "action" of the texts through hints and indications. This is what we referred to earlier as "logographic necessity": in the interplay of the "argument and the action," a new argument or teaching emerges, the esoteric teaching, which, as such, is necessarily an argument in and of political philosophy, as Strauss understands this term. What Strauss disallows in the name of historical exactitude is that there is a history to texts: for instance, that disagreements can be explained by authorial development or that intellectual or political or historical context might crucially inform what an author is doing.

Among contemporary schools of intellectual history, the standpoint most at variance with Strauss's interpretive approach is the Cambridge School, whose most prominent exponent is Quentin Skinner. The Cambridge School can be seen as the dominant school of interpretation of the history of political thought in the English-speaking world. Skinner established a very different method for interpreting the texts that form the history of political thought in the western tradition. Strauss's ahistorical, essentially textual approach that seeks to discern a hidden, true teaching is the target of a number of Skinner's methodological writings, but especially his most important essay, "Meaning and Understanding in the History of Ideas."[2] According to Skinner, Strauss engages in a set of mythologies that distort the process of recovering the meaning of texts written in very different times. Skinner advocates a contextualist account, which he argues is uniquely able to recapture what any given thinker from the past is "doing" in writing their text. Only in this fashion, according to Skinner, do we have access to the real historical meaning of the text, rather than a construct that is more the product of the mind of the scholar than that of the mind of the historical figure. Over the last several decades, debates between Straussian and Cambridge School interpretations have occasionally been undertaken, though for the most part the two "schools" ignore one another. One notable exception to this was Myles Burnyeat's review of Strauss's posthumously published collection of essays, *Studies in Platonic Political Philosophy*, under the title "The Sphinx without a Secret."[3]

While there is clearly a deep antithesis between Skinner's contextualist and Strauss's textualist accounts, and between Skinner's historicism and Strauss's ahistoricism, nonetheless there is also a remarkable concurrence between the two approaches. Both claim to have the same object: understanding a thinker from the past as that thinker understood themselves. Further, both see the texts involved as not simply propositional (making arguments that are truth claims); rather, both see an inherently performative character within these texts: both see these texts as "political." They agree that *scribere est agere* ("to write is to act"). Skinner, building on the thought of J. L. Austin and Ludwig Wittgenstein, insists that we read texts as "speech acts." Similarly, Strauss asks us to see what a writer is "doing" in a text – and in texts (especially ones with dramatic action, such as dialogue) insists that we look to both "the

---

[2] Quentin Skinner, "Meaning and Understanding in the History of Ideas," *History and Theory*, 8 (1), 1969, pp. 3–53.
[3] Myles Burnyeat, "The Sphinx without a Secret," *The New York Review of Books*, May 30, 1985. See as well the responses, several by prominent students of Strauss: *The New York Review of Books*, October 10, 1985.

argument and the action." For both Strauss and Skinner, then, the recovery of authorial intention is attained by the reader being able to decipher or read these linguistic "actions." Certainly, one can assimilate such practices to the ancient practice of rhetoric, but is it best to understand philosophical argument and truth as being recovered under the methodologies of rhetorical interpretation? Can such methodologies or rules ever in fact stabilize meaning?

Strauss's Writings as Practicing the Art of Esoteric Writing

Some of the difficulties inherent in Strauss's interpretive strategy, and above all in his claims about recovering the esoteric meaning of texts, are exposed by scholarly efforts to understand Strauss himself. We need not sort through the various interpretations of Strauss to appreciate the irony that students and apologists for Strauss's thought, as well as critics, can apply an "esoteric" approach to Strauss, in ways that seem to undermine that approach. Far from stabilizing Strauss's meaning by getting to its apparently stable inner teaching, we have a plethora of readings that can appear arbitrary or plausible depending on one's assumptions.

There is a great deal of unclarity about whether it is legitimate to use Strauss's own techniques, or some approximation of them, to bring out a more shocking or radical teaching underlying Strauss's own exoteric professions. Strauss himself indicates in his correspondence that he does use esotericism, or at least engages in the practice of not fully disclosing his own standpoint (OT 257). For some who discover an esoteric teaching in Strauss it is, in today's context, of a fairly mild sort: for example, Strauss does not explicitly state his atheism in published texts, yet declares it in a perfectly straightforward way in correspondence. For others, Strauss's esotericism is more complete and often more insidious: for instance, that Strauss appears to be an opponent of Nietzsche, but is in fact fully supportive, except in opposing Nietzsche's boldness – or that Strauss presents himself as a friend of liberal democracy, but is in fact seeking to undermine liberal democracy from within. We will consider this latter charge in more detail in chapter 6. But it is certainly a blow to Strauss's claims that the art of reading between the lines increases historical exactness, given the difficulties in stabilizing the meaning of the author as he understood himself when contemporaries or near-contemporaries apply principles of esotericism to Strauss himself.

The primary difficulty that manifests itself in Strauss's claims about esoteric reading and writing is the self-reflexive character of interpreting this forgotten kind of writing. In the interplay of irony, it can never be the case that one can find a non-ironic stable ground. In his account of deconstruction, Jacques Derrida points to the issue of an endless deferral of meaning with which esotericism seems potentially burdened.[4] This is doubly the case in Strauss, who himself not only violates the secrecy of the tradition of esotericism by publicly stating its presence, but outlines the techniques by which any scholar exercising historical exactitude might make open to all this *"terra incognita,"* as he described it. Is this disclosure in fact Strauss's repudiation of the art of esotericism by Strauss, as Catherine and Michael Zuckert suggest in their defense of Strauss ("Straussians," 136–54) – or is it rather the most explicit instruction from Strauss himself about how he intends his own writings to be read?

This book argues that we are in possession of sufficient unpublished writings to be fairly clear about what Strauss is saying and doing in his published writings. In general, it seems reasonable to say that Strauss is often not fully transparent, and is sometimes willing to mislead, in order to make his own teaching appear more conservative and traditional than in fact it is. But while I think one can have reasonable hope of establishing the basic structure of Strauss's thought, the controversy about even the most basic claims of his position – aided in good measure by the question of its esotericism – does suggest that Strauss's apparent confidence about his use of a forgotten kind of reading as an agent of historical exactitude is at least questionable. Strauss himself was aware of this difficulty in interpreting the thoughts of political philosophers, ancient and modern. His suggestion that more conventional scholarly approaches are also subject to such interpretive disagreement is hardly persuasive here, as surely the art of reading between the lines, practiced with the radicality that Strauss engages in it, adds more than just a further dimension to scholarly dispute: it seems to disable the very possibility of a shared scholarly enterprise at all.

---

[4] There are some striking parallels between Strauss's art of esoteric reading and Derrida's deconstructive approach: both recognize the play of irony in texts. See Catherine H. Zuckert, *Postmodern Platos: Nietzsche, Heidegger, Gadamer, Strauss, Derrida* (University of Chicago Press, 1996).

4

Recovering Classical Political Philosophy

In this chapter we will investigate what Strauss described as his recovery of classical political philosophy. At first, Strauss's position appears to be an effort to ground politics and morality in metaphysical realities, so as to correct the turn to moral relativism and moral nihilism that seems to be a consequence of the modern foundation of moral and political life in human will and history. Certainly, Strauss can give the impression that this is his object – and, if it were so, his standpoint would closely resemble positions of various other conservative critics of modernity, such as the neo-Thomists.

What we need to see is that this is not Strauss's strategy, nor is it his aim. His recovery of classical political philosophy, and of the concept of "natural right" is, as we argued in chapter 1, effected in a non-metaphysical manner; it is crucially inspired by Husserl's phenomenology. Our goal here will be to outline that recovery, and we will focus specifically on a close reading of the chapter entitled "Classic Natural Right" from Strauss's most important book, *Natural Right and History* (1953). But before turning to that book, and as a way to enter into Strauss's recovery of classical political philosophy, we will briefly consider the first book Strauss published after he emigrated to the United States, *On Tyranny* (1948).

On Tyranny

Throughout his career Strauss often called for a revival of the "la querelle des anciens et des modernes," "the quarrel of the ancients and the moderns." Originally, this phrase described the debate that took place in France and elsewhere in Europe in the late seventeenth and early eighteenth centuries over the relative merits of ancient and modern literature. At issue was the presumption that ancient or classical writing represented an inherently superior standard of literary excellence that moderns could at best imitate. Those who sought to contest this presumption were not only arguing for the equal or even greater excellence of modern writers; they contended that modern writers need not conform to ancient standards of literary excellence but rather should be judged relative to modern principles. Strauss sought to revive this quarrel, now locating it in the field of philosophy, and particularly political philosophy.

Strauss's invocation of the quarrel of the ancients and the moderns was not without irony. He was perfectly aware that, unlike the original debate, what was being criticized in his time was not the thought of the moderns, but that of the ancients – and that the standards being applied to argue against the ancients were now those of the moderns. Against this modern prejudice, Strauss sought to revive ancient – or, better, "natural" – standards. Strauss's initial and most deliberate effort to begin the revival of this debate was his first American book, *On Tyranny*. It was also his first book dedicated to an ancient text, and consisted of a very detailed and complicated interpretation of a short dialogue by Xenophon. In this book, Strauss sought to engage his intellectual friend Alexandre Kojève, famous for his recently published lectures on Hegel's *Phenomenology of Spirit*. Kojève and Strauss had met in Paris in 1932, and they maintained a lively correspondence after fate drew them apart. Strauss saw in Kojève the finest living expositor of the "modern" standpoint. In 1949 Kojève wrote an extended review of *On Tyranny*, later entitled "Tyranny and Wisdom," to which Strauss replied in a "Restatement" (1950), thereby providing a living document reviving the old "querelle."

It would not be possible here to go into the details of the complicated and multilayered debate between Strauss and Kojève, but implicit everywhere in Strauss's defense of classical political philosophy is a critique of modern political philosophy, and of modernity more generally. The basic form of the critique contained in *On Tyranny* is one we are already familiar with from our discussion of the exoteric/esoteric distinction in chapter 3 – namely, that modern political philosophy seeks to dissolve the distinction between philosophy and the city that is so fundamental to Strauss's account of the classical standpoint. By contrast, Kojève presents a Marxist-Hegelian account of truth as fundamentally historical, and a vision of history as arriving at its completion in a universal and homogeneous state inclusive of all human beings. For Kojève, theory and practice, philosophy and the city, unite in history. Strauss's strategy in the whole debate with Kojève is to take a two-sided approach to the question of the relation of philosophy and the city. On one side, Strauss is always looking at the question by emphasizing the theoretical nature of classical philosophy: for him, only in its separation from concern for the city, morality, and history can philosophy *be* philosophy. At the same time, Strauss looks at the question from the practical side, the side of the city: only in the city's independence from philosophy can its natural moral horizon come to light. In this way, Strauss sees the modern project as destructive of both philosophy and the city: the turn to a historical project in modernity resulting in the universal homogeneous state is destructive of all human goods, both practical and theoretical, and can only result in what Nietzsche identified as the world of "last men" and ultimately destructive of philosophy: "Kojève would seem to be right although for the wrong reason: the coming of the universal and homogeneous state will be the end of philosophy on earth" (R 77).

The self-awareness of political philosophy that we have seen being discovered through the theological-political problem includes an awareness of the need to maintain the separation of philosophy and the city. In order to have this awareness, classical political philosophy needs to think the unity of philosophy and the city and discover it to be impossible. Strauss interprets a number of ancient texts, most notably Plato's *Republic*, that appear to argue for the need of philosophy to become political, and Strauss argues that the esoteric teaching of those texts in fact demonstrates the opposite – namely, the distinction of philosophy from the city. This exoteric/ esoteric approach can also be seen in Strauss's consideration of Xenophon's dialogue *Hiero* or *Tyrannicus* in *On Tyranny*.

At the beginning of *On Tyranny*, Strauss calls for a return to pre-modern moral and political awareness. He writes of the moral failing of modern political science, incapable of recognizing even Hitler's and Stalin's horrific regimes for what they were: tyrannies. Strauss states: "A social science that cannot speak of tyranny with the same confidence with which medicine speaks, for example, of cancer, cannot understand social phenomena as what they are. It is therefore not scientific. Present-day social science finds itself in this condition" (OT 177). So it appears that Strauss returns to ancient philosophy in order to ground a common sense that can see both tyranny and cancer for what they are. The explicit or, for Strauss, exoteric teaching of the ancients seems to provide this ground through a metaphysical or cosmological justification of this "common sense." Strauss's whole work is both to recover this common-sense standpoint, and to give to it a validity in relation to what Strauss calls "the fundamental and permanent problems" (WIPP 39). What kind of validity this actually entails for Strauss will be the task of this chapter to clarify.

Strauss's careful reading of Xenophon's *Hiero* (which is considerably longer than the brief dialogue itself) is meant to be a model for reading esoteric texts. On the surface, Xenophon's dialogue appears to be a simple exchange between the poet Simonides and the tyrant Hiero about the life of the tyrant. It is divided into two parts: the first part consists primarily of Hiero recounting the miseries of being a tyrant, in contrast to the pleasures of a private life. The second part is Simonides' recommendation of beneficial deeds that would radically improve the lot of the tyrant by making him beloved of his people. The message of the dialogue would seem to be that tyranny can be made good, for both the people and the tyrant, if the tyrant enacts things that are for the public good. This seems to suggest that there can be "good tyranny" (perhaps in contrast to "good cancer") if the tyrant follows the advice of a wise man such as Simonides.

However, Strauss wants to argue that the dialogue is altogether more complex and more interesting than this superficial account suggests. Strauss reads under the seemingly bland surface of Xenophon's text a complex dynamic interchange between Hiero and Simonides that points to a hidden teaching. The most basic claim that arises from Strauss's complicated reading is this:

> The "tyrannical" teaching – the teaching which expounds the view that a case can be made for beneficent tyranny, and even for a beneficent tyranny which was originally established by force or fraud – has then a purely theoretical meaning. It is not more than a most forceful expression of the problem of law and legitimacy. (OT 76)

The notion that philosophy can or should rule the city is, then, not a practical proposal in Xenophon's dialogue – any more than it is (according to Strauss's later account) in Plato's *Republic* (CM 137–8). The actual object of the dialogue is to contrast "*the* two ways of life: the political life and the life devoted to wisdom" (OT 79). So

Strauss takes us from his initial claim, which blames modern social science for being unable to recognize what appears to be an inherently bad regime, to an apparent justification of this regime under certain conditions, to a repudiation of "good tyranny" as a purely theoretical proposal that in truth points to the tension between philosophy and the city. All of this is to imply that Xenophon has somehow already thought through the modern project that seeks to make philosophy politically and historically effective, and has rejected it as impossible from both sides of that equation. In his review of Strauss's reading, Kojève responds that modernity can, in fact, make the "tyrannical teaching" of the *Hiero* historically actual and effective in the world. He sees this already is the case, in a provisional way, in, for example, Salazar's Portugal or Stalin's Soviet Union (OT 139). Kojève's ultimate vision is of a universal homogeneous state that brings history to an end. Strauss agrees that this is the goal of the modern project, but argues that it is not a dream, but a nightmare, a vision of nihilism and "the end of philosophy on earth."

Philosophy as Knowledge of Causes vs. Philosophy as Knowledge of Problems

In contrast to Kojève's vision of philosophy fulfilling itself in history, Strauss offers an account of classical political philosophy. In *On Tyranny*, he provides two different formulations, in tension with one another, of what that philosophy is. Each formulation creates a specific distinction from the city. The first one articulates philosophy as the knowledge of "eternal causes":

> The philosopher's dominating passion is the desire for truth, i.e., for knowledge of the eternal order, or the eternal cause or causes of the whole. As he looks up in search for the eternal order, all human things and all human concerns reveal themselves to him in all clarity as paltry and ephemeral, and no one can find solid happiness in what he knows to be paltry and ephemeral. (OT 198)

The stance of philosophy is one of theoretical knowledge, above all, of that which is eternal and does not change. As such, the ancient account of philosophy is radically independent from action or the political: it does not seek or pursue political ends. For Strauss, this is the crucial point of distinction between the ancient and the modern: the ancients divide philosophy from politics and political ends, whereas the moderns unite them by seeking philosophically to transform the political world of human interests. In doing this, the moderns shift the object of philosophy from eternity to history.

Of course, as we already know from Strauss's account of esotericism, his portrayal of philosophy's lack of concern for human things as we have just outlined it is too stark. Strauss immediately modifies it by pointing to a number of ways in which the philosopher is drawn back into the city and must engage in its concerns. He writes, as we already noted in chapter 3, that "philosophic politics" consists in "satisfying the city that the philosophers are not atheists, that they do not desecrate everything sacred to the city, that they reverence what the city reverences, that they are not subversives, in short that they are not irresponsible adventurers but good citizens and even the best of citizens" (OT 206). However, at the level of philosophy concerned with eternal causes, philosophy transcends all moral and political concern with good and evil. In this sense philosophy is amoral: it is concerned with what eternally is. But this concern with "eternal causes" seems to be a metaphysical concern. So this theoretical standpoint would seem to have been won only to become subject to Nietzsche's and Heidegger's critiques of metaphysics.

Strauss provides an alternative account of philosophy in his "Restatement on Xenophon's *Hiero*," in which he posits that philosophy does not arrive at knowledge of eternal causes, but rather is properly the Socratic knowledge of ignorance. What it comes to are not "causes," but "problems":

> But philosophy in the original meaning of the term is nothing but knowledge of one's ignorance. The "subjective certainty" that one does not know coincides with the "objective truth" of that certainty. But one cannot know that one does not know without knowing what one does not know. What Pascal said with anti-philosophic intent about the impotence of both dogmatism and skepticism is the only possible justification of philosophy which as such is neither dogmatic nor skeptic, and still less "decisionist," but zetetic (or skeptic in the original sense of the term). Philosophy as such is nothing but genuine awareness of the problems, i.e., of the fundamental and comprehensive problems. (OT 196–7)

It is important to see that Strauss's account of philosophy here is in some tension with his other description in the "Restatement" of philosophy as knowledge of eternal causes. The latter account appears to be in accord with a more traditional understanding of ancient philosophy as metaphysics, that which Heidegger would call knowledge of the Being of beings or "ontotheology." Indeed, Kojève, in line with Heidegger, calls such an account "religious" (OT 151–2), thereby suggesting that, against his own intentions, Strauss has not attained a philosophical standpoint based on unassisted reason. From this perspective, Strauss is presenting a view that our capacity to know or seek to know eternal causes points to realities that precede human will and action, and in some manner act causally upon them. But these implications are avoided in Strauss's alternative account of what philosophy is – namely, "awareness of the fundamental problems" – an account Strauss repeats in various other writings, and most extensively in *Natural Right and History*. This way of describing philosophy is in tension with the more metaphysical account. Causes are not problems. Problems cannot be prior to or independent of the human: problems are problems for someone, presumably the philosopher. There is an inherently self-reflective character to the language of problems, which goes along with the Socratic account of philosophy as "knowledge of ignorance": ignorance is a state of the knower, not of an independent reality, and further suggests that whatever knowledge is attained in this "knowledge of ignorance," it is not and cannot be knowledge of "eternal causes" – which would surely bring an end to the zetetic, questioning, work of philosophy. Further, the Socratic account of philosophy points to a relation to human things as not simply paltry: philosophy seems to be informed and determined by a reflection upon human ignorance.

The easiest way to resolve this apparent disjunction between Strauss's two accounts of philosophy within a single text would seem to be with reference to Strauss's own doctrine of esoteric writing. The "metaphysical" account that accords with a more traditional view of ancient philosophy – where Plato's ideas are understood as eternal, metaphysical causes and not permanent problems – could be understood as the exoteric teaching of Strauss. On the other side, the zetetic, and therefore more destabilizing, account of philosophy would then be his esoteric account. This exoteric/esoteric way of accounting for Strauss's two descriptions of philosophy certainly is consistent with much of what Strauss writes and is, I would argue, largely correct.

But it is not simply correct. A curious feature of Strauss's account of zetetic philosophy is that he calls it the "original meaning" of philosophy, while being perfectly aware that Greek philosophy did not begin with Socrates and his knowledge of ignorance. Rather, it began with the Pre-Socratics. As we shall see, not only in *Natural Right and History* but also in *Socrates and Aristophanes*, Strauss argues that Pre-Socratic philosophy sought too directly to know nature and, in bypassing and downgrading the human and the political, claimed a metaphysical knowledge it could not attain. Instead, Pre-Socratic philosophy produces a variety of competing metaphysical claims, which in turn gave rise to a sophistic critique denying that such knowledge is humanly available.

As we shall see when we turn to *Natural Right and History*, Strauss argues that the Socratic turn to philosophy as political philosophy – as phenomenological and not metaphysical – avoids this problem of Pre-Socratic philosophy. But his shift to political philosophy is not a complete repudiation of Pre-Socratic philosophy. Strauss ends his "Restatement" by invoking once more the language of "eternal causes":

> Philosophy in the strict and classical sense is quest for the eternal order or for the eternal cause or causes of all things. It presupposes then that there is an eternal and unchangeable order within which History takes place and which is not in any way affected by History. It presupposes in other words that any "realm of freedom" is no more than a dependent province within "the realm of necessity." It presupposes, in the words of Kojève, that "Being is essentially immutable in itself and eternally identical with itself." This presupposition is not self-evident. (OT 212–13)

Strauss is both acknowledging classical philosophy's presupposition of an eternal order, of a Being identical in itself, and recognizing that this presupposition is not self-evident: it is problematic. What are we to make of this? Is Strauss confessing that his return to classical philosophy must take up the metaphysical standpoint rendered problematic by the critiques of Nietzsche and Heidegger, not to say by its own internal problems? But we saw in Strauss's account of esotericism that Plato's apparently metaphysical teaching, especially of the "ideas," is an exoteric teaching. In his account of Plato's *Republic* Strauss remarks: "The doctrine of ideas which Socrates expounds to his interlocutors is very hard to understand; to begin with, it is utterly incredible, not to say that it appears to be fantastic" (CM 119). Strauss understands that the true meaning – the esoteric teaching – of Platonic ideas is as "fundamental and permanent problems" (WIPP 39).

From the standpoint of the ideas or true objects of philosophy as "fundamental problems," it seems that philosophy – or at least political philosophy – need not be committed to any specific metaphysics or cosmology. Strauss makes precisely this point about Socratic philosophy in his essay "What Is Political Philosophy?":

> Classical political philosophy viewed man in a different light. It was originated by Socrates. And Socrates was so far from being committed to a specific cosmology that his knowledge was knowledge of ignorance. Knowledge of ignorance is not ignorance. It is knowledge of the elusive character of the truth, of the whole. Socrates, then, viewed man in the light of the mysterious character of the whole. He held therefore that we are more familiar with the situation of man as man than with the ultimate causes of that situation. We may also say he viewed man in the light of the unchangeable ideas, i.e., of the fundamental and permanent problems. (WIPP 38–9)

In this passage, Strauss seems to be arguing that classical political philosophy does not presuppose a cosmology. In particular, then, it should not presuppose the eternal order or the eternal causes. What are we to make of this apparent contradiction, or at least tension, about the status of "eternal causes" in Strauss's account? Strauss is actually walking a very fine line. The passage from "What Is Political Philosophy?" states that Socrates is not "committed to a specific cosmology" and instead cites the elusive character of the whole. This works perfectly well when the whole is perceived to be crucially informed by fundamental problems. But these problems as fundamental and permanent, in turn, "presuppose" eternal causes or an eternal order, which the philosopher may seek to know, but can never make "self-evident." This presupposition is not a commitment to a specific cosmology – but it is necessary to establish as a basis for the fundamental problems, a basis that is more than human and so more than historical. In this very limited and indirect sense, Strauss does affirm in this "presupposition" a humanly unknowable "metaphysics." For Strauss, the Socratic "turn" was the crucial reconception of philosophy from being directly cosmological to being cosmological in and through "man," in and through the fundamental problems.

Natural Right and History

The two central chapters of *Natural Right and History* provide Strauss's most developed account of the Socratic turn. *Natural Right and History* is a complex and multilayered work, perhaps Strauss's greatest piece of writing. We will not be able to do justice to the entire work here, but in the argument of his chapter 3, "The Origin of Natural Right," and chapter 4, "Classic Natural Right," Strauss outlines a history of Greek thought, and in so doing takes us through a series of stages, bringing to light the context in which natural right as a knowable reality can appear. The crucial moment in this is, for Strauss, to be found in the figure of Socrates and his relation to the pre-philosophical world of the city.

In *Natural Right and History*, as well as in some other writings, Strauss sees philosophy emerging from a pre-philosophic context, in which the basis for determining what one should do or how one should live one's life is the customs or the "ways" of one's society (IPP 159–66). As Strauss puts it, "'Custom' or 'way' is the prephilosophic equivalent of 'nature'" (NRH 83). The notion of "way" applies equally to human and non-human phenomena: all have their "ways." For pre-philosophic humans, our particular way is right in both being ours and being ancient: "Prephilosophic life is characterized by the primeval identification of the good with the ancestral" (NRH 83). For Strauss, this involves a further identification of the ancestral with the gods and with the "first things." Philosophy arises out of a certain break with this comprehensive world or horizon, as the diversity of ways among different peoples becomes observed and (at least in Greece) gives rise to the demand that one seek to know not this or that way, but what is the true "way" or the "way" that is best by nature. Here is born philosophy: philosophy and the discovery of "nature" occur together. Strauss locates the discovery of philosophy in a crisis in moral and political life: the ancestral way is governed by authority, and philosophy arises with a questioning of authority – and, with that, shifts from acceptance to "quest," the quest for what is true or right by nature.

In a number of writings, Strauss makes clear the parallels between this account of the emergence of philosophy from pre-philosophic "common-sense" life, and phenomenological accounts of the emergence of science or reflection from the "life world" (Husserl) or "being-in-the-world" (Heidegger) (CM 11). While Strauss justifies this account by making reference to ancient texts, his actual terms of discussion are largely of his own devising, and clearly have a certain phenomenological character. We begin engaged in a pre-philosophic world of "common sense" and ancestral ways; this world is then disrupted, and out of it a more external and reflective standpoint emerges. This is the emergence of philosophy, together with philosophy's proper object, "nature" – that is, a reality behind conventions and appearances, behind "ways." The diversity of, and contradictions among, various ancestral ways as they become aware of one another brings about this moment of skepticism or doubt about one's own ways: "The emergence of the idea of natural right presupposes, therefore, the doubt of authority" (NRH 84). For Strauss, as we have seen, the most fundamental human question – the question that orients his "phenomenology" – is the question of what is the best way of life. The crisis of the conflict among ancestral ways is then to turn to nature to determine this best way. A reasonable question to ask of Strauss's account here is why, from out of this basic human problem, philosophy emerges only in Greece. As we have seen, Strauss understands Judaism as an alternative response to the basic problem: in Judaism, God and not nature is what stands beyond the many ways. But what of other peoples? Strauss does not really address this question.

Strauss argues that what first develops from the crisis of alternative "ways" is not in fact a real resolution of the moral or ethical problem. The nature first discovered by Pre-Socratic philosophy is not productive of "natural right." The basic response of Pre-Socratic philosophy to the diversity of ways is conventionalism. Nature is both what is first, and what is always. Convention is changeable and variable, and is the work of the "city." "Nature," then, functions here as a term of distinction, in contrast to the conventional or artificial, and also as a standard, a term of assessment. The natural is superior to and prior to the conventional. The natural replaces conventional authority with the good, "that which is good by nature" (NRH 91).

While Strauss is critical of it, conventionalism is a very important and intellectually powerful standpoint for him. It is the great alternative to natural right, and it is that against which the natural right standpoint formulates its own position. One of the most important things to keep in mind in terms of the larger argument of *Natural Right and History* is the difference Strauss sees between conventionalism, especially in its Epicurean formulation, and historicism. Both are making relativistic accounts of morality; both point to the variability and artificiality of conventions as a way to criticize claims to a natural right. But, crucially, conventionalism belongs to the pre-modern standpoint in which philosophy and politics are kept distinct. Nature, not history, is the standard for the conventionalist as much as it is for the natural right thinker. Strauss writes:

> The adherents of the modern historical view, on the other hand, reject as mythical the premise that nature is the norm; they reject the premise that nature is of higher dignity than any works of man. On the contrary, either they conceive of man and his works, his varying notions of justice included, as equally natural as all other real things, or else they assert a basic dualism between the realm of nature and the realm of freedom or history. In the latter case they imply that the world of man, of human creativity, is exalted far above nature. (NRH 11)

We will need to keep this in mind when in chapter 5 we turn to Strauss's view of the modern project.

As was mentioned earlier, for Strauss, the Pre-Socratic turn to nature is cosmological in its character: "The philosophic quest for the first things presupposes not merely that there are first things but that the first things are always and that things which are always or are imperishable are more truly beings than the things which are not always" (NRH 89). This claim parallels the passage from Strauss's "Restatement" that classical political philosophy presupposes an eternal order or eternal causes. Philosophy's original turn is toward nature as cosmology. But here the very problematic that produced the discovery of nature repeats itself: Pre-Socratic philosophy produces a variety of mutually exclusive cosmologies or metaphysics. This gives rise to sophistry, as opposed to philosophy (NRH 115–18). In this way, the power of human reason turns upon itself. Socrates' turn to political philosophy is generated out of this crisis in Pre-Socratic philosophy, as a way to philosophize without presupposing a cosmology.

Socrates

At the very center of Strauss's thought is the figure of Socrates. It is in relation to Socrates that Strauss's "positive" philosophical standpoint is constituted. Strauss cites Cicero in outlining something of the shift effected by Socrates: Socrates turns from nature or the cosmos to human things (NRH 120). In this sense, Socrates can also be seen to be at the origin of "political philosophy" as a specific branch or form of philosophy. Strauss certainly sees the Socratic turn as involving a shift in philosophy; more fundamentally, however, for him it is more a shift in method or approach than a shift in subject matter. As Strauss makes clear, Socratic political philosophy remains a philosophy of all beings: "Socrates' study of the human things was then based on the comprehensive study of 'all things.' Like every other philosopher, he identified wisdom, or the goal of philosophy, with the science of all the beings: he never ceased considering 'what each of the beings is'" (NRH 122). The Socratic turn, for Strauss, is a shift from trying to engage in the humanly impossible task of directly confronting the cosmological question of what is, to a reframing of what is in and through what is first for the human: this involves turning to speeches or opinion, and to the engagement of citizens in their ordinary pre-philosophic life. Philosophy as political is therefore also philosophy as phenomenological. As Strauss wrote in *The Political Philosophy of Hobbes*, "Plato 'takes refuge' from things in human speech about things as the only entrance into the true reasons of things which is open to man" (PPH 142). It is crucial for Strauss's whole position that the privileged form of openness to the whole is reason as present in speeches (*logoi*), in contrast to other ways in which one can be phenomenologically open to the world. For instance, moods are a more fundamental form of disclosure in Heidegger. This role of reason as disclosive is why Strauss can find in philosophy the highest form of openness. For Strauss, philosophy in this Socratic form is above all the effort to move from opinion to knowledge – but this is to occur through opinion, and not through a radical negation or break from opinion, which Strauss sees as more characteristic of modern political philosophy.

The fundamental discovery of *Natural Right and History* – and Strauss's fundamental claim for classical political philosophy – is, as we have seen, the discovery of the permanent problems. Strauss makes clear that this is the basis of his claim to a standpoint beyond historicism. He articulates this crucial point early in the book:

> Philosophy is possible only if there is an absolute horizon or a natural horizon in contradistinction to the historically changing horizons or the caves. In other words, philosophy is possible only if man, while incapable of acquiring wisdom or full understanding of the whole, is capable of knowing what he does not know, that is to say, of grasping the fundamental problems and therewith the fundamental alternatives, which are, in principle, coeval with human thought. (NRH 35)

Much is at work here. The object of philosophy is not, or not directly, nature understood as cosmos or metaphysical reality. Rather, the object of philosophy is the unchanging problems that, together with their alternative solutions, are "coeval with human thought." The problems form a "natural horizon," in contrast to the historically contingent horizons of the "cave," or of individual cities or regimes or civilizations.

What, then, constitutes the "naturalness" of the horizon formed by "fundamental problems"? Strauss is not straightforward here. In part, he discovers or recovers this horizon by a return to the ancients, and above all to Greek and, more specifically, Socratic philosophy. But Strauss is perfectly aware that such a return is full of difficulties: why do we not encounter a Greek view of nature as just another contingent or historical horizon? So he needs also to claim that, in this return, we are also returning to what is first, or natural in itself, but that our basis of access to this nature is through what is natural *for us*. The return to the Greeks gives us access to nature, to the natural horizon. But how does Strauss justify such a claim?[1] To answer this question we need to explore Strauss's account of classical political philosophy.

Strauss's Account of Dialectics

Strauss emphasizes that awareness of the tension between philosophy and the city is fundamental to classical political philosophy. Further, he argues that this tension consists in the distinction between what belongs to the nature of opinion, and what belongs to the nature of philosophy.

But what, according to Strauss, is the content of opinion, and what is the content of philosophy? How is this content generated?

As we have already noted in chapter 1, Strauss follows Husserl in returning to pre-philosophic life. For Strauss, there is especially the need to return to ancient pre-philosophic life, where the emergence

---

[1] Strauss indicates an answer to this question in "What Is Political Philosophy?": "A human being is said to be natural if he is guided by nature rather than by convention, or by inherited opinion, or by tradition, to say nothing of mere whims. Classical political philosophy is non-traditional, because it belongs to the fertile moment when all political traditions were shaken, and there was not yet in existence a tradition of political philosophy" (WIPP 27).

of philosophy from this life can be observed. But it is specifically the emergence of Socratic political philosophy (in contrast to metaphysical Pre-Socratic philosophy) that Strauss "discovers" to be in conformity with Husserl's phenomenology. The crucial beginning of this Socratic approach is to open the relation of humanity to the world, through the question "what is ... ?" This is important because it exposes the beginning of philosophy to the pre-philosophic encounter with "essences" – a term found in Husserl's phenomenology – which Strauss equates with the *eidos* or idea of a thing, the "look" of a thing, as Strauss calls it elsewhere – referring to the Greek etymology of "idea" (IPP 196). To ask about the "what is ... ?" of a phenomenon is to ask about it in a non-causal form (NRH 123). It is to *not* seek a cosmological or metaphysical explanation of that phenomenon, thus avoiding metaphysical causality:

> Socrates seems to have regarded the change which he brought about as a return to "sobriety" and "moderation" from the "madness" of his predecessors. In contradistinction to his predecessors, he did not separate wisdom from moderation. In present-day parlance one can describe the change in question as a return to "common sense" or to "the world of common sense." That to which the question "what is?" points is the *eidos* of a thing, the shape or form or character or "idea" of a thing. It is no accident that the term *eidos* signifies primarily that which is visible to all without any particular effort or what one might call the "surface" of the things. Socrates started not from what is first in itself or first by nature but from what is first for us, from what comes to sight first, from the phenomena. (NRH 123–4)

The beginning point of philosophy is with these irreducible "essences" or "ideas," the "what" of phenomena. As Strauss notes, the "whole" is "articulated" in and by these various "essences" (NRH 123). Strauss will describe this situation as one of "noetic heterogeneity" (RCPR 132). There are a variety of "whats" that can be neither causally reduced – as the Pre-Socratics and modern science seek to do (WIPP 38) – nor simply synthesized into a whole or homogenized:

> The "what is" questions point to "essences," to "essential" differences – to the fact that the whole consists of parts which are heterogeneous, not merely sensibly (like fire, air, water, and earth) but noetically: to understand the whole means to understand the "What" of each of these parts, of these classes of beings, and how they are linked with

one another. Such understanding cannot be the reduction of one
heterogeneous class to others or to any cause or causes other than the
class itself: the class, or the class character, is the cause *par excellence*.
Socrates conceived of his turn to the "what is" questions as a turn, or a
return, to sanity, to "common sense": while the roots of the whole are
hidden, the whole manifestly consists of heterogeneous parts. (CM 19)

In this passage Strauss makes clear the irreducible character of
the "essences." Unlike Husserl, Strauss does not seek to explain
how there are such "essences." Strauss uses a language of humans
being "open" that echoes aspects of Husserl's account of inten-
tionality but, like essence, is left unexplained and unthematized.
Strauss does regard the status of these noetic essences inherent
in pre-philosophic awareness as impervious to any alteration
of a wider cosmological understanding, such as the collapse of
Aristotelian physics or the development of evolutionary theory
(CT 92–3). Strauss here does speak of the essence, or at least of the
class character, as "the cause *par* excellence." It is important to see
that this is not metaphysical causality. An essence does not cause
the instantiations of that essence. Rather Strauss is somewhat coyly
indicating the kind of causality that does belong to essence: the
cause *par excellence*. That is to say, for Strauss, there is implicit in
every essence, every "what," an excellence that derives from its
class character. The class character is not only a description but also
a specific excellence, the goodness of that class: belonging to the
class "human" is, then, the excellence of the completeness of human
nature. As Strauss notes elsewhere, it is fundamental to humans to
"look up to something" (CT 99–100). In the language of positivism,
essences like human or justice or courage are not "value neutral,"
but "value laden." Strauss brings out the significance of the Socratic
turn to essences, natures, or ideas in this way:

Socrates, it seems, took the primary meaning of "nature" more
seriously than any of his predecessors: he realized that "nature" is
primarily "form" or "idea." If this is true, he did not simply turn
away from the study of the natural things, but originated a new
kind of the study of the natural things – a kind of study in which,
for example, the nature or idea of justice, or natural right, and surely
the nature of the human soul or man, is more important than, for
example, the nature of the sun. (IPP 165)

What is absolutely vital to Strauss is that in this "pre-modern"
standpoint, the essences are not made or constructed by the human

self or consciousness. That would be to re-enact the disaster of the modern turn to human making, and lead to nihilism.[2]

This realm of heterogeneous essences – justice, courage, humanity, animal, and so on – is the beginning point of opinion, according to Strauss. These essences become the subject matter of philosophy in and through their appearance in opinion:

> But the being of things, their What, comes first to sight, not in what we see of them, but in what is said about them or in opinions about them. Accordingly, Socrates started in his understanding of the natures of things from the opinions about their natures. For every opinion is based on some awareness, on some perception with the mind's eye, of something. Socrates implied that disregarding the opinions about the natures of things would amount to abandoning the most important access to reality which we have, or the most important vestiges of the truth which are within our reach. He implied that "the universal doubt" of all opinions would lead us, not into the heart of the truth, but into a void. Philosophy consists, therefore, in the ascent from opinions to knowledge or to the truth, in an ascent that may be said to be guided by opinions. (NRH 124)

So opinions are opinions about the "essences." This is the sense in which the city is "open" to nature or the whole. But it is also closed to that whole. In order to *be* opinion, opinion is necessarily fixed and incomplete, and therefore it is false as well as true. This is not only what allows for, but what actually generates, the various different opinions about essences such as justice or piety. So we now have not only heterogeneous essences that are not reducible to one another, but further in opinion we have opposed views about these essences. Strauss notes that if there were no essences, there could not be disagreement about questions such as "what is justice?" or "what is a god?" The task of philosophy in asking the "what is?" question is to seek to "ascend" from opinion to knowledge of essences or ideas. Thus, the philosophical process is "dialectics":

---

[2] An alternative moral phenomenology that has much in common with Strauss's can be found in the communitarian thinkers Charles Taylor and Alasdair MacIntyre. But, as we briefly noted in chapter 3, Strauss's approach requires a given identity, such as belongs to an essence, whereas for Taylor and MacIntyre, with their debts to Wittgenstein and Heidegger, a moral teleology can emerge from practices and involvements.

Philosophy consists, therefore, in the ascent from opinions to knowledge or to the truth, in an ascent that may be said to be guided by opinions. It is this ascent which Socrates had primarily in mind when he called philosophy "dialectics." Dialectics is the art of conversation or of friendly dispute. The friendly dispute which leads toward the truth is made possible or necessary by the fact that opinions about what things are, or what some very important groups of things are, contradict one another. Recognizing the contradiction, one is forced to go beyond opinions toward the consistent view of the nature of the thing concerned. That consistent view makes visible the relative truth of the contradictory opinions; the consistent view proves to be the comprehensive or total view. The opinions are thus seen to be fragments of the truth, soiled fragments of the pure truth. In other words, the opinions prove to be solicited by the self-subsisting truth, and the ascent to the truth proves to be guided by the self-subsistent truth which all men always divine. (NRH 124)

In this passage from *Natural Right and History*, Strauss seems to be invoking Plato's image of the line from the *Republic*, where the pursuit of knowledge seems to require a separate, transcendent realm of ideas that are the metaphysical cause of all that participates in them. But, as we have seen, in his account of Plato's *Republic*, Strauss explicitly repudiates such an account of the ideas as "incredible" and "fantastic" (CM 119). As Strauss brings out in *The Political Philosophy of Hobbes*, the transcendence that Plato is referring to is not metaphysical transcendence but the transcendence found in speech (the universal), and specifically in philosophic speech or dialectics as it inquires into the "what is" of an essence. So dialectics is not, as Socrates suggests in the *Republic*, a dialectics of transcendent ideas in relation to one another. It is instead a limited or human dialectics: "The dialectics which is possible will remain dependent on experience" (IPP 220). But this way of putting things seems to suggest that there is a realm of beings – noetic essences – that are available through human openness to the world, and that philosophy is seeking to recover those essences.

At the same time, however, Strauss wants to argue that the ideas or essences are "fundamental and permanent problems" (WIPP 39). According to this understanding of the ideas or essences, it is the task of dialectics to reveal the inherently unresolvable character of "what is." The source of the problematic character of "what is" rests at two levels: (1) the heterogeneity of essences; and (2) the necessary orientation of the human to the whole, of which the heterogeneous essences form parts. In Plato, this turns out to be the distinction between the "what is" question and the question of the Good. So, in the *Republic*, Socrates is to answer not only what justice is, but why it is better than injustice, the latter being a question of the goodness of justice. The quest of philosophy is to have a comprehensive account that holds together these two aspects: the "what is" and the Good, the heterogeneous part and the whole: "All knowledge, however limited or 'scientific,' presupposes a horizon, a comprehensive view within which knowledge is possible. All understanding presupposes a fundamental awareness of the whole: prior to any perception of particular things, the human soul must have had a vision of the ideas, a vision of the articulated whole" (NRH 125). But fundamental to Strauss's whole project is that, by the nature of things, such a comprehensive standpoint is not humanly available. So, from the human standpoint, the whole remains elusive, and thereby so do all its parts, even as we can come to more limited understandings of each – specifically of the limits of the city. But while it is vital to look at Strauss's claim to a certain insight into the city to understand how he establishes the problem of natural right, we first need to focus on Strauss's overarching account of philosophy to consider more precisely what dialectics or philosophy in fact consists in.

In an important passage from "What Is Political Philosophy?" Strauss addresses the question of whether a knowledge of the whole, a cosmology, is available:

> The knowledge which we possess is characterized by a fundamental dualism which has never been overcome. At one pole we find knowledge of homogeneity: above all in arithmetic, but also in the other branches of mathematics, and derivatively in all productive arts and crafts. At the opposite pole we find knowledge of heterogeneity, and in particular of heterogeneous ends; the highest form of this kind of knowledge is the art of the statesman and of the educator. The latter kind of knowledge is superior to the former for this reason. As knowledge of the ends of human life, it is knowledge of what makes human life complete or whole; it is therefore knowledge of a whole. Knowledge of the ends of man implies knowledge of the human soul; and the human soul is the only part of the whole which is open to the whole and therefore more akin to the whole than anything else is. But this knowledge – the political art in the highest sense – is not knowledge of *the* whole. It seems that knowledge of the whole would have to combine somehow political knowledge in the highest sense with knowledge of homogeneity. And this combination is not at our disposal. (WIPP 39)

In this passage, Strauss makes clear what is the basis for the incapacity of humans to unite openness to the whole with knowledge of the heterogeneous parts. There is a more fundamental difference at work even than that among the heterogeneous ends or parts: there is an irreducible distinction between heterogeneity and homogeneity based on a difference between knowledge of ends and knowledge of mathematics and the productive arts. According to Strauss, this more fundamental difference between homogeneous and heterogeneous thinking determines the possibility and character of philosophy. It means that "the situation of man ... includes then the quest for cosmology rather than a solution to the cosmological problem" (WIPP 39). Strauss tells us that this understanding "was the foundation of classical political philosophy" (WIPP 39). So Strauss is identifying very precisely the reason that part and whole can never be brought into a single cosmological or metaphysical standpoint: there is an incapacity in the human to unite thinking of ends and mathematical thinking. The striking thing about this claim – which Strauss simply asserts as true – is that it so directly opposes what Plato, or more accurately Plato's Socrates, says explicitly or exoterically in the *Republic*. There, in the allegories of the line and the cave, Socrates outlines a movement of knowing from images to the idea of the Good. In this ascent, mathematical thinking is followed by dialectics, or the knowledge of the forms or ideas – the knowledge of ends. According to Plato's Socrates, mathematical thinking is both a step to knowledge of the forms and is taken up in the ascent to knowledge of the forms or ideas.[3] In the *Republic*, Socrates appears to argue that mathematical thinking (homogeneous thinking) and thinking of ends (dialectics or heterogeneous thinking) are fully capable of being connected and united. Strauss, on the other hand, is denying such a cosmological or metaphysical thinking is humanly available.

As we have noted a number of times, Strauss's denial of metaphysics leaves us with a zetetic or questioning form of philosophy. As he tells us: "To articulate the problem of cosmology means to answer the question of what philosophy is or what a philosopher is" (WIPP 39). It is important to clarify Strauss's standpoint as "non-metaphysical," the term with which I have been labeling it: it is non-metaphysical in denying the possibility of metaphysical knowledge, or knowledge free of "opinion" or of the pre-philosophic world. But Strauss is not suggesting a simple

---

[3] See *Republic* 509d–520a.

abandonment of cosmology or a knowing of the whole. In this sense, one could speak of a zetetic or phenomenological "metaphysics" still at work in the "quest for cosmology," which is at once futile or "Sisyphean," according to Strauss, and yet "sustained and elevated by *eros*" and "graced by nature's grace," by the aspiration for the whole (WIPP 40). But it is more accurate, and accords with Strauss's general practice, to avoid the language of metaphysics, and instead describe his account of philosophy as being the quest or love for knowledge. As such, philosophy is adumbrated by the "fundamental and permanent problems," that "natural horizon" that includes the "problem of cosmology," and so excludes the claim of metaphysics to resolve those problems into knowledge.

For Strauss, philosophy or dialectics begins in the contradictions at work in opinion, and is not able simply to resolve those contradictions in a more comprehensive, completed whole. Rather, every "resolution" of a contradiction in opinion is itself inherently problematic. One way of capturing this is to say that every resolution of a "what is" question is achieved (to the extent it is possible) on the basis of an abstraction. Strauss commends Plato's dialogues as a whole because he sees them as an imitation of the whole and of nature. Any specific dialogue can consider a part, address a "what is" question, by abstracting from the whole. It can therefore only present a partial understanding of that part, because every part belongs essentially to the whole. This means that any dialogue, even in its esoteric teaching, is problematic. Strauss's account of Plato's *Republic* is again exemplary. In the *Republic*, Strauss argues, Socrates abstracts from *eros* in his construction of the *kallipolis*, the ideal city. What this means for Strauss is that a proper reading of the dialogue – a reading aware of the esoteric nature of Plato's writings – recognizes that in fact *eros*, which is largely absent from the text, is central to it (CM 137–8). So what is excluded is precisely what is vital to the interplay of dialectics; the separation or distinction necessary to dialectics is always also an inclusion or connecting. (Benardete, "Strauss on Plato," 413).

That dialectics means that philosophic openness to the whole is unresolvably problematic has many implications. Most fundamental for Strauss is the way this constitutes the very character of political philosophy, and why political philosophy is "first philosophy." The self-awareness of political philosophy is that philosophy arises from the city and is a separating out from, or transcendence of, the city. We have seen Strauss emphasize this in terms of both its character – questioning – and its standpoint, a theoretical thinking of nature. But what makes political philosophy political is that it has the awareness that, in this separating out, there remains a connection of philosophy to the city, through both its beginning point in opinion and its context as a civic act, if only in the effort to connect with potential philosophers. So Pre-Socratic philosophy is precisely philosophy as abstracted from the political, as if the philosopher does not remain human with a human soul:

> Even Socrates is compelled to go the way from law to nature, to ascend from law to nature. But he must go that way with a new awakeness, caution, and emphasis. He must show the necessity of the ascent by a lucid, comprehensive, and sound argument which starts from the "common sense" embodied in the accepted opinions and transcends them; his "method" is "dialectics." This obviously implies that, however much the considerations referred to may have modified Socrates' position, he still remains chiefly, if not exclusively, concerned with the human things: with what is by nature right and noble or with the nature of justice and nobility. In its original form political philosophy broadly understood is the core of philosophy or rather "the first philosophy." It also remains true that human wisdom is knowledge of ignorance: there is no knowledge of the whole but only knowledge of parts, hence only partial knowledge of parts, hence no unqualified transcending, even by the wisest man as such, of the sphere of opinion … The elusiveness of the whole necessarily affects the knowledge of every part. Because of the elusiveness of the whole, the beginning or the questions retain a greater evidence than the end or the answers; return to the beginning remains a constant necessity. (CM 20–1)

Natural Right

We have just made our way through Strauss's account of Socratic classical political philosophy; this account forms the first of three parts to chapter 4 of *Natural Right and History* (120–6). The other two parts are the classic natural right teaching (126–46), and the three forms of the classic natural right standpoint (146–64): the Socratic-Platonic-Stoic (146–56), the Aristotelian (156–63), and the Thomistic (163–4).

As we turn to these last two parts we should bear in mind Strauss's account of classical political philosophy, and, in particular, two aspects of it: (1) the common-sense standpoint of opinion; and

(2) the dialectical, philosophical reflection upon opinion that exposes it as problematic. The final two parts of his chapter 4 parallel these two aspects of classical political philosophy. The classic natural right teaching considers natural right from within the standpoint of the city, the sphere of opinion. The three classic natural right schools engage in the question of the deduction or grounding of the classic natural right teaching. We must keep in mind Strauss's statement in *Natural Right and History*: "The possibility of philosophy does not require more than that the fundamental problems always be the same; but there cannot be natural right if the fundamental problem of political philosophy cannot be solved in a final manner" (NRH 35). It will be important to determine whether Strauss in fact provides such a solution.

However, the first task we have is to try to clarify what Strauss might mean by "natural right." The phrase is somewhat awkward or unusual; Strauss uses the term "natural right" as a translation of the Greek *physei dikaion*, or "what is just by nature" (SPPP 138). Elsewhere Strauss indicates that the idea of justice and natural right are "identical at least for all practical purposes" (TNRH 223).

For Strauss the term "natural right" is held in contrast to (1) modern natural rights; (2) medieval or Thomistic natural law; and (3) ancient conventional right. In chapter 5 we will look in more detail at Strauss's understanding of modern natural rights. However, a simple distinction is that modern natural rights are subjective claims grounded in the passions and will, whereas classic natural right has a more objective character, functioning as a standard or end for human action. We will consider the distinction between natural right and natural law shortly when we look at Strauss's account of Aquinas. The most significant distinction between the two is that natural law functions as a body of law that "determines what is right and wrong and which has power or is valid by nature, inherently, hence everywhere and always" (SPPP 137). The standpoint of natural right, by contrast, argues that "There is a universally valid hierarchy of ends, but there are no universally valid rules of action" (NRH 162). Finally, since (as we have already seen) conventional right or conventionalism was the original philosophic position according to which right is established not by nature, but by convention or as arbitrary, it is that standpoint against which natural right first established itself in the ancient world.

For conventionalism, justice or right is artificial and thus of both lesser reality and lower rank than what is natural. In chapter 3 of

Natural Right and History, Strauss brings out certain basic features of conventionalism: it tends to a reductionist, materialist account that suggests that the natural good for humans is pre-social and pre-political, above all aimed at the natural (i.e., not the social or political) good of pleasure. In conventionalism, there is no "common good" as distinct from this natural good. Because the city is artificial, it is reducible to its natural parts: the individual humans. So there is no good that is not individual. Humans unite in cities by convention for the sake of those individual goods. Insofar as justice or right belongs to the city as a whole, justice or right is only good to the extent that it serves that individual good. It is not hard to see how Thrasymachus' account in Plato's *Republic* derives from a sophistic interpretation of the conventionalist account: "justice is in the interest of the strongest," or even more fully, "injustice is better than justice." This latter claim makes sense because, for the conventionalist, justice understood as what is commanded by the laws of the city necessarily will function as a prohibition upon the pursuit of an individual's pleasure. So the individual who can get away with injustice is better or wiser than one who believes in the justice of the city: to believe otherwise is folly and needs correction by the sophistic art. Strauss connects this conventionalist account to Epicureanism, not to denigrate conventionalism, but to display its philosophic power and continuing presence in the ancient and the modern world, where a renewed and transformed Epicureanism comes to dislodge the natural right teaching begun by Socrates and Plato (NRH 170).

Conventionalism, a standpoint connected originally to Pre-Socratic philosophy, claims to discern a nature knowable through a break with pre-philosophic, ordinary citizen opinion. Conventionalism is shocking to the opinion of the city, whereas classic natural right will both begin with and preserve this opinion: "How adequate this account of justice is, is said to appear from the fact that it 'saves the phenomena' of justice; it is said to make intelligible those simple experiences regarding right and wrong which are at the bottom of the natural right doctrines" (NRH 105). So the recovery of natural right begins from the involvement of citizens in moral and political life, in questions of right and wrong and good and bad, oriented by the ways of the city in determining the best way of life. As we have seen in this chapter, this is the beginning point of Strauss's Husserl-inspired approach to political philosophy. Natural right, at least in its classical form, is not going to be viewed as a product of some underlying source, whether desire (pleasure) or will (values) or history (*Weltenschauungen*) or metaphysics. As we have already seen, the world that appears in moral and political life is irreducible: it is constituted of "ideas" or "essences" that become available in opinion expressed in and by speech. As moral and political – as virtues – these ideas or essences appear as "ends" belonging to ways of life.

Strauss argues that to establish natural right, it was, however, insufficient to simply directly engage dialectically with what is said in the speeches (*logoi*) of citizens. Because of the claim of conventionalism that the content of such speeches was merely conventional, natural right needed to be established through "facts" (NRH 126). The classic natural right teaching, which comprises the second part of chapter 4 of *Natural Right and History*, is the presentation of those facts that preserve the phenomena found in the speeches of citizens, and as such preserves and explains citizen morality. After we have listed these seven "facts" we will briefly consider how, on their basis in human nature, they serve to justify natural right:

1. "the hierarchic order of man's natural constitution which supplies the basis for natural right as the classics understood it" (NRH 127);
2. "man is by nature a social being" (NRH 129);
3. the city as the classics conceived it is a "closed society" (NRH 130);
4. the city is a "coercive society" (NRH 132);
5. the city is established by a "founder" whose goal is "human perfection or virtue" (NRH 133, 134);
6. that such a city is founded as a "regime" (*politeia*) as the most basic structure determining human ethical life (NRH 135); and
7. the variety of possible regimes points to the guiding thought of the "best regime" as the most fundamental question of right or justice. So, Strauss can conclude, "The classic natural right doctrine in its original form, if fully developed, is identical with the doctrine of the best regime" (NRH 144).

It is crucial to see that the whole movement of thought through these "facts" is guided by the Socratic question concerning the right way of life. Strauss moves from the initial Socratic insight into "essences" revealed in opinion, to a more direct consideration of the human constitution available through the observation of man's natural constitution as a "natural order of wants." These wants show the "What," the essence of the human. As we saw earlier, an "essence" or "nature" is not merely descriptive but points to an excellence. This is Strauss's way of describing the higher human ends, arising from specifically human wants, that the life of the city promotes and protects. At the end of his chapter 4, Strauss will find a common claim by both Plato and Aristotle that there is a "universally valid hierarchy of ends" (NRH 162). In turn, such a hierarchy of wants or ends can be seen to issue in a hierarchy of virtues. All of this is really an account of human nature or the human soul, revealed in the opinions of citizens. As Strauss argues, the account of "facts" is confirmed by "opinions" (NRH 126). These are the "facts" that constitute the sphere of opinion and so are embodied in that sphere. Strauss here is engaging in what Daniel Mahoney calls a "phenomenology of the human soul" (Mahoney, "L'Expérience du totalitarisme et la redécouverte de la nature," 121). Such an account can determine what is "right" by nature, because it is based on the observable nature of the human. Further, this right will take the form of duties and not simply of passions or desires. The virtues or higher activities are then not reducible to pleasure or the rational means for pleasure. As Strauss notes, "there are things which are admirable, or noble, by nature, intrinsically" (NRH 128). To interpret and reduce such acts to pleasure or mere desire "distorts the phenomena" (NRH 128).

This account of the "facts" of the "phenomena" as they appear to the citizen can look like an articulation of a conservative, perhaps nostalgic, defense of traditional morality fully in line with the metaphysics of Thomism or a teleological Aristotelianism. Strauss, in part, intends his account at this stage to be just that. He sees his argument as compatible, at this point, with a number of "deductions" that he will consider later to ground or justify or explain the phenomena or "facts" being described in this part of his chapter 4. At this point, his account is neutral, balancing between the problematizing non-metaphysical dialectics that belongs to the Socratic-Platonic approach and the more teleological and hence more metaphysical accounts of Aristotle and Aquinas.

In bringing out the inherently social and then political character of natural right, Strauss is crucially framing the horizon of the more general claims he has made thus far. He is arguing that these higher powers or activities of the soul not only are made available by social and political life, but are crucially constituted by it, specifically by the life of the founder or statesman and more fully by the regime. This is why it is important to note the phrase "in its original form" when Strauss says, "The classic natural right doctrine in its original form, if fully developed, is identical with the doctrine of the best regime" (NRH 144). The identity of natural right with the doctrine of the best regime can only be true if the Socratic question about the best way of life can be answered by the best regime. Why might this appear to be the case? Strauss wants to argue that the phenomenon of a completed human nature attained by virtues and fulfilling the hierarchy of wants is an inherently social and political possibility – the realization of which depends upon the character of that social and political life. For Strauss, that is the question of regimes. He argues that for the ancients, in contrast to the moderns, "regime" (*politeia*) is a term that captures the whole way of life of a city or, more broadly, of a country. Strauss argues that the common translation of "constitution" for *politeia* is inadequate; "constitution" suggests a merely formal structure or even a set of functional legal arrangements. For Strauss, "regime" is connected to a determinate answer to the question of how a human life should be lived: it forms and is in turn effected through the whole formation of its citizens. This is the sense in which the ancients saw the question of the perfection or completion of human nature as inherently connected to the question of regime. Different kinds of regime (such as democracy or aristocracy) produce different interpretations of human nature – the democratic soul, the aristocratic soul, and so on. However, within the idea or essence of regime lies the notion of excellence, and so also the question of the best regime.

For Strauss, the fundamental question for natural right, at least "in its original form," is apparently answered by the doctrine of the best regime. The doctrine of the best regime seems to make fully actual the claim to natural right:

> But the best regime, as the classics understand it, is not only most desirable; it is also meant to be feasible or possible, i.e., possible on earth. It is both desirable and possible because it is according to nature. Since it is according to nature, no miraculous or non-miraculous change in human nature is required for its actualization; it does not require the abolition or extirpation of that evil or imperfection which is essential to man and to human life; it is therefore possible. And, since it is in accordance with the requirements of the excellence or perfection of human nature, it is most desirable. (NRH 139)

So the best regime is the real possibility of the realization of human excellence, and so is inherently right by nature: it is natural right. Precisely because we are beginning with essences, with natures and specifically human nature, for Strauss there is an objectivity to the best regime: it can be known. Because of the noetic character of the best regime, the quality required in its ruler is necessarily wisdom. In order to be truly best, the best regime requires "the rule of the wise" (NRH 140).

The Problematic Status of Natural Right

Strauss concludes his account of the best regime by seemingly untying, or rather problematizing, this standpoint that equated natural right with the question of the best regime. What brings about this problematization is the tension central to Strauss's understanding concerning the relation of philosophy to the city. His crucial claim is that the only natural basis for rule is wisdom, because it is only the wise who are able to rule so as to ensure that what is by nature good for humans – natural right – can be established. But as he develops the Socratic-Platonic account, Strauss will bring out deep tensions and problems with this apparently simple claim. How is natural right to be made present or effective in the city?

To try to meet this challenge, Strauss argues that the classical account of natural right modifies the best regime from both sides. The "wise" are in fact philosophers, those who seek or pursue wisdom but do not possess it. They are, as such, given over to that pursuit, and would only rule if compelled by the unwise. Equally, the citizens (the unwise) would refuse to be ruled by the wise – who are too few to rule by force – and so their consent is required in the government of the regime. To the extent that both these claims are true, the best regime is made impossible, and is reduced to the "best possible regime" (NRH 138–40) – namely, the rule according to good laws by "gentlemen," that is, those non-philosophers experienced in "things noble and beautiful" (NRH 142). So the very effort to realize or live the right way of life, the best regime that most fully perfects or completes human nature, encounters the problematic character of reality as heterogeneous and disrupts the possibility of this realization. We see here the ineliminable conflict between philosophy, as the highest human life that seeks an end beyond the city, and the city itself, which fails to realize its own wants and ends because of the absence of the rule of the wise. The concern with the relation of philosophy to the city, in turn, leads Strauss to a radical formulation: "If man's ultimate end is trans-political, natural right would seem to have a trans-political root. Yet can natural right be adequately understood if it is directly referred to this root? Can natural right be deduced from man's natural end? Can it be deduced from anything?" (NRH 145). The "doctrine of the best regime" has turned into the problem of the best regime. It seems that the pursuit of the best regime has in fact destabilized the whole question of natural right.

Further, our seemingly easy deduction of natural right from human nature – or the human soul, or the hierarchy of human wants or ends – is itself cast in doubt by Strauss's next point:

> Human nature is one thing, virtue or the perfection of human nature is another. The definite character of the virtues and, in particular, of justice cannot be deduced from human nature. In the language of Plato, the idea of man is indeed compatible with the idea of justice, but it is a different idea. (NRH 145)

Strauss tells us that virtue, the perfection of human nature, exists not in "deed" – not as a "fact" we can "see" the way we can see human nature – but in "speech" and as an object of aspiration (IPP 124, NRH 34). The whole apparently given world of human excellence with which we began explicating Strauss's account of natural right seems to be coming apart before us. What is emerging is a kind of ungroundedness of natural right, at least at the level of the city and of opinion. The three schools of natural right that Strauss is to consider face this problem in different ways. However, before tackling this question, we should review briefly where we have got to.

A Pause to Clarify Natural Right at the Level of the City

Strauss has presented a vision of natural right that preserves the "phenomena" of the city, of the ordinary citizen – namely, that there is a right or justice in the city, and that there are goods the city makes possible. These are the goods made available and fulfilled, at least in part, by civic life, the higher goods that arise from the "hierarchy of wants" and point to a "hierarchy of ends." Such an account is in contrast to conventionalism's reductionist view of civic goods. The realization of the higher civic and moral ends is achieved in and through virtues. Corresponding to human wants and ends are "essences" by which these virtues and ends are knowable and are available as objects of moral and civic aspiration – for example, the "look" or essence of justice or courage (IPP 196). In this sense, these essences are causes: they function as irreducible goods pursued for their own sake. They "cause" not metaphysically, but rather in and through human moral desire and activity. The virtues are developed as integral to realizing these aspirational ends and forming the soul to this purpose. For this to be the case, the citizen must discern the good in question: justice or courage or piety. Such discernment is a function of reason, because these essences are noetic essences. The passions must be subject, through the virtues, to this reason so that they can be ordered to serve the goods discerned. This is the classical account of how a human ethical life is lived.

What makes this ethical life possible, according to classic natural right, is the city. The regime is the structure of the city that both makes the ethical life of the citizen possible and shapes that life. In this sense every regime is an interpretation of the ethical life: it is a way of being ethical. In the case of right or justice, the regime is a way of being just. Justice is the most comprehensive of civic virtues. The best regime, then, is the best way of being right or just. In this sense, natural right coincides with the best regime. Political philosophy is the activity of discerning what is just by nature: the best regime discerned by philosophy is what is just by nature.

This is the vision of natural right that Strauss outlines as the classic natural right teaching. In the following section of the chapter (NRH 146–64), Strauss gives an account of the three schools of natural right (the Socratic-Platonic-Stoic, the Aristotelian, and the Thomist) and looks at three different ways in which to deduce or ground this teaching. The problems he raises just before turning to the three schools – the problems we have just outlined – show the need to do this. As we will see, what distinguishes the Socratic-Platonic approach, according to Strauss, is that instead of solving the problems raised, it deepens them. This deepening of the problems arises from the application of Socratic dialectics to the idea or essence of justice present in the citizen's understanding of right or justice. The outcome of dialectics will not be to undermine or seek to negate the citizen standpoint, but rather to recognize its limits; it is, in fact, only an inadequate and partial reflection of the full problem of natural right or justice. Dialectics turns the "look" or essence of justice into the problem of justice. Or, to put it better: dialectics discerns the problem of justice inherent in the "look" or essence of justice. Through dialectics the deep-seated logic of noetic heterogeneity is revealed: it reveals essences as inherently problematic. Because the essences or "looks" or "ideas" are inherently implicated in and by noetic heterogeneity, they are irresolvably problematic: they are "fundamental or permanent problems" (WIPP 39).

A city, even the best city, will necessarily be a mixture of the natural and the conventional, the true and the false. Every regime is, to varying degrees, open to the whole through the essences derived from human nature and necessary to its full activity, and at the same time closed, a cave, insofar as it must determine and interpret these essences in accord with its character as a specific regime. Precisely in order that it may produce the goods that belong to the city and to the human nature of its citizens as a hierarchy of wants, every regime must present to its citizens a "noble lie," as Plato describes it, so that those citizens may seek their purpose in the life of the city. The city *qua* city can never be fully open to nature or to the fundamental problems inherent in the being of things. The only being capable of that is the philosopher.

The Schools of Natural Right

At first sight, Strauss's account of the three schools of natural right appears to be a purely historical survey of standpoints. However, Strauss is doing much more than this: there is a distinctive shape to his survey, in which he outlines a history of natural right. First is the Socratic-Platonic standpoint, within which Strauss includes Stoic natural right. Second, there is Aristotle and, finally, Thomas Aquinas. We will only remark in passing upon what Strauss says about Aristotle and Aquinas; to varying degrees, the positions of both for Strauss represent a philosophical decline. In both he sees a limiting of the radical interplay of philosophy and the city, and an effort to stabilize the realm of moral life from the full dialectics of philosophy. The fullest expression of this tendency he finds in Aquinas, who, for Strauss, provides a rigid and inflexible account of natural law (in contrast to natural right), one that has as a correlate an account of conscience, and is inherently tied to theological claims (NRH 163–4). It seems fairly clear that, in Strauss's mind, the abstract universalism of natural law as Aquinas develops it leads to, or at least supports, the development in the later Middle Ages and Renaissance of those tendencies that will instigate the modern break with classic natural right. Strauss remarks that "modern natural law was partly a reaction to this absorption of natural law by theology" (NRH 164). Strauss's conclusion here is a preparation for the transition to his next chapter, "Modern Natural Right," where he will outline the character of modern natural law. Strauss's book *Thoughts on Machiavelli*, written and published later in the 1950s, explains the rise of the modern project out of Machiavelli's response to "pious cruelty" made possible by principles of natural law and conscience briefly outlined here in the account of Aquinas (TM 157, 186–7).

Aristotle's account of natural right represents for Strauss a middle position between original Socratic-Platonic natural right and Thomistic natural law. One way to formulate Strauss's problem with natural law teaching, especially in Thomistic Christian form, is that it seeks to answer the problem of natural right too definitely or theologically. Strauss recognizes that Aristotle retains the problematic character of natural right, but in a modified and more limited form than Plato. According to Strauss, Aristotle makes the political sphere, or whole, altogether more complete and separate from philosophy as a way of life. While for Plato, the life of the city is severely compromised by its exposure to dialectical philosophizing, appearing as merely "political or vulgar virtue" (CM 27), for Aristotle, the life of the city represents a sphere of "moral virtue" that has its own inherent nobility (NRH 151). As Strauss puts it in his 1968 article "On Natural Law," "It is in accordance with the general character of Aristotle's philosophy that his teaching regarding natural right is much closer to the ordinary understanding of justice than is Plato's" (NL 80). As Strauss sees it, Aristotle reduces the deeply problematized character of civic natural right that comes to light in Plato by more completely distinguishing the practical from the theoretical, and so he is able to treat the city as a natural whole. In *The City and Man*, Strauss writes:

> Aristotle is the founder of political science because he is the discoverer of moral virtue. For Plato, what Aristotle calls moral virtue is a kind of halfway house between political or vulgar virtue which is in the service of bodily well-being (of self-preservation or peace) and genuine virtue which, to say the least, animates only the philosophers as philosophers. (CM 27)

According to Strauss, while for Aristotle the philosophic life is the highest life, its radical character has been circumscribed and its effect on the city limited. Aristotle allows the seeming completeness of civic virtues and the life of the city as an end for the human to stand.

Strauss sees that the cost of this move for natural right is that natural right becomes "changeable" (NRH 157). The source of the changeableness of natural right in Aristotle is that because for Aristotle the idea or form of justice or right is not transcendent, the changeability that belongs to the world must be attributable to natural right itself in any instance. Strauss concludes his account of Aristotle on natural right by noting, "There is a universally valid hierarchy of ends, but there are no universally valid rules of action" (NRH 162). For Aristotle, natural right or natural justice requires practical wisdom or *phronesis* in its exercise in any given instant (SPPP 139–41, NRH 157–63). For Strauss, Aristotle preserves the ordinary world of the city and its excellences – above all, those of the "gentleman." Strauss points to Aristotle's "sobriety," which he opposes to "the divine madness of Plato" (NRH 156).

In order to understand what Strauss sees as the most philosophical account of classic natural right, we must now turn to what he says about Plato's "divine madness." Strauss takes the kind of dialectical problematization of the pre-philosophic that earlier we saw characterized his discussion of Socratic political philosophy, and here applies it to the problem of natural right. For him, Plato's Socrates exposes the contradictions and instabilities of the realm of opinion, the world of the city and its account of justice, much more radically than does either Aristotle or Aquinas. Strauss sees that Aristotle and (even more completely) Aquinas ground their accounts in a teleological or theological metaphysics. Strauss's analysis of the Socratic-Platonic account aims to show it is without such a standpoint.

In the section of *Natural Right and History* dedicated to the Socratic-Platonic-Stoic account (NRH 126–46), Strauss makes what one commentator has described as two ascents – that is, two ways in which dialectics problematizes the standpoint of justice as the city understands it. One of these ascents is by following the "idea of justice," and the other is by following the "idea of man" (Kennington, "Strauss's *Natural Right and History*," 77). In his discussion of both cases of "ascent," Strauss brings out a radicalization of natural right, a transcendence of its instantiation in the city. In Strauss's analysis, the source of the instability of natural right and the idea of justice rests in its having a double aspect: on the one hand, justice is giving each his due (above all, what is due according to the law of the city); on the other hand, justice is what is good for each. As we saw earlier, this doubleness is a form of the dialectics of part and whole that Strauss sees as characteristic of the human condition. It is the second aspect, the relation of justice to the good – of part to whole – that is so destabilizing and leads to what Richard Kennington calls the two "ascents."

The first ascent (NRH 148–50) occurs through reflection on the contradiction between the demands of the idea of right or justice and the requirements of the city as a specific city. This is achieved, in accord with the pure requirements of the idea of justice, by retracting any arbitrary limitations that might contradict justice. As Strauss pushes at the idea of justice here, he expands it to become a principle of universal justice requiring divine providential guidance or the rule of wise citizens over all of humanity. Every limit on justice in time or space seems arbitrary, and so is a source of injustice. If we follow Strauss's logic of justice here, we must arrive at a universal state under the rule of wisdom. Strauss connects this development to the way that Stoicism and its cosmopolitanism are implied by the demand that justice be good, be the whole. But the resulting divinely sustained cosmopolitanism is, as Strauss notes, something that "obviously transcends the limits of political life" (NRH 151).

The second ascent (NRH 151–3), the ascent according to the idea of man, begins with the need for the city to be ruled by the wise, but at the same time breaks through the limits of the city in pursuing justice as what is good for the human. What emerges in Strauss's argument here is that philosophy transcends the good of the city; it is apparent that the only true realization of natural right is the life of the philosopher and not the life of the citizen. Strauss draws upon his reading of Plato's *Republic* in arguing that for Plato – for the Socratic turn – the philosophic life is the only fully just life, the only fully human life. The standpoint of the philosopher-king, as described in the *Republic*, brings with it a knowledge of the tension between the idea of justice and natural right, and the limitations inherent in the city:

> In descending into the cave, the philosopher admits that what is intrinsically or by nature the highest is not the most urgent for man, who is essentially an "in-between" being – between the brutes and the gods. When attempting to guide the city, he knows then in advance that, in order to be useful or good for the city, the requirements of wisdom must be qualified or diluted. If these requirements are identical with natural right or with natural law, natural right or natural law must be diluted in order to become compatible with the requirements of the city. (NRH 152)

The justice of the city is, then, necessarily riddled with convention and with what is, from the standpoint of the idea of justice, unjust. This is the standpoint of "vulgar or popular virtue" (NRH 151). Strauss radicalizes this claim: "From this point of view the man who is merely just or moral without being a philosopher appears as a mutilated human being. It thus becomes a question whether the moral or just man who is not a philosopher is simply superior to the nonphilosophic 'erotic' man" (NRH 151). In the context of the *Republic*, the "erotic man" refers to the tyrant, the figure who overthrows the just order of the city. Strauss appears to argue that, from the standpoint of the philosopher, the moral or just citizen and the erotic tyrant are indistinguishable. From this perspective, it becomes difficult to see whether Strauss is affirming moral and political life at all. In what way is the Platonic standpoint, as Strauss has outlined it, any different from that of the sophist or, more significantly, from that of the Epicurean philosopher for whom all civic morality is merely conventional, driven by the calculations and necessities of human needs and pleasures?

At this point, Strauss's account of Socratic natural right can seem to open the door to the very moral nihilism for which Strauss presents his position as the remedy. That is: how is Strauss's philosopher, who dialectically rises above civic morality, not just another form of Nietzsche's *Übermensch* ("Overman"), beyond good and evil? Certainly, in his "philosopher," Strauss seeks – as Nietzsche does in his "philosopher of the future" – a standpoint beyond the moralizing humanism that he sees everywhere in the modern project (RCPR 40–1). But in contrast to the Nietzschean "philosopher of the future," the Straussian philosopher, open to the fundamental and permanent problems, does not seek to transform the standpoint of the city. In fact, for the sake of his own philosophic reflection and self-understanding, Strauss's Socratic political philosopher seeks to preserve and protect the standpoint of the city and its limited, but still noble, moral horizon.

This is, of course, just another form of the question we asked in terms of the status of the Socratic or Platonic philosopher. Strauss is looking at the "in-between" status of human moral and political life from two sides: the dilution of natural right means the city is necessarily, to a lesser or greater extent, both just and unjust, both natural and conventional. This inescapable "in-between" status of civic moral life is another aspect of the problematic character of the heterogeneous whole. For Strauss, the great merit of the Platonic standpoint, in contrast to either the Aristotelian or the Thomistic standpoint, is the clear and perspicuous awareness that civic moral life, civic justice, is problematic. What distinguishes the philosopher from the citizen in this Platonic account is precisely the capacity to live in and through this awareness of the fundamental problems, and to love the pursuit of a more complete understanding of these problems. The self-referentiality of the philosophic life is the place where awareness, and that of which one is aware, unite: such union is attained in Socratic ignorance (OT 196). For Plato, according to Strauss, the best life, the most just life, and the most self-sufficient life is the philosophic life. So the city is simultaneously vulgar, from the perspective of the philosopher *qua* philosopher, and noble, from the perspective of the citizen *qua* citizen, a standpoint that the philosopher *qua* political philosopher also has a share in.

According to Strauss's account of the Socratic-Platonic standpoint, pure natural right, the idea of justice, is "dynamite for civil society" (NRH 153). We have already seen the explosive capacity of natural right in the two ascents Strauss describes. Natural right exceeds the city in terms of both the limits and determinations inherent in the city, and the life most in accord with natural right: the life of the philosopher. But what this recognition of the problem of natural right for the city is, of course, returning us to is the tension and opposition between the life of the city, which requires opinion, political opinion, as constitutive of its way of life, and the life of the philosopher, which is constituted by the dialectical, zetetic questioning of that opinion. The horizon of the city cannot be the natural or absolute horizon of the philosopher. Strauss returns us, then, to the primacy of the political philosopher, in both pursuing the philosophical ascent from the opinions of the city and securing the way for philosophy to co-exist with the city.

In his correspondence with Eric Voegelin, Strauss states that, in *Natural Right and History*, "I do nothing more than present the *problem* of natural right as an unsolved problem" (FPP 74). Yet in *The City and Man*, at the end of his long chapter on Plato's *Republic*, he can also say:

> The teaching of the *Republic* regarding justice can be true although it is not complete, in so far as the nature of justice depends decisively on the nature of the city – for even the trans-political cannot be understood as such except if the city is understood – and the city is completely intelligible because its limits can be made perfectly manifest: to see these limits, one need not have answered the question regarding the whole; it is sufficient for the purpose to have raised the

question regarding the whole. The *Republic* then indeed makes clear what justice is. As Cicero has observed, the *Republic* does not bring to light the best possible regime but rather the nature of political things – the nature of the city. Socrates makes clear in the *Republic* of what character the city would have to be in order to satisfy the highest need of man. By letting us see that the city constructed in accordance with this requirement is not possible, he lets us see the essential limits, the nature, of the city. (CM 138)

According to Strauss, then, justice – the idea of natural right – entails and is the essence of the relation between the city and philosophy. In *Natural Right and History*, Strauss states that "there cannot be natural right if the fundamental problem of political philosophy cannot be solved in a final manner" (NRH 35). Natural right precisely as a problem also reveals the limits and, thereby, the nature of the city. The problem of natural right reveals itself in the irreconcilable opposition between philosophy and the city, and in doing so it reveals the natural or eternal or "final" character of philosophy as political philosophy. It is in this sense that Strauss indicates that "in a final manner" the problem of natural right solves "the fundamental problem of political philosophy" (NRH 35). In short, justice, or natural right, embodied in and as the revival of the tension between philosophy and the city, brings to light and reveals itself as "political philosophy."

Recovery or Project?

As a conclusion to this chapter, we should clarify what I would argue is the most fundamental claim at work in Strauss's whole project. His account of classic political philosophy, which we have just worked through, is in Strauss's understanding a recovery of what belonged to the ancient world, and not a projection of a contemporary standpoint upon ancient writings. At the beginning of *The City and Man*, Strauss makes it clear that the motivation for his return is contemporary: "It is not self-forgetting and pain-loving antiquarianism nor self-forgetting and intoxicating romanticism which induces us to turn with passionate interest, with unqual-ified willingness to learn, toward the political thought of classical antiquity. We are impelled to do so by the crisis of our time, the crisis of the West" (CM 1). But while his motivation may be contem-porary, Strauss argues that what he has learned about the nature of philosophy from Husserl and Heidegger opens him up to what is at work in the original philosophizing of Socrates and Plato, Xenophon and Aristotle. Strauss finds a distinctive non-historicist "phenomenology" (using the term very broadly), inspired above all by Husserl, to open up what is at work in Plato or Aristotle. Strauss leaves behind the egological character of Husserl's "constitutive phenomenology," breaking with what he sees as a residual modernity in Husserl's account. Nonetheless, the philosophic project Strauss outlines in its own right, and which he discovers more concretely in the ancients, bears striking and obvious parallels to Husserl and, to a certain extent, to Heidegger.[4]

Strauss needs to claim three things:

1. Socratic political philosophy coincides with the phenomenological approach opened up by Husserl and Heidegger.
2. This understanding of Socrates, available through Plato and the other Socratics more generally, is a true return to these thinkers as they understood themselves.
3. Socratic political philosophy, so recovered, gives access to nature as an absolute horizon of fundamental problems.

It is worth pausing at this point to ask whether what Strauss is engaging in is in fact a phenomenological projection upon Socrates, or a "recovery." Is Strauss really finding the Socratic standpoint? Is he really reading these texts as their authors understood them? And has he, in doing all this, really recovered the horizon of nature? As we have seen, Strauss is clearly conscious of his use of the general approach Husserl applied to philosophy in his appropriation of classical political philosophy. That a phenomenological approach also coincides with a recovery of ancient thought arises from Strauss's account of the circularity of the western development: Strauss sees that nihilism opened up the possibility of a "radical" contemporary recovery of the healthy "roots" of philosophy itself. In turning to these origins, free of a self-destroying historicism, nature is made accessible.

Certainly, Strauss does not develop an independent contemporary philosophical standpoint and then apply it to earlier thought,

---

[4] So, even in the quotation cited above that speaks of a "natural horizon," the language of "horizon" is an obviously significant aspect of phenomenological analysis that has no ancient equivalent. When Strauss compares the "cave" to changing historical "horizons," this is obviously an interpretation.

as one could accuse Heidegger of doing. Rather, he "discovers" in these pre-modern texts this standpoint. One could equally argue, however, that this very "discovery" is already predetermined by its contemporary beginning point in the "crisis of our time." In short, there is a hermeneutical circle here: the only question is whether it is an open or a closed one.

5

The Critique of Modernity

Perhaps the most compelling aspect of Leo Strauss's thought is his critique of the modern world. As we have seen, like Nietzsche and Heidegger, Strauss understands the West to be in the grip of a profound spiritual crisis. And, also following Nietzsche and Heidegger, Strauss sees that this crisis itself opens up the possibility of a release from modernity. Such a release, for Strauss, both brings to light a principle or reality forgotten by modernity, and at the same time points to a return to those origins, free from and prior to the sources of modernity.

As we saw in chapter 1, unlike Nietzsche or Heidegger, Strauss does not trace modernity to the metaphysical turn that began with Socrates and Plato, nor to what Nietzsche called "the slave revolt of morality" that received its most decisive impetus from Judaism and then Christianity. Rather, Strauss sees the roots of contemporary nihilism in the deliberate reformulation of political philosophy achieved by the great early modern thinkers, particularly Machiavelli and Hobbes (WIPP 40–9, 172). The source of modernity, according to Strauss, lies not in a metaphysical, religious, or even scientific transformation, but rather in a fundamental alteration of how political and moral things were understood (PPH 129). He sees the history of modernity above all as a history of the further development of this initial alteration in political philosophy.

This development culminates in what Strauss called the "cave beneath the cave," an unnatural cave below the cave described in Plato's *Republic*. As we learned in chapter 4, the Platonic cave – the city, the world of opinion – is the beginning point of philosophy, a beginning open to nature and to the problem of natural right. The modern construction of this second, deeper cave, cut off from nature, is, then, a condition of our loss of contact with what is naturally "first for us." In this second cave, we moderns have lost contact with "those simple experiences regarding right and wrong which are at the bottom of the natural right doctrines" (NRH 105). According to Strauss, it is modern political thought that has constructed the second cave: for him, historicism, and the nihilism that arises from it, are the outcome of modern political philosophy. It is Strauss's understanding of the source of this nihilism that we need to sketch in this chapter.

For Strauss there is a history or development to historicism itself. Historicism by no means arises simply from the fact of historical and cultural diversity that seems to point to the conventional character of natural right or human opinion; this was known by the ancients, and actually was the basis for the discovery by classical philosophy of natural right in contrast to the seeming variety of opinion. Strauss will point instead to features of Machiavelli's and Hobbes's founding of modern political philosophy as constituting the basis for historicism. In this way, he sees historicism as arising from certain aspects of modernity as a project, and as the culmination of modernity.

The full realization of the culmination of modernity, which Strauss calls radical historicism, he finds in Nietzsche, and more completely in Heidegger. We saw in chapter 1 that Strauss identified in Nietzsche's principle of a will to power not only a radical historicism, but also an intention beyond it in a return to nature (WIPP 55, RSM 153). What characterizes "radical historicism" in the hands of Heidegger is, for Strauss, that it makes the human (*Dasein*) inherently historical in its very being. The term Heidegger uses to describe this more radical stance is "historicity." That is, history is understood not simply to be the factual and contingent changes that happen in human life and to human institutions and collectivities, but to mean that the very being of the human – what Heidegger calls the "existential" – is temporality. The implication of this is that the human exists only in and through time. There is no truth that is not temporal truth. For Strauss this means that philosophy, and specifically political philosophy, is impossible: there can be no quest for truth or wisdom per se; all "truth" is historically contingent and radically relative. There can be no access to nature. All knowing is only in, by, and through a dispensation that is finite, contingent, and changeable. For Strauss, this radical historicism exposes and accepts the apparent self-contradiction that if historicism is true, then it itself is subject to history and cannot be true for all times and places: it cannot be simply true. Strauss sees that Heidegger builds this tension into his whole standpoint.

For Strauss, the self-negating character of historicism points not so much to its intellectual refutation as to its impossibility for humanity:

> Modern thought reaches its culmination, its highest self-consciousness, in the most radical historicism, i.e., in explicitly condemning to oblivion the notion of eternity. For oblivion of eternity, or, in other words, estrangement from man's deepest desire and therewith from the primary issues, is the price which modern man had to pay, from the very beginning, for attempting to be absolutely sovereign, to become the master and owner of nature, to conquer chance. (WIPP 55)

As Strauss puts it elsewhere, "the crisis of modernity is then primarily the crisis of modern political philosophy" (IPP 82). It is for him the crisis of our time because it brings into question the moving principle of modernity: this crisis "consists in the fact that the West has become uncertain of its purpose" (CT 42). That purpose Strauss terms "the Modern Project" (CT 41), and he describes that purpose or project as "the universal society, a society consisting of equal nations, each consisting of free and equal men and women, with all these nations to be fully developed as regards their power of production, thanks to science" (CT 42). Strauss equates the project of modernity with the realization of a revolutionary humanism, a humanism released from the constraints of an older institutional order (SPPP 143–4). The revolutionary politics of the nineteenth century was animated by just such a vision, whether in a liberal or socialist form. The revolutionaries presumed that the substance of the nineteenth-century nation state would pass into the hands of an emancipated humanity.

It was of course Karl Marx who argued most forcefully that the European nation state, with its capacity to form citizens to higher moral and political ends, had the roots of its dissolution in early modern Europe. It is perhaps ironic that Strauss follows Marx in locating the source of revolutionary humanism in the early modern period. Strauss and Marx agree that the origin of this revolutionary result must be found in the beginnings of modernity. For both Marx and Strauss, there is a revolutionary innovation at the origins of modernity that cannot be contained within the traditional structures of European social and political life, but that is necessarily antithetical to them. However, Strauss finds the source of this revolutionary modernity in the political philosophy of the period, whereas Marx sees that philosophy as only the "epiphenomenon" of more fundamental material causes – the new modes of production. The revolutionary result is, for Strauss, not the outcome of the unconscious working of history; it is, rather, the self-conscious project of certain fundamental political philosophers whose thinking crucially reoriented political life.

Strauss's claim about the origins of modernity has two elements: a causal element, and a hermeneutical element. The causal element – that modernity could be caused by the thoughts and writings of certain political philosophers – is an extraordinary claim, but it cannot be considered in this chapter (IPP 83–4, OT 206–7). The more fundamental element of Strauss's position is his hermeneutical claim that thinkers such as Machiavelli, Hobbes, Spinoza, and Locke held the revolutionary standpoint he attributes to them. As Strauss himself recognized, it is not immediately obvious that these thinkers advocated a fully radical, atheistic humanism. Here Strauss uses his recovery of the exoteric/esoteric distinction, which we discussed in chapter 3, to establish this is in fact their position (PAW 22–37, WIPP 221–2). The exoteric face of these early modern texts hides an esoteric radicality: early modern texts seem at once to exhibit both a departure from the tradition and a conformity to it. Strauss's critique of much of the scholarly literature on these texts is that complacent commentators have failed to recognize the consistent radicality behind their apparently contradictory face.

In order to understand better Strauss's account of what constitutes modernity, it can be useful to distinguish three aspects of his account. They are: (1) the critique of religion; (2) the critique of the pre-modern account of nature and its replacement by a modern conception of nature; and (3) modernity in its positive content, or what Strauss calls the "modern project," which culminates in the vision of what I have called a revolutionary humanism, or what Strauss's friend Alexandre Kojève called the universal, homogeneous state (OT 255). The subsequent failure of the modern project, according to Strauss, is the crisis of moral nihilism. He sees his own contemporary moment as two-sided: it is both the fullest realization of modernity and at the same time the failure of the modern project. As we saw in chapter 1, it is this ambiguity that issues in Strauss's own recovery of classical political philosophy.

We shall look at each of these three themes or aspects of Strauss's account of modernity in turn.

The Critique of Religion

All three of these themes were part of Strauss's critique of modernity from the 1930s onward. But the primary emphasis in his first formulations of what determined modernity in the early 1930s was the critique of religion. This theme was also part of Strauss's later formulations of modernity; for example, he wrote in *Thoughts on Machiavelli* (1958) of "anti-theological ire" as formative of Machiavelli's break with pre-modern forms. But by the 1950s and 1960s, in describing the rise of modernity Strauss tended to put more emphasis on the break with, or the alterations to, ancient thought. This certainly could be more a matter of emphasis than of substance, but there may be some significance in these changes in emphasis. In fact, I will argue that Strauss's later formulations continue to rely upon his earlier formulations, but that his failure to make this sufficiently clear compromises the lucidity of his later accounts of what modernity is. We will look at an example of this when we consider his account of Machiavelli, later in this chapter.

The fundamental role of the critique of religion in the shape and character of modernity arises naturally enough from Strauss's concerns in the 1920s. His involvement with Zionism and his work on *Spinoza's Critique of Religion* helped to establish in Strauss's mind not only the distinction between orthodox belief and modern thought, but also the way in which this opposition informed modern thought. The argument of Strauss's first book, *Spinoza's Critique of Religion*, was that modern rationalism had tried but failed to refute the claims of orthodoxy, and its awareness of this failure had pushed modernity instead to seek to bring about historical conditions by which the claims of orthodoxy would no longer be practically compelling. In *Philosophy and Law* (1935), Strauss spoke of the strategy of modern rationalism in military terms:

> Animated by the hope of being able to "overcome" orthodoxy through the perfection of a system, and hence hardly noticing the failure of its actual attack on orthodoxy, the Enlightenment, striving for victory with truly Napoleonic strategy, left the impregnable fortress of orthodoxy in the rear, telling itself that the enemy would not and could not venture any sally. Renouncing the impossible

direct refutation of orthodoxy, it devoted itself to its own proper work, the civilization of the world and of man. (PL 32)

Strauss sees the intellectual failure of modern rationalism as a motivation for the modern project *as* a project, as engaged in a polemical stance. As we saw in chapter 1, the modern project is, for Strauss, implicated in the orthodoxy it seeks to refute in practice, by seeking to humanize the world and, thereby, to desacralize that world. The revelation opposed by modernity defines and determines the secularity that would replace it. The logic of this inner negative relation between modern rationalism and religion, specifically revealed religion, is made more explicit in Strauss's work on Hobbes in the early 1930s. Prior to writing the book he published in 1936 as *The Political Philosophy of Hobbes*, Strauss wrote an unpublished manuscript entitled *Hobbes's Critique of Religion*. In this text, Strauss finds in Hobbes an even more radical grounding of modernity than that of Spinoza, arising from the confrontation of modern rationalism with religious belief. Strauss finds in Hobbes (and Descartes) a move to a radical skepticism that seeks to confront and overcome divine omnipotence from within modern thought (HCR 94–9). The method in both Hobbes and Descartes is to build a radical skepticism into the beginning point of modern thought such that, even if there is an omnipotent God, what is knowable cannot be doubted. Religious claims cannot destabilize the realization of modern rationalism. For Strauss, what distinguishes Hobbes from Descartes and marks Hobbes as the beginning of modernity (as Strauss held it at this time) is the cognitive principle that we can know only what we make (HCR 109–14). We can never know the world of given realities, whether nature or God's creation, but we can know what we have constructed. This turn to construction allows the production of a purely human, purely secular knowledge, which is at the same time world-altering: it is both knowing and making. In this synthesis of knowledge and practice, Strauss sees the origins of the modern project.

What is to be noted is the constructed character of this project. In his analysis of Hobbes, Strauss sees that the crucial ground in nature or the passions that effects this transformation is the "fear of violent death" (PPH 57). In his writings from the 1930s, Strauss frames the activity of this fear in broadly Hegelian terms of self-consciousness (PPH 57–8). The fear of death brings about this self-consciousness. The modern world is the world constructed in and by self-consciousness. It is this self-consciousness that constitutes what Strauss refers to as the "cave beneath the cave," an artificial or constructed cave. Strauss recognizes that this self-consciousness, in its profoundly unnatural character, is fundamentally shaped by its opposition to revelation. The modern self is then the image – the negative image – of the creative God, standing omnipotent over all nature. Further, this constructed character of modernity demands its progressive realization in the world. We will consider this more when we consider the modern project in its own right, but it is important to see the negative impetus at work: modernity needs progress precisely in order to overcome or evade the compelling, competing demands of orthodoxy.

Another way to state that modernity is negatively implicated in biblical revelation is through the terms Strauss uses in *Spinoza's Critique of Religion*. There Strauss argues that modernity framed religious belief as "prejudice" and, in contrast, framed its own self-understanding in terms of the "positive mind" (SCR 93–7, 146). The positive mind is self-grounding and establishes its claims, inadequately as a comprehensive system and more effectively as progress, as the positive mind remakes or humanizes the world and dissolves the hold of religious "prejudice" through mockery:

> The reversionary character of modern philosophy shows itself much more fundamentally in the fact that is decisive for the whole span of the 17th and 18th centuries: in the *fight against prejudices* that fills these centuries. The word "prejudice" is indeed the Enlightenment's polemical keyword – it is met with so to speak on every page of every writing of the Enlightenment. One must *free* oneself from prejudices, and this freeing is accomplished by *retreating* to a plane, or even a point, from which one can finally free progress of prejudice once and for all. (RLS 247)

As we saw in our discussion of the theological-political problem in chapter 2, there is for Strauss a total opposition between religious faith and enlightenment reason. And enlightenment reason is itself inscribed by the very prejudice it seeks to overthrow:

> With a view to the radical meaning of revealed religion it must be said: there exists *the* prejudice pure and simple. Therefore freedom – falling away from revelation – also exists. Therefore, the struggle of the Enlightenment against prejudice has an absolute meaning. For this reason the age of prejudice and the age of freedom can stand opposed to one another. For the age of freedom it is essential that it be preceded by the age of prejudice. "Prejudice" is an

historical category. This precisely constitutes the difference between the struggle of the Enlightenment against prejudices and the struggle against appearance and opinion with which philosophy began its secular journey. (SCR 181)

What Strauss is bringing to light here is the instability at work in modern rationalism. This instability is present first in its self-assertive, self-grounding beginning, which arises in its very "positive" character from its need (and yet failure) to refute the claims of faith. Second, it is shown in its undoing, as the confidence in "progress" in the modern project gives way to the crisis of our time. Modernity's "Napoleonic strategy" fails (PL 32). For Strauss, it is this instability, the need to assert itself and dissolve religious prejudice by establishing a secular, free humanity, that pushes the modern project forward, but equally leads to its undoing in nihilism.

It is important to distinguish Strauss's account of the religious grounds of modernity from that of his contemporary and correspondent Karl Löwith, who in *Meaning and History* (1949) provided one of the most compelling versions of what is called the "secularization thesis." Secularization is the claim that modernity occupies religious – above all Christian – standpoints, but in secular or this-worldly forms. The general thesis of secularization can be traced through Nietzsche back to Feuerbach and Hegel. But this is not what Strauss is claiming, and his later formulations can be understood as efforts to further distance his account of modernity from secularization claims. Strauss is clear that, rather than continuing religious standpoints in secular forms, modernity (at least in its initial formulation) seeks to fundamentally break with religion and specifically with Christianity: it is anti-theological. Strauss is arguing that because of this oppositional relation, modernity, against its deepest intentions, is nonetheless marked by the religion it opposes. It is marked in its negativity, in its radicality, in its turn from nature and the ordinary speech by which nature manifests itself. Strauss will elsewhere describe modernity as a "lowering of horizons" and, in various ways, a diminishment of what the ancient world was open to. While such an alteration is necessary to modernity as Strauss understands it, modernity cannot simply be a diminishment of the pre-modern. To understand the nihilistic dynamic of modernity's course, the inwardness and negativity of modernity must be seen to arise more specifically from its origins in opposition and antagonism to revelation.

Strauss is arguing that while modernity is not the secularization of religious, and specifically Christian, claims or stances, it is crucially determined by its negative relation to those claims and stances. In fact, Strauss will bring out a deepening appearance of this religious formation as modernity develops into its second and third waves. Strauss was both sensitive to and critical of the religious aspects of Nietzsche's and Heidegger's radical modernity, and in both cases saw this religious inflection as inhibiting a proper return to the ancients or to nature. The difficulty for Strauss with the account of modernity arising from the critique of religion is that that account's profound sense of the transformative power of the modern world endangers Strauss's more basic claim that this modern standpoint comes to nothing. This may be why Strauss tends in his later writings to put more weight on modernity's break with the classical account of nature.

The Rejection of the Ancient Account of Nature

Alongside the critique of religion, Strauss points to a break with ancient philosophical accounts of nature or the whole in the formation of modernity. This break is above all and in the first instance a break with how nature is conceived in political philosophy. For Strauss, the history of political thought in the West is broken in two: the thought of the ancients, and that of the moderns. As an anti-historicist, Strauss does not characterize this break as a result of historical causes; rather, he sees it as the result of a reconception of moral and political thought, a fundamental restructuring by political philosophy of how we conceive moral and political life.[1] At the center of our moral and political self-understanding, for Strauss, is the notion of "nature," that is,

---

[1] Strauss's conception of historical causality is not without subtlety. The source of modernity is the thought of Machiavelli and other political philosophers and not larger historical events. However, that thought can be crucially conditioned, not only in its influence upon history, but in its very conception. For example, Machiavelli's thought was not caused by the surrounding Christian culture, but was conditioned by it in both motivation (anti-theological ire) and content (the central place of propaganda); see WIPP 44–5. However, Strauss sees these conditions as not touching upon the fundamental possibility and character of political philosophy, which rest rather on the permanent problems and not on historical conditions; see WIPP 63–77 and OT 212.

what is given prior to human willing. Beginning with his writings in the 1930s, Strauss characterized the division between modern and ancient in terms of a distinction concerning what is meant by "nature." In "Comments on *Der Begriff des Politischen*," Strauss points to two fundamental concepts of nature: "whether as an order seen as a model or whether as disorder which is to be removed" (SCR 336). In *The Political Philosophy of Hobbes*, Strauss writes: "Traditional natural law is primarily and mainly an objective 'rule and measure,' a binding order prior to, and independent of, the human will, while modern natural law is, or tends to be, primarily and mainly a series of 'rights,' of subjective claims, originating in the human will" (PPH vii–viii). The ancients in one way or another conceived of nature as a restraining order within which human beings lived out lives of lesser or greater virtue; the moderns saw nature as an alien other, to be overcome through human activity. For Strauss, the distinction between the ancients and the moderns lies in determining which is the central grounding principle for moral and political life – nature's order, or humanity's will (IPP 85–6). The simplicity of this opposition is what gives such force to Strauss's account of the history of political thought. Implicit in it is the assumption that any position that argues for a synthesis of these two sides is inherently contradictory. The originators of modernity – the early modern thinkers – appear to argue for such a synthesis, and so, for Strauss, either they were contradictory, or their apparent contradictions hid a deeply consistent radical, atheistic humanism.

From within Strauss's moral and political phenomenology, the emergence of modernity must begin with a new conception of nature, so that it will no longer be understood as "the hierarchic order of man's natural ends," but rather as a source of "terror and fear" (SPPP 144, 223). In his first writings on Hobbes, what Strauss wanted to clarify was that the nature relative to which modernity takes its point of departure is not simply the mechanical necessity of modern natural science; rather, nature is itself the source of this terror (PPH 169–70). Strauss later came to see that this same notion of nature had its first articulation in Machiavelli (SPPP 223, TM 279–80). For Strauss, nature as terror and as a moral phenomenon is more primal to the definition of modernity than is nature as mechanical (WIPP 47).

With this shift in the conception of nature, a whole realignment in the structure of the moral and political imagination has occurred – or, rather, as Strauss sees it unfolding, the destruction of that imagination (PPH 152). Nature is no longer a whole that structures the moral and political, providing a schema by which to give content to good and evil, a connection between "is" and "ought." Nature is no longer a system of ends or perfections that is realized and gives meaning to notions of virtue (WIPP 90). In modernity, nature acts not as an end to be realized, but rather as a beginning from which one must escape (NRH 180, 249–50). Nature is to be conquered or mastered, and this conquest or mastery is at the same time the realization of human culture (WIPP 46–7, NRH 201, IPP 85). Nature now stands over and against humanity:

> Man can be sovereign only because there is no cosmic support for his humanity. He can be sovereign only because he is absolutely a stranger in the universe. He can be sovereign only because he is forced to be sovereign. Since the universe is unintelligible and since control of nature does not require understanding of nature, there are no knowable limits to his conquest of nature. He has nothing to lose but his chains, and, for all he knows, he may have everything to gain. Still, what is certain is that man's natural state is misery; the vision of the City of Man to be erected on the ruins of the City of God is an unsupported hope. (NRH 175)

Like Heidegger, Strauss sees the turn to a self, external to the world, not as a step toward greater objectivity and freedom from illusions, but rather as a construct unable to find an integrated relation to the "other" it is necessarily opposed to. Indeed, the "other," the object, is objective precisely in order that it might be available for conquest or mastery and thus for culture. As Strauss said in his commentary on Carl Schmitt, "'Culture' is to such an extent cultivation of nature that it can be understood as a sovereign creation of the mind only if the nature being cultivated is taken to be the *opposite* of mind, and has been *forgotten*" (SCR 336). From the standpoint of classical political philosophy, both modern nature with its indifference to humanity, and the culture that becomes the necessary response to it, are constructs: that is, they are constructed upon and over the natural world as envisioned by the ancients (OT 192). Strauss contrasts the immediacy or concreteness of classical political thought, which takes its orientation from the standpoint of the city and the structures of "natural" moral and political imagination, to the abstractness of modern political philosophy (WIPP 28). For Strauss, modern political philosophy nevertheless retains an implicit relation to that natural structure (WIPP 181). As the development of modernity more and more completely undermines this connection, humanity comes to find itself lost in a directionless void. This, for Strauss, is the crisis of our time.

Of course, a movement beyond the horizon of the city, the pre-philosophic awareness of moral and political things, belongs to the philosopher in the classical period. The skeptical dissolution of the city's horizon did not lead the classical philosopher to nihilism insofar as he discovered nature lay beyond the city, and the philosopher did not step beyond nature.[2] However, for the moderns, nature is beyond the city only insofar as it is below the city. As Strauss states in his discussion of Hobbes,

> Hobbes's view of man, as far as it is essential to his political teaching, expresses how the new view of the whole affects "the whole man" – man as he is understood in daily life or by the historians and poets, as distinguished from man as he is to be understood within the context of Hobbes's natural science. "The eternal silence of these infinite spaces frightens" man: the mood generated by the truth, the true mood, is fear, the fear experienced by a being exposed to a universe which does not care for it by properly equipping it or by guiding it. (WIPP 181)

According to Strauss, the realization of modernity requires that not just philosophers but citizens in general step outside pre-philosophic awareness: they must become enlightened, atheistic individuals (WIPP 46). What distinguishes these modern citizens from philosophers is that their detachment is the result of a dogmatic skepticism, not a zetetic skepticism motivated by love of wisdom (NRH 171–2). In modernity, further, philosophy itself becomes changed; its end is no longer wisdom for its own sake, but rather is "to relieve man's estate, or to increase man's power" (TM 296). When nature "lacks intelligence," philosophy becomes effective (WIPP 181, PPH 163–4).

If nature no longer provides guidance to moral and political life, except as that from which humanity must escape in order to establish itself, then what is the source of the principles that structure the modern moral and political imagination?

The culmination of modernity as Strauss sees it brings to light the

---

[2] For Strauss, this stepping outside of or beyond nature is deceptive. Moderns presuppose as given that there is a moral sphere; they do not question the possibility of political philosophy. In this sense moderns can take up a detached standpoint while assuming the very being of the moral and political. Moderns, for Strauss, fail to ask the fundamental question: "What is virtue?" See PPH 152 and WIPP 92–4.

answer: it is the contentless human will (PPH 165). In this moment of nihilism, we can see how Strauss's critique of modernity intersects with the critique of religion. The nihilism of the modern will, its loss of all standards, arises from the move outside of nature by which modern nature as source of terror, or lack, arises. This movement outside can be seen to be one with the negation and inwardness Strauss sees arising from the critique of religion, from "anti-theological ire" as he calls it in his discussion of Machiavelli. In a way, the human has posited for itself the place of the creative God but has also discovered its incapacity to give content to that space. For Strauss, this insight into the emptiness or oblivion of the human moral or political will is only the culmination of modernity, not its beginning point. Modernity begins with a project.

The Modern Project and its Culmination or Failure in Nihilism

For Strauss, modernity does not begin with contentlessness – or, at least, in the beginning this lack of content remains implicit. Machiavelli and Hobbes assume a certain notion of the good, namely, the fulfillment of human need (TM 294). While Strauss describes the foundations of modernity negatively, as a lowering of horizons, a removal of restraint, and a turning to pleasure as the highest good, the philosophers who were moved to initiate modernity were motivated not simply by these reductions, but more directly by an affirmation: the desire to effect the fulfillment of human needs, and above all those most fundamental and pervasive needs, the passions. Strauss tells us that Machiavelli "achieves the decisive turn toward that notion of philosophy according to which its purpose is to relieve man's estate or to increase man's power or to guide man toward the rational society, the bond and the end of which is enlightened self-interest or the comfortable self-preservation of each of its members" (TM 296). In Strauss's eyes, what is crucial about needs or passions for the early modern philosophers is that they are immediately and fully actual, and do not require the recognition of a "hierarchy of ends" to give them structure and significance (NRH 162). These needs exist in the state of nature, outside the moral and political imagination of the ancients. In this turn to the body, the early moderns do not simply reduce humanity to animality. The idealism or "political" nature of the hedonism of the early moderns is that it is premised upon a need less easily satisfied than the need for food or protection. That need is the requirement that the fulfillment of these ends be guaranteed. The call for guaranteed effectiveness points to an endless will at the heart of modernity. Strauss tells us that, for the moderns, "there is a guarantee for the solution of the political problem because a) the goal is lower, i.e., in harmony with what most men actually desire and b) chance can be conquered" (IPP 87). By removing all ends inherent in political life, the early moderns make the end simply the fulfillment of human need. The whole, nature, must serve humanity in the givenness of its needs (TM 207–8).

Because the whole order of the world is to serve humanity in its needs and desires, the truth of the early modern is a revolutionary humanism:

> Man is effectively emancipated from the bonds of nature, and therewith the individual is emancipated from those social bonds which antedate all consent or compact, by the emancipation of his productive acquisitiveness, which is necessarily, if accidentally, beneficent and hence susceptible of becoming the strongest social bond: restraint of the appetites is replaced by a mechanism whose effect is humane. (NRH 248)

For Strauss, the modern project is not fulfilled in a single moment, in the single founding act of Machiavelli. Rather he sees both a development and an instability within the modern project. Its instability lies in the interaction of the two sources or roots of the modern project: its opposition to Athens and its opposition to Jerusalem. The opposition to Athens (to the ancient conception of nature) is to enable that the modern project be established in the world. The opposition to Jerusalem (to the standpoint of revelation) is to displace the omnipotent God by establishing a point beyond the world from which to transform it. These two negations – the lowering of horizons and anti-theological ire – are fused in modernity as Strauss conceives of it. Though Strauss is by no means explicit in this matter, it appears that the logic of his position requires a development to modernity because of the unstable interaction of these two sources or roots. Strauss characterizes this development as a series of three "waves," or stages, of modernity, culminating in the crisis of our time. Within each stage or wave there is further development.

According to Strauss, the first wave began with Machiavelli, and was crucially modified by Hobbes and Locke to produce the modern doctrine of natural right. Its contemporary correlate is capitalist liberalism, the acquisitive consumer society dedicated to fulfilling human needs (NRH 246, PPH 121). The second wave, initiated by Rousseau, absorbed nature as a standard by taking it into human history, which now served as the source of moral and political guidance (NRH 274). Freed from notions of a natural necessity, this wave produced a more radically utopian – and hence more deeply alienated – form of humanism. Its contemporary correlate is communism (WIPP 54). The third wave, which Strauss sees as our contemporary crisis, began with Nietzsche's questioning of the rationality or "humanity" of both history and nature: humanity finds itself in the midst of a terrifying existence, free to create the values by which to live. The contemporary correlate of this wave is fascism (IPP 98).

The three waves by which Strauss defines the historical stages of modernity all take form in contemporary political standpoints. But while Strauss sees these positions as distinct, they also belong together as a common development. The waves of modernity expose with increasing explicitness the nihilism at the heart of modernity. The assumption that the human will has a positive content is thereby shown to be simply the residue left by the tradition, due to an inadequate liberation from that tradition in the preceding waves. The second wave dissolves the assumption of a human nature adumbrated by a fundamental guiding passion that could form the basis of natural right. The third wave dissolves the assumption of a human right or rational right that came to replace natural right. The third wave brings to light that the sole basis of humanity's guidance is its own free activity or, equally, submission to the dispensations of fate – beyond both nature and reason. The whole development is then premised upon humanity's turning to history to fulfill itself in deepening stages: this leads to the reversal of this project when humanity discovers itself given over to a histo-ricity or historicism that proves morally nihilistic, Strauss's "second cave," in which the deepest longings of humanity for the eternal are occluded.

But let us now look at each wave in more detail.

The First Wave

In the 1940s Strauss came to revise his earlier judgment that Hobbes was the originator of modernity. Rather, "it was Machiavelli, that greater Columbus, who had discovered the continent on which Hobbes could erect his structure" (NRH 177). In 1951, Strauss described this shift in his judgment concerning "the originator of modern political philosophy" from Hobbes to Machiavelli as an "easily corrected error" (PPH xv). His great scholarly work that argued for this new claim was his much-disputed *Thoughts on Machiavelli* (1958). There are various ways in which Strauss's correction can be seen to represent a subtle alteration in his account of modernity, though perhaps it may seem more an alteration of emphasis than of substance.

The most important alteration Strauss makes at this point is that he comes to emphasize the "lowering of horizons" as the crucial character of modernity, and in so doing makes primary the break with the classical conception of nature, in contrast to his earlier emphasis on the critique of religion. Strauss writes from this later perspective:

> In fact, however, Machiavelli does not bring to light a single political phenomenon of any fundamental importance which was not fully known to the classics. His seeming discovery is only the reverse side of the oblivion of the most important: all things necessarily appear in a new light if they are seen for the first time in a specifically dimmed light. A stupendous contraction of the horizon appears to Machiavelli and his successors as a wondrous enlargement of the horizon. (TM 295)

Strauss seems to be suggesting here that the break with the ancients is really a reduction. Certainly, in his later account of modernity, Strauss continues to insist on the simultaneous break with Jerusalem and the atheistic character of modernity. But it is a mark of Strauss's change of emphasis that we no longer find in his writings the sustained use of the metaphor of modernity as a "cave beneath the cave," a metaphor that in the 1930s he found especially illuminating (SKC 29, 38, 40, 42, 45–8, 51–3). It is clearly a reference to Plato, and what Strauss's image of a second cave does is to suggest that the construction of modernity (the second cave) occurs *beyond* the limits of the ancient world, and is not simply a reduction or diminishment within that world. The image thus points to something outside of Athens – that is, the opposition to Jerusalem – as necessary to the construction of such an unnatural cave.

In Strauss's later writings the image of the second cave is dropped, and the role of the critique of religion is not emphasized so firmly as in his earlier formulations of the formation of modernity. This is not to say, however, that a "theological" account of modernity has entirely disappeared from Strauss's newer account, the account that now begins with Machiavelli. However, I would argue that the logic of this later account of modernity seems to be somewhat less cogent than the earlier formulation, and in fact appears to rely upon the earlier account.

Strauss's treatment of Machiavelli includes the role of religion in two specific ways: (1) in what Strauss refers to as Machiavelli's "anti-theological ire," itself instigated by the emergence of a "pious cruelty" in the Christian pre-modern world; and (2) in the use by Machiavelli of "propaganda," a technique Machiavelli associates (according to Strauss) with Christianity's "unarmed" conquest of the ancient world. Strauss tells us explicitly that "the only element of Christianity which Machiavelli took over was the idea of propaganda. This idea is the only link between his thought and Christianity" (WIPP 45).

Strauss puts such emphasis on the break with the ancient account of nature in Machiavelli's account of modernity that the only continuity with Christianity is "propaganda," and the only opposition is a matter of "anti-theological ire." But in fact, in *Thoughts on Machiavelli*, immediately after stating that Machiavelli brings to light no political phenomenon not already known to the ancients, Strauss points to the crucial repositioning of philosophy that occurs in Machiavelli, and that Strauss had established in his earlier writings through the critique of religion. In order to conquer chance and guarantee the fulfillment of the lowered horizons (the human needs that now are the object of political philosophy), modern political philosophy needs to attain "an Archimedean point outside of nature" (TM 297) to bring about the means to fulfill these human ends. Strauss tells us, "the narrowing of the horizon which Machiavelli was first to effect, was caused, or at least facilitated, by anti-theological ire" (WIPP 44). It is from the Archimedean standpoint motivated by ire that the union of theory and practice that characterizes modern political thought is both effected and made effective in the world, in and by propaganda:

> Propaganda is to guarantee the coincidence of philosophy and political power. Philosophy is to fulfill the function of both philosophy and religion. The discovery of the Archimedean point outside of everything given, or the discovery of a radical freedom, promises the conquest of everything given and thus destroys the natural basis of

the radical distinction between philosophers and non-philosophers.
(TM 297–8)

It appears, then, that modernity, far from being a simple narrowing of horizons, is altogether transformed by an antagonistic relation to religion. But, insofar as "anti-theological ire" is the explanation for the discovery or construction of this "Archimedean point," Strauss seems to ascribe the possibility of modernity to a merely personal psychological state, "a passion which we can understand but of which we cannot approve" (WIPP 44). Strauss seems to speak of the world-transforming event of modernity as due to contingent and, indeed, purely personal causes. So Strauss's account of the origins of modernity in Machiavelli seems to have a certain instability: there is nothing in modernity unknown to the ancients, and yet it brings about a wholly new relation of philosophy and practical life; it is a massive cultural change, and yet its origins rest in a personal passion.

Another way to formulate the criticism I am raising about Strauss's new emphasis on the "lowering of horizons" as the primary characterization of the modern project, as he speaks of it in the 1950s and 1960s, is to ask a question Strauss himself both asks and answers explicitly: what is the difference between the modern project and ancient conventionalism? Both can be said to be lowering the horizon from the perspective of the citizen. But as Strauss notes, the lowering of horizons connected with conventionalism is relative to a nature that stands higher than the conventional, whereas the modern lowering of horizons in fact raises the human above nature: it raises history above nature (NRH 10–12). Or as Strauss puts it, the modern project involves fusing hedonism with idealism (NRH 169). The ancient lowering of horizons in conventionalism separates the philosopher from the city: it is a private affair. The modern unites philosophy with the city: it produces historical change and seeks universal "enlightenment" achieved by propaganda. The problem with all of these formulations is that they are only descriptions of the difference between ancient conventionalism and the modern project. What they fail to do with sufficient clarity is to *explain* the modern project as a project arising from an "Archimedean" point that can master nature and realize human freedom. In the Strauss of the 1930s, it was the critique of religion that provided this explanation. Here, by reducing the role of the critique of religion in his account of Machiavelli, Strauss instead provides a variety of formulations that do not appear to fully cohere with one another as accounts of the modern project.

These different formulations or descriptions of Machiavelli's founding of modernity point to tensions in Strauss's broader conception. His whole account of modernity needs to walk a fine line between history and historicism. In order to assume a standpoint beyond modernity, but in contrast to Nietzsche and Heidegger, Strauss must avoid the grip of historicism. However, as we saw from the conclusion to chapter 1, Strauss's recipe for avoiding this fate requires that he engage in a history of that historicism, a history of modernity. But is a standpoint to write such a history available to us? Strauss's claim is that the power of modernity is such that it in fact cuts us off from nature, the standpoint beyond history, and that we can become free of modernity's effect only in its self-destruction in nihilism. In this way, modernity seems to be a transformative event by which history is actually altering, if not human nature, then the human condition: we now live in a cave below the natural cave, a second cave that did not previously exist. Modernity, then, seems to have a nearly all-embracing power in terms of our human ability to phenomenologically gain access to nature. On the other side, modernity, and above all the historical consciousness with which it culminates, must be a contingent event that can collapse once its nihilistic emptiness becomes manifest. Strauss's different accounts of modernity, as at once all-transforming and yet bringing about nothing new, at once civilizational and yet the result of a passion, arise from this deeper issue in Strauss about the status of historicism as simultaneously powerful and fragile.

A similar ambivalence is at work in Strauss's assessment of the status of philosophy in modernity. Are the modern political philosophers – Machiavelli, Hobbes, Rousseau, and so on – philosophers in the original or proper sense? That is, do the modern philosophers maintain the Socratic stance of "knowledge of ignorance," where fundamental problems are affirmed over any solution to those problems? The fusing together of theory and practice in service of the modern project would seem to pervert the inner character of philosophy as Strauss conceives it, a way of life given to ceaseless questioning in the pursuit of wisdom. As Strauss says in *Thoughts on Machiavelli*: "Instead of saying that the status of philosophy becomes obscured in Machiavelli's thought, it is perhaps better to say that in his thought the meaning of philosophy is undergoing a change" (TM 295). In seeking to resolve the fundamental problems, do modern philosophers not necessarily degrade philosophy so that it becomes dogmatism – the very antithesis of philosophy for Strauss – even if it is (to quote one of his formulations of modern philosophy) a "dogmatism based on skepticism" (LAM 26)? Strauss seems to say that modern political philosophers are seeking to secure the freedom of philosophizing, and at the same time that their philosophy is a fundamentally compromised standpoint that entraps philosophy, so that even thinkers of the rank of Nietzsche and Heidegger fail in their efforts to escape modernity. We will see this ambivalent sense of modernity's reality and power as we continue to follow Strauss's account of its development.

But the lowering of horizons and anti-theological ire are, in fact, not the only motivations Strauss suggests are at work in Machiavelli's founding of modern political philosophy; Machiavelli is also moved by the passion that he recommends to his readers as crucial for effective political life: glory. The modern project is the glorious project of making political life effective by lowering the horizons to render them effectively achievable, and then harnessing a transformed political philosophy to create the conditions that will guarantee the fulfillment of these ends. In Strauss's analysis, glory is the crucial motivation because it unites selfishness with the common or public good. Glory exemplifies and makes effective the basic Machiavellian insight that selfish means and non-virtuous ends can and must be harnessed to attain common, public, or ideal ends.

The modern project initiated by Machiavelli is the release of human selfish passions in the service of realizing human need in and through institutions founded on this premise to overcome chance and use unjust means to bring about effectual just results – namely, the fulfillment of actual human needs. The necessary stance of philosophy in this project is to subordinate itself to the modern project, by turning reason and inquiry to both the mastery of chance and the enlightenment of all – that is, through propaganda. Philosophy is to be united with the city; theory and practice are to become one. In short, Strauss discovers in Machiavelli the origins of technological humanist modernity that has as its fulfillment what Kojève called the universal and homogeneous state, or the realization of a revolutionary humanism. Like Nietzsche and Heidegger, Strauss will argue that this end will prove illusory, and that its truth is more in accord with what Nietzsche calls the "last man" (OT 239).

While the continent of modernity was discovered by Machiavelli, according to Strauss, its effective occupation was carried out according to the principles of Hobbes. For Strauss, Hobbes (who nowhere mentions Machiavelli) crucially modifies Machiavelli's founding by purging it of "glory" (WIPP 48). This purgation occurs through Hobbes's effort to make the modern project even more effective, less reliant on human greatness and thus more reliable, grounded on an inescapable human passion: the fear of violent death and desire for self-preservation. In doing so, Hobbes founded natural rights liberalism as the truly effective politics grounded in the first true political science. On the basis of Hobbes's political science, free historical humanity has been made a matter of natural necessity.

In the early modern period, according to Strauss, this revolutionary humanism is established by Hobbes in terms of the relationship between natural right and natural law (PPH 156–7). What distinguishes modern natural right from classical natural right is that it is a subjective claim – namely, the claim to the fulfillment of one's most pressing passion: self-preservation. According to Strauss, for both Hobbes and Locke natural law acts not as a limit to this right, but rather as a set of calculated principles by which that right might most readily be realized: "Through the shift of emphasis from natural duties or obligations to natural rights, the individual, the ego, had become the center and origin of the moral world, since man – as distinguished from man's end – had become that center or origin" (NRH 248).

Strauss makes use of his hermeneutical method (the exoteric/esoteric distinction) to eliminate all apparent constraints upon natural right that appear in the texts of Hobbes and Locke. In the case of Locke, where the text seems to give priority to natural law over natural rights, Strauss engages in complex arguments to demonstrate that Locke means the opposite of this (NRH 202–20, WIPP 197–220). And not only is it inherent in this "early modern" revolutionary humanism that there are no natural constraints upon it; equally, for Strauss, there must be no supernatural constraint. Atheism is necessary to modern natural right: God's existence would limit, give significance to, and provide consolation from the expansive, technological society. As Strauss says, "if we do not permit ourselves to be deceived by ephemeral phenomena, we realize that political atheism and political hedonism belong together. They arose together in the same moment and in the same mind" (NRH 169). Again, Strauss expends considerable effort in eradicating from the inner teaching of early modern political philosophers every apparent aspect of theism belonging to their texts (WIPP 183–96, SPPP 220–3). Strauss uses the word "revolutionary" to describe the thought of Machiavelli, Hobbes and Locke (TM 62–9, 131, NRH 169, 183, 246–8, IPP 60, 88).

While Hobbes and Locke participate in the Machiavellian revolution through the turn to natural rights founded on self-preservation, both thinkers make this revolution stable, practical, and settled. According to Strauss, it is in the Hobbesian-Lockean form that the first wave of modernism becomes liberalism. While Hobbes lays the groundwork for this, its fullest and historically most effective form is attained in Locke's formulation. Hobbes's grounding is attained by founding rights in self-preservation itself, discovered by the fear of violent death, and these rights arise relative to nature understood as lack or source of fear and terror. This negative grounding of natural rights means that the realization of natural rights occurs in and through an analysis of power importantly made neutral, manageable, and dynamic. Strauss notes: "Power, as distinguished from the end for which power is used or ought to be used, becomes the central theme of political reflections by virtue of that limitation of horizon which is needed if there is to be a guaranty of the actualization of the right social order" (NRH 195–6).

In Locke, Hobbes's grounding of politics in the natural right of self-preservation is crucially modified by his expanding natural rights to include property or (better yet) by expanding self-preservation to mean "comfortable self-preservation" (NRH 228, 26, 238). But, as Strauss notes, neither the comfort nor the property is understood in the classical sense as a fixed requirement for the exercise of virtue, but they are crucially made dynamic through Locke's account of the state of nature. What Locke then means by the right to property is the right to acquisitiveness. Strauss notes that the crucial operational principle in Hobbes's account of natural rights is power, but power transformed into a dynamic, controllable phenomenon. So also in Locke, property is transformed into the dynamism of modern expansive bourgeois capitalism. As Strauss notes concerning this Lockean reworking of Hobbes's reworking of Machiavelli's founding of modernity:

> Thus the desire for self-preservation turns into the desire for property, for acquisition, and the right to self-preservation becomes the right to unlimited acquisition. The practical consequences of this small change are enormous. Locke's political teaching is the prosaic version of what in Hobbes still had a certain poetic quality. It is, precisely on Hobbes's premises, more reasonable than Hobbes's

own political teaching. With a view to the resounding success of
Locke, as contrasted with the apparent failure of Hobbes, especially
in the Anglo-Saxon world, we can say that Machiavelli's discovery
or invention of the need for an immoral or amoral substitute for
morality, became victorious through Locke's discovery or invention
that that substitute is acquisitiveness. Here we have an utterly selfish
passion whose satisfaction does not require the spilling of any blood
and whose effect is the improvement of the lot of all. In other words,
the solution of the political problem by economic means is the most
elegant solution, once one accepts Machiavelli's premise: economism
is Machiavellianism come of age. (WIPP 49)

With Locke, Strauss sees the founding of the economy and society
as separate spheres of human interaction. This was to become one
of the crucial themes of eighteenth-century political philosophy,
perhaps most notably in Montesquieu, but also, of course, in Hume,
Adam Smith, and a number of Enlightenment figures (WIPP 49–50).

However, it is the very accomplishment and realization of the
Lockean vision of bourgeois economic and social life – or what
Strauss describes as the "joyless quest for joy" (NRH 251) – that
leads to the first crisis of modernity, the crisis of natural right
formulated by Jean-Jacques Rousseau. This brings about the second
wave of modernity.

The Second Wave

As Strauss sees it, the crucial work of the second wave is to negate
or dissolve the assumption of nature still operative in the first
wave. The first wave rejected or refused to assume the standpoint of classical natural right, where nature was understood as
a hierarchy of wants or ends that provided a positive or ends-
oriented conception of human life. The first wave replaced the
classical conception with a negative conception of nature as a realm
of lack, or even a source of fear or terror, but one that still provided
a (negative) purpose for human life as the overcoming of this nature
for the fulfillment of basic human need. While this was a profound
"lowering of horizons," nature nevertheless remained as a standard
that preceded human will and human history even as it stimulated
humanity to enter into history in the conquest of nature. The first
wave justified political life, but also limited it relative to certain
"natural rights" that were trans-political and trans-historical. By
contrast, the second wave is premised on the recognition that any

such rights are themselves the product of history and of human will and reason, not of a nature that precedes human will. The "immanent" character of human nature or right or justice is, then, much more radically brought to light in this second wave. There humanity does not precede history but is rather itself the work and outcome of history.

For Strauss, the great figure who began the second wave and engaged in the first profound internal critique of modernity was Rousseau. As Strauss sees it, there are three aspects to the transition to the second wave that are at work in Rousseau's account:

1. Rousseau criticizes the first wave from the standpoint of the ancient city and ancient virtue; however, this critique leads not to a retraction of the modern project but rather to its radicalization.
2. Rousseau's radicalization of the modern project involves his acceptance of "Hobbes's premise" (NRH 266) of a state of nature, but Rousseau moves more consistently than Hobbes to a view of the state of nature as prior to any assumptions belonging to social or historical life.
3. From this standpoint, Rousseau outlines two trajectories that are in fundamental tension with one another. One is the "political" standpoint that seeks to realize a more completely human modernity, one that establishes itself in history as the realization of human freedom. The other is a standpoint beyond both politics and history, found in "solitary contemplation" as achieved by the "feeling of existence" (NRH 291–2).

One way to describe what Strauss takes to be the basis of Rousseau's critique of the first wave of modernity is that modernity reduces humans to a merely material or commercial existence: "They lack the greatness of soul of the ancients. They are bourgeois rather than citizens" (NRH 253). The ancient republic points to a greater human fullness found in a standpoint of virtue that points to ends beyond the merely material. According to Strauss, Rousseau's response to this is to seek not to recover the pre-modern account of nature and natural right, but rather to overcome the apparent reductionism of the first wave by discovering in humanity a standpoint free of the seemingly naturally given ends – the human needs – that are the standard for the first wave. The fullness of humanity lacking in the bourgeois humanity of the first wave is to be found by a release, not a constraint, of human activity. So instead of looking to the constraint of ancient virtue, Rousseau seeks more completely to release humans from even the very limited constraint imposed by the needs found in Hobbes's state of nature. According to Strauss, this is precisely what Rousseau attains by pursuing, more consistently and rigorously than Hobbes, a pre-social, pre-historical human existence.

Rousseau sees that, while making humans "asocial," Hobbes failed to free them sufficiently from the effects of social formation. In contrast, Rousseau's natural humanity is not only without society, but also without language or reason. As Strauss puts it, "natural man is subhuman" (NRH 271). There are a number of implications of this claim, which according to Strauss functions as both a "fact" and a standard. What natural man does have, and what inform human history, are two passions (self-preservation and compassion) and a capacity for what Rousseau calls "perfectibility," which Strauss interprets as malleability. The passions and malleability of the subhuman humans mean that full humanity, rationality, and community are accidentally acquired over the course of history, and so are experienced from the perspective of natural man as sources of constraint and misery. Central to Strauss's analysis is Rousseau's declaration at the beginning of *On the Social Contract*:

> Man is born free, and everywhere he is in chains. One believes himself the others' master, and yet is more a slave than they. How did this change come about? I do not know. What can make it legitimate? I believe I can solve this question. (Rousseau, *The Social Contract and Other Political Writings*, 39)

Strauss wants to draw our attention to the two levels implied in this quotation. The first level is the legitimation of historical life provided by Rousseau's account of the social contract and the general will. The second level is implied by the word "chains": even this legitimation is itself a constraint, and so the freedom achieved by even the most legitimate regime is still an enchained or limited freedom. This suggests that there is a more complete freedom outside of politics and history. We will turn to this second level in a moment.

According to Strauss's account of Rousseau, at the first level, the level of human history, the crucial turning point is the promised change from illegitimacy to the legitimacy achieved by the social contract:

> At that moment, which is Rousseau's moment, man will no longer be molded by fortuitous circumstances but rather by his reason. Man,

> the product of blind fate, eventually becomes the seeing master of his
> fate. Reason's creativity or mastership over the blind forces of nature
> is a product of those blind forces. (NRH 273)

This, for Strauss, is the distinctive principle of the second wave:
human history is redeemed with the rise to a self-knowledge that
history and human life generally need not be externally determined
or limited, even by nature itself. Hobbesian self-making is released
from all external and internal constraint. Human freedom, and not
nature, is the new basis of historical existence. Human indeter-
minacy or malleability means that human history and human being
are entirely in human hands. Strauss writes of Rousseau's vision
of human freedom: "Man has no nature in the precise sense which
would set a limit to what he can make out of himself" (NRH 271).

In Rousseau, the means by which humanity comes to govern and
shape itself is the "general will," the capacity within the human
for free collective self-determination. In Strauss's view, the malleability of humanity means that there is no inherent limit to this
self-determination. We do not need to go into the details of Strauss's
exegesis here, but it is necessary to bring out the general principle
Strauss sees at work in Rousseau's general will: the principle
of generalizability. The way that the general will functions as a
limit or basis of right is by reference not to a "vertical" or hierar-
chical structure of ends inherent in human nature, but rather to a
"horizontal" principle by which human freedom is limited only
by human freedom: a formal, not substantive limit. Further, this is
an accomplishment occurring within human history in which "is"
and "ought" are united and there is no need to refer positive right
to natural law or natural right: according to Rousseau, the general
will does not err.

Strauss points to a number of aspects that belong to this second
wave. One is the Machiavellian character of the logic that the
accidental, amoral, or even immoral can lead to the standpoint
of freedom (WIPP 54). This Machiavellian account of human
agency, Strauss sees, is worked out more fully by Kant, Hegel, and
Marx as philosophies of history in which an "invisible hand" or
the "cunning of reason" shows how the accidental movement of
history brings forth the accomplishment of freedom or rationality
or human progress more generally: "According to this view, the
rational or just society, the society characterized by the existence of
a general will known to be the general will, i.e., the ideal, is necessarily actualized by the historical process without men's intending

to actualize it" (IPP 91). Strauss also sees in this shift from natural right to rational right or the law of freedom a connection to a whole series of nineteenth-century phenomena, including the rise of concepts of culture and nationalism, concerns about social and political conformism, and the doctrine of progress: "For a moment – the moment lasted longer than a century – it seemed possible to seek the standard of human action in the historical process. This solution presupposed that the historical process or its results are unambiguously preferable to the state of nature or that that process is 'meaningful'" (NRH 274).

For Strauss, the second wave of modernity is the high point of the modern project. In it, a fully free, self-determining humanity has come into possession of itself and the world. In this sense, Karl Marx represents the culmination of this standpoint. Kojève's Hegelian-Marxist standpoint, with its vision of a universal and homogeneous state, was understood by Strauss to be the finest contemporary defense of this fulfillment of modernity. But even in this moment of fulfillment, Strauss points to issues that lead to the crisis of the second wave, which in turn becomes the crisis of modernity. The most direct way to capture the instability of the modern project is this: in its fulfillment is also its decline. For Strauss, this is a feature built into the historical character of modernity. The source of it is the historicism implicit in second-wave modernity: precisely by making "right" immanent in history, it becomes subject to history. Strauss's interest in Hegel's under-standing of the "End of History" illustrates this point: Strauss sees implicit in the notion of "end" or completion the necessary decline from this end. Equally for Strauss, a liberal or Marxist vision of infinite progress toward an end is vulnerable to the actual events of history, above all to the cataclysmic events of the twentieth century, which seem to point to the failure to realize any progress except in a technical or scientific sense. A loss of confidence in a Hegelian or Marxist culmination to history joins with growing concerns about conformity, shallowness, and relativism: "Post-Hegelian thought rejected the notion that there can be an end or peak of history, i.e., it understood the historical process as unfinished and unfinishable, and yet it maintained the now baseless belief in the rationality or progressive character of the historical process. Nietzsche was the first to face this situation" (IPP 95).

But before we turn to the third wave of modernity, we need to take note of Strauss's claim that besides history's resolution in the general will there is "another fundamental thought of Rousseau, no less important than the one indicated" (IPP 92). This second "fundamental thought" is the one captured by the stance of solitary contemplation in Rousseau that, according to Strauss, views the realm of "freedom" constructed by the general will as still only legitimated "chains." From this standpoint, there is a fuller freedom found in an experience of existence to be had in "reverie," a recollection, at the level of feeling, of the goodness of existence. Strauss connects this trans-political experience of existence to Romanticism and, more specifically, to its transformation into the infinite striving found in the figure of Goethe's Faust. In all of this, there is the reappearance of a religious dimension, but one now inwardly experienced. Strauss describes this stance: "Faust's goodness is unrest, infinite striving, dissatisfaction with everything finite, finished, complete, 'classic'" (IPP 94). In this standpoint beyond historical development, Strauss is drawing out a more deeply negating stance that he will connect to Nietzsche and Heidegger where the striving comes to be experienced relative to an abyss and no longer to the goodness of human existence. In this we are seeing the roots of the more radical historicism and nihilism that will emerge in modernity's third wave. But we can also detect here the religious character that Strauss sees at work in Nietzsche and Heidegger. Strauss's critique of religion helps to make sense of what is at work here. The "Archimedean point" that Strauss found in Machiavelli, and that he earlier characterized as the "self-consciousness" that emerged out of Hobbes's critique of religion, has, in the second wave, been made the inner center of human freedom and existence. The higher freedom that Rousseau discovers in the feeling of existence is the direct "religious" experience of the assumption that sustains the conception of the underlying rationality and humanity of history.

What is crucial about German idealism is that it sought to unite what for Rousseau were two distinct conditions – romantic existence and social life: "The German philosophers who took up [Rousseau's] problem thought that a reconciliation is possible, and that reconciliation can be brought about, or has already been brought about, by History" (WIPP 53). The conjunction of romantic inwardness and history produces what Strauss calls the historical consciousness of the nineteenth century. When, for Nietzsche, history is no longer the space in which human inwardness and social life can be rational, reconciled in and by history, he does not abandon historical consciousness, but instead radicalizes it. Nietzsche "taught then that all human life and human thought ultimately rests on horizon-forming creations which are not susceptible of rational legitimization" (WIPP 54). The second wave's turn to history dissolves the claim to the rationality or indeed the humanity of that history: the second wave dissolves into the third wave.

The Third Wave

In none of Strauss's accounts of the modern project does he give more than very limited space to an account of the third wave. In a sense, he has already dealt with it (as have we) in the consideration of positivism and especially historicism. So texts such as *Natural Right and History* or "What Is Political Philosophy?" that begin with accounts of positivism and historicism have returned to their beginning when their histories of natural right or political philosophy turn to the third wave. But in another way, a remarkable feature of Strauss's writings is his apparent evasion of confronting the two thinkers, Nietzsche and Heidegger, who mark for him the most profound philosophic reflections of and about this third wave, and who are, at the same time, a significant inspiration for his own project.

For Strauss, what most basically constitutes the third wave is that it has drawn the conclusion that the rationality and humanism of the second wave are an unsustainable presupposition. In Nietzsche's declaration of nihilism and of the death of God, the irrationality, the arbitrary and accidental character, of existence are faced directly:

> This last epoch was inaugurated by Nietzsche. Nietzsche retained what appeared to him to be the insight due to the historical consciousness of the 19th century. But he rejected the view that the historical process is rational as well as the premise that a harmony between the genuine individual and the modern state is possible ... He taught then that all human life and human thought ultimately rests on horizon-forming creations which are not susceptible of rational legitimization. The creators are great individuals. The solitary creator who gives a new law unto himself and who subjects himself to all its rigors takes the place of Rousseau's solitary dreamer. For Nature has ceased to appear as lawful and merciful. The fundamental experience of existence is therefore the experience, not of bliss, but of suffering, of emptiness, of an abyss. (WIPP 54)

The greatness of Nietzsche and Heidegger, then, was not only to recognize and face the nihilism brought forth by the crisis of the third wave, but to strive to formulate new ways of being that could overcome this nihilism without denying it. In Nietzsche, this appears in his teachings of the will to power, the overman, and the eternal return of the same. In Heidegger, this occurs through the effort to overcome the forgetfulness of Being and to move beyond the metaphysical, technological standpoint toward a new kind of thinking.

Strauss's relation to these efforts is ambivalent, as we have already seen in his encounters with the nihilism prevalent in the Weimar Republic. He recognizes that Nietzsche and Heidegger cannot simply be identified with the nihilism they are bringing to light, but that they are also confronting and seeking a release from it. As we have seen, in Nietzsche's and Heidegger's effort to get beyond nihilism, Strauss sees real possibilities in their pointing to an ancient or a natural standpoint. Yet, in Strauss's judgment, their incapacity to liberate themselves from historicism fundamentally disables these efforts to get beyond nihilism. The terrible irony – an irony Strauss detected also in Rousseau's critique of modernity (NRH 253) – is that, in their very effort to be free of nihilism and modernity, they only deepen and radicalize it.

Strauss reads the modern project as fundamentally a uniting of theory and practice such that human life becomes historical. Each of the three waves is a deepening development of modernity from nature to history to historicity (or radical historicism), as the world becomes more deeply willed or transformed by humans, so that humanity itself becomes historical and temporal. For Strauss, what is lost sight of in this is what he calls "eternity" – his general term for realities that are beyond history – whether nature or God.

The inadequacy of Nietzsche's and Heidegger's profound and thoughtful insight into the nihilism of modernity is that they misdiagnose this nihilism, and so their critique of modernity remains (like Rousseau's earlier) an internal critique that can only deepen modernity. Like Rousseau, Nietzsche and Heidegger look to the ancients for a vision of human fullness and, also like Rousseau, they see that the escape from modern emptiness is by negating what appears to be leveling or reductionist in the second wave: its rationality and humanism. The nature of their misdiagnosis has to do with a focus in Nietzsche and Heidegger on the rationality of modernity, or what Heidegger calls "technology." In Strauss's analysis, this is an incomplete account that misinterprets not only what modernity consists in, but also the premodern world and, more specifically, Socrates. Even more problematic is that it means that Nietzsche and Heidegger seem to think they can only get beyond modernity through radicalizing historicism and temporality by releasing it from rationality or technological thinking. Certainly this has the effect of "de-humanizing" modernity, liberating it from the technological and metaphysical – but, equally, as Strauss notes, this anti-humanist development erases the political and ethical, precisely as what Nietzsche calls "human-all-too-human" (OT 212). In engaging in this dehumanization, the deeper sources of modernity in political philosophy are lost sight of rather than overcome, and so modernity becomes "postmodern" in the form of radical historicism.

One sign of this deepened modernity is that Nietzsche and Heidegger continue to look for historical solutions to the problem of nihilism. A crucial claim that distinguishes Strauss's analysis of the crisis of our time from both Nietzsche and Heidegger is that Strauss does not think there is a historical standpoint "beyond nihilism" or a dispensation or stance of willing that builds nihilism into itself as an historical moment and then transcends it. Rather, for Strauss (as we have seen) nihilism puts into question modernity and points to a pre-modern rationalism that is more fully human and more deeply open to the whole. Crucial to this is that Strauss, in contrast to Nietzsche and Heidegger, does not think that history or temporality is ontological, a fundamental dimension of existence. Strauss thinks that the claim to "historical consciousness" is delusional.

From this point of view, neither Heidegger's turn to Being nor Nietzsche's turn to the will to power can function directly as a model or be assimilated by Strauss. Claims that Strauss is a Nietzschean or Heideggerian fail to pay attention to the whole force and tenor of Strauss's account of the modern project. Of course, Strauss's position does have an array of characteristics that parallel aspects of Nietzsche's and Heidegger's thought. Nevertheless, because of its liberation from historicism, Strauss's "whole" or "nature" cannot be Nietzsche's will to power or Heidegger's Being.

Another way that Strauss characterizes his difference from Nietzsche's and Heidegger's standpoints is that he finds in them a religious dimension. Fundamental to Strauss's turn to classical political philosophy, according to his understanding, is its existing prior to and so free of the claims of revelation or the modern effort to polemically confront those claims. The synthesis or fusion of philosophy and religion in Nietzsche and Heidegger is, as we have seen, another aspect of the continuing modernity inherent in these positions. From this point of view, historicism and historical consciousness are just such a construct: for Strauss they are premised on the claim of historical transformation and as such are delusional in the face of an abiding nature.

Does this mean, then, that the whole modern world, premised on historical consciousness, is itself delusional? By no means. This is a very tricky aspect of Strauss. Does his critique of modernity imply an undoing of the modern world? And does it imply, for example, an undoing of American liberal democracy? This is where it is so important to remember Strauss's basic stance that he discovers in classical political philosophy. For him, philosophy is the pursuit of the fundamental and permanent problems. The problem with the modern project is that it makes primary a solution to the permanent problems. Strauss is often ambivalent about whether (or to what extent) the philosophers responsible for that project were themselves dogmatic or still retained (or even sought to retain) in the modern project the freedom of philosophizing. Such ambivalence suggests that one can be a philosopher in the classical sense, and yet still affirm or at least not seek to undo the construction of modernity as a set of historical circumstances. This possibility is at work in the question of how Strauss, or at least his students and followers – the Straussians – came to act and intervene in the contemporary world, above all in contemporary America. This will be the subject of our next chapter.

6

Strauss, the Straussians, and America

Leo Strauss was a figure of controversy during his life, but the controversy has grown exponentially since then, as have his influence and place in contemporary scholarship and thought. In this chapter, I shall say something about the multidimensional phenomenon that is Strauss's influence and legacy. We have already had some opportunity in earlier chapters to consider briefly Strauss's contribution to Jewish thought, and the ways in which his account of esoteric writing have informed reflections on hermeneutics and intellectual history. Here we will look at his more widely felt influence and significance and, above all, examine the controversies that have gathered around his thought and around the most notable contributions made by his students and followers, the "Straussians."

Perhaps most important has been the influence of Strauss's thought on American political thought and political life. In order to address this aspect of Strauss's influence, we will need to spend some time discussing what he made of American liberal democracy. Considering how remarkably little Strauss wrote about American politics, it is striking how much has been said about his views and their influence upon American political life. We will conclude this chapter by looking at the most notable public dispute on the subject of Leo Strauss: the connections that have been made between the influence of Strauss's thought and the decision of the George W. Bush White House to invade Iraq some thirty years after Strauss's death. Though this controversy happened nearly twenty years ago, recalling it will allow us to crystallize the more fundamental question of the influence of Strauss upon American political life and the relation of his thought to practical political realities more generally.

During his intellectual career Strauss's writings were at once highly respected and highly controversial within scholarly circles. But for much of his intellectual life, those circles were pretty small. It is really only with his arrival at the University of Chicago in 1949, and the appearance of a number of his most notable works in the early 1950s, that Strauss came to broad recognition and became a subject for wider scholarly debate. His books and articles met with a mixed reception, often including significant confusion and misunderstanding. Perhaps most controversial was Strauss's publication of "Persecution and the Art of Writing," first as an article and then as the title chapter of a book that appeared in 1952. *Persecution and the Art of Writing* solidified the sense that Strauss's scholarship refused to adhere to the standards of his profession.

But it was really by engaging in debates with social science in various publications in the early 1960s that Strauss came into open dispute particularly with his colleagues in political science. His most provocative act was his involvement in a book edited by his colleague and former student Herbert Storing, *Essays on the Scientific Study of Politics* (1962), which concluded with an epilogue written by Strauss himself. Strauss's "Epilogue" built upon the critiques written by the volume's other contributors concerning the methods and results of the positivist approach to political science. Very much in line with Strauss's earlier critiques of positivism (as found, for instance, in *Natural Right and History*), this "Epilogue" was a strident attack on the assumptions and inconsistencies he found in the positivist approach to political science. He argued that positivism both repudiates the standpoint of "common sense" in its orienting role in political and moral life, and yet at the same time relies on common sense to provide any sense of relevance for its supposedly more scientific or exact methodology. Strauss's "Epilogue" builds to a conclusion hardly calculated to win the support of the positivists:

> Only a great fool would call the new political science diabolic: it has no attributes peculiar to fallen angels. It is not even Machiavellian, for Machiavelli's teaching was graceful, subtle, and colorful. Nor is it Neronian. Nevertheless one may say of it that it fiddles while Rome burns. It is excused by two facts: it does not know that it fiddles, and it does not know that Rome burns. (LAM 223)

The book was reviewed by John Schaar and Sheldon Wolin in the *American Political Science Review* (March 1963) with considerable hostility and at great length, which review was responded to by Strauss and the other contributors to the original book with further vehemence. It seems that this exchange may have crystallized the sense that Strauss and his students, a number of whom were contributors to Storing's *Essays on the Scientific Study of Politics*, were outside the norms of academic life. This was to play out in the growing hostility toward Strauss's students: as they began to be hired at universities and colleges in the United States in various departments – including Political Science, Classics, and Philosophy – they began to be seen as sectarian and cliquish. There was a growing sense that the Straussians respected and promoted "their own." One among many signs of this hostility was the failure of one of Strauss's most prominent students, Thomas Pangle, to gain tenure at Yale in 1979. There were a number of other such incidents. Strauss's scholarship was coming to be more directly contested and rebutted, often with little evidence and in shockingly high-handed ways. The intellectual ability and formation of his students were sometimes recognized, and other times denied. That Strauss's students were often associated with conservative standpoints in the predominantly liberal or left-of-center world of the American academy only exacerbated the growing animosity toward Strauss, his students, and – subsequently – *their* students. Beginning in the 1950s, something like the sense of a "school" began to emerge, and, with time, this became more of a problem. "Straussian" – a label that Strauss's students wear awkwardly and recognize as often tinged with hostility and contempt – has become widely used in both the academic world and the popular press.

A particularly important alteration in Strauss's reputation occurred when, after his death, he began to be labeled as a Nietzschean. As we have seen, this is not in itself a position without foundation, but in the hands of a number of critics (above all Shadia Drury), this position became the basis for establishing the claim that Strauss and his students were engaged in a project fundamentally opposed to American liberal democracy. Before we explore the charge of Strauss as an anti-democratic thinker, it is worth pausing to notice the shift that happened in the opposition to Strauss. In the debate in the 1960s over *Essays on the Scientific Study of Politics*, the primary concern was that Strauss was advocating a pre-modern or traditionalist, moralistic attachment to one's regime, and in so doing was displaying a Cold War type of Americanism. Since

Strauss's death in 1973, the charge has been the opposite: Strauss and his school are secret Nietzscheans seeking to undermine the American regime of liberal democracy.

We have already discussed the place of Nietzsche in Strauss's thought, and the need to see the role Nietzsche plays in Strauss's intellectual formation. We have also seen that, in seeking a return to classical rationalism, Strauss builds a distinctive post-Nietzschean standpoint, and so points toward an alternative way to address the "crisis of our time." But in order to assess how Strauss's Nietzschean or post-Nietzschean position might influence American political thought and politics, we need to have a better sense of Strauss's own relation to American liberal democracy. This is not a straightforward matter. Strauss wrote very little about American politics; even in his classes – for many of which we have verbatim transcripts made from recordings – he says very little. He never wrote at length about the American founding or the American constitutional order. Notably, he began *Natural Right and History*, his most comprehensive book, with an invocation of the Declaration of Independence and the natural rights cited there as fundamental to the greatness of the American order (NRH 1). The book seems to present itself as a defense and recovery of these natural rights – but the Declaration of Independence is never mentioned again. Further, a fundamental thesis of Strauss's book is that what the modern understands as natural "rights" (such as those of life, liberty, and the pursuit of happiness) are both a falling away from classical natural right, and an expression of the series of waves or stages that will lead to contemporary nihilism.

At the same time, Strauss speaks of himself as a friend and ally of democracy (IPP 344), and a number of his students have written to defend his claim. But it is a somewhat curious form of self-description, for to call oneself a "friend of democracy" is to both establish one's support for democracy and at the same time step back from identifying oneself as a democrat. Further, while Strauss seems as a practical matter to have displayed unhesitating support for American as well as British democracy and liberalism, his attitude to liberal democracy prior to his arrival in the English-speaking world was far less positive. We will turn shortly to Strauss's Weimar views, in particular a now-infamous letter he wrote to Karl Löwith in 1933, to illustrate this. But let us first articulate how, given his larger account of modernity, Strauss might be a friend of American liberal democracy.

As with all of Strauss's positions, the meaning of his claim to be a friend of democracy, and specifically the American form of democracy, is complex and multilayered, and involves balancing a series of considerations. The first and most important of these considerations is that, insofar as there is a necessary and ineliminable tension between the philosopher and the city, Strauss (to the extent that he identifies himself with the philosopher) cannot be attached to any regime. But as we have seen in his account of classical natural right, this very detachment is itself attenuated by his attachments both as philosopher and as citizen. So Strauss must be attached to his city, even if it is (or perhaps especially *because* it is) his city of refuge. Strauss is clear in saying that classical political philosophy is superior to modern political philosophy, and even that classical political forms are superior to modern political forms. For Strauss, the best regime belongs to the ancient city, not to the modern state. As he wrote to Karl Löwith in 1946: "I *really* believe, although to you this apparently appears fantastic, that the perfect political order, as Plato and Aristotle have sketched it, *is* the perfect political order" (LCM 107). Strauss clearly did not intend Plato and Aristotle's "perfect political order" to be a practical goal; but he does see it as the best regime, as we saw in chapter 4. However, even as it is important to recognize that both at the level of philosophy and at the level of the best regime Strauss points to the superiority of the ancients, we need to also recognize the difference between philosophy and history for Strauss. The historical realities of modern political life may not be subject to the same critique as modern political philosophy is.

Strauss is reasonably clear that American liberal democracy belongs to the first wave of modernity, or at least is deeply informed in its founding by the thought of John Locke. There is an ambivalence built into this. On the one hand, the United States is a modern regime, which for Strauss means it is part of the lowering of horizons endemic to the modern standpoint. In this sense, for him the United States would be given over to the leveling and dehumanizing tendencies built into the modern project. On the other hand, because it is constitutionally grounded in the first wave, the United States is established against the second and third waves of modernity, when modernity loses all contact with nature and so gives political and moral life over to history. Strauss's identification of American liberal democracy with the first wave suggests that it is the best regime available in the modern world, where the classical polity can have no historical reality.

It is this standpoint, what could be called "conservative

modernity," that explains much of Straussian political involvement. The Straussian is pulled in two directions at once. The struggle at the practical level is between preventing the further development and radicalization of modernity in American political life, and yet intellectually recognizing that such radicalization is the ineluctable inner logic of modernity. The Straussian is caught in a kind of tension: intellectually such radicalization belongs to the deeper logic of modernity and would – if followed through – expose, historically and politically, the nihilism at the heart of the modern project. But, historically and politically, this would be destructive of human good. So Strauss and his students see that the corruption of moral and political life in the name of progressivism and moral relativism is inevitable – and at the same time must strive to inhibit that inevitability.

There are still further complications. Strauss seems to point to ways in which modern liberal democracy can have forms and institutions and practices that re-enact ancient principles of natural right. That is to say, a number of pre-modern traditions and practices persist within the American regime – above all, religious belief. As well, the structures of American political life, including its constitutional order, can be seen to promote and sustain an "aristocracy" within democracy that makes possible a certain imitation of "the rule of gentlemen" belonging to the best practicable regime according to the ancients. In this context, Strauss gave two lectures about the role of a "liberal education" – that is, an education in the great books – as preparatory to and supportive of a democratic aristocracy (LAM 3–25). Insofar as the American founders built such ancient principles into the American regime, that regime can and should be supported. Strauss would thus see tensions at work in the American regime between its modernizing, leveling tendencies and its ancient, aristocratic ones. The work of the Straussian statesman would be, in general, to strengthen the latter tendencies.

But to say even this much is to go beyond anything explicitly stated by Strauss in his writings. However, the way in which what Strauss sees as the interplay of ancient and modern tendencies may influence the course of American political life is not straightforward. Many of Strauss's students have developed these ideas in different and often conflicting directions – and certainly, Strauss's position is by no means necessarily simply to support reactionary forces. The underlying standpoint, for Strauss, is not the past or tradition, but natural right. Abraham Lincoln is taken up by a number of Strauss's students as the great example of natural right: an exemplary American statesman who refashions, perhaps even refounds, America, disrupting the aristocratic aspects of the South connected to and sustained by slavery. It is important, then, to see that the "conservatism" of Strauss is a secondary and strategic position. It belongs to an overall standpoint that would make an ahistorical (and therefore non-traditional) natural right the abiding standard.

All of these points can certainly support the claim that Strauss was perfectly right to say he was a friend and ally to liberal democracy, and to American liberal democracy more specifically. However, critics have been less convinced about the sincerity of such attestations. This skepticism has become outright denial in light of two phenomena: (1) growing claims about Strauss's secret Nietzscheanism; and (2) the number of Strauss students (or those connected to his students) who have been involved in American political life, largely on the right, and above all as neo-conservatives. We will look at this second aspect toward the end of this chapter. It is important to note here, however, that while the neo-conservatives would see themselves as firm supporters of liberal democracy, many who see Strauss as a Nietzschean connect his students' involvement in apparently anti-liberal and anti-democratic right-wing politics to that Nietzscheanism.

As we have seen, Strauss himself connected Nietzsche to anti-democratic and, indeed, even fascistic politics. While Strauss warns against "reductio ad Hitlerum" arguments, he makes strong connections between both Nietzsche's and Heidegger's philosophical standpoints and fascism or Nazism as political movements. So, by Strauss's own standards, to identify him as a "Nietzschean" suggests that he was no friend of liberal democracy. Some of Strauss's admirers, such as Laurence Lampert and Stanley Rosen, see his thought as Nietzschean or as having Nietzschean tendencies. However, it has belonged to Strauss's accusers to make the most notable cases in this direction. Shadia Drury's *The Political Ideas of Leo Strauss* was the first sustained and influential account of Strauss as a secret, anti-liberal Nietzschean. Others have followed in her footsteps; perhaps most thorough in his research is William H. F. Altman, whose *The German Stranger* is a far more scholarly work than Drury's in seeking to portray Strauss as a "Jewish Nazi" inspired by Nietzsche. We have already had a chance in chapter 1 to consider the relation of Strauss to Nietzsche, the extent to which there is a basis for this claim in Strauss's thought, and the crucial differences between their positions, at least from his "reorientation" in the 1930s forward.

In 1933, Strauss wrote a letter that problematizes the portrait of him as a friend and ally to democracy as I have sketched it above. On May 19, 1933, shortly after Hitler came to power, Strauss wrote from Paris to his friend Karl Löwith, who was still in Germany. This letter has come to wider attention fairly recently, and for many it is the "smoking gun" whose publication reveals the hidden agenda of Strauss's teaching. In fact, an entire book – *Cloaked in Virtue: Unveiling Leo Strauss and the Rhetoric of American Foreign Policy* by Nicholas Xenos (2008) – is dedicated to interpreting all of Strauss's thought and scholarship through the lens of this letter. I have reproduced the relevant portions of the letter below in Altman's translation as it appears in *The German Stranger*:

> And, as to the substance of the matter: i.e., that Germany having turned to the right does not tolerate us, that proves absolutely nothing against right-wing principles. On the contrary: only on the basis of right-wing principles – on the basis of fascistic, authoritarian, *imperial* principles – is it possible with integrity, without the ridiculous and pitiful appeal to the *droits imprescriptables de l'homme*, to protest against the money-grubbing bedlam. I am reading Caesar's *Commentaries* with deeper understanding, and I think about Virgil: *Tu regere imperio ... parcere subjectis et debellare superbos* [You rule by power ... to spare the conquered and to subdue the proud]. There exists no reason to crawl to the cross, to liberalism's cross as well, as long as somewhere in the world there yet glimmers a spark of the *Roman* thought. And even then: better than any cross, the ghetto.
>
> I therefore do not fear the emigrant's destiny – at the most *secundum carnem* [according to the flesh]: hunger and the like – . In a sense our kind is *always* "emigrant"; and what concerns the rest, the danger of embitterment, which certainly is *very* great, [Jacob] Klein, who in every sense was always an emigrant, is for me the living proof that it can be defeated. *Dixi, et animam meam salvavi* [I have spoken and have saved my soul]. (Altman, *The German Stranger: Leo Strauss and National Socialism*, 227–8)

Strauss makes a very similar statement to Gerhard Krüger, in very similar terms, on July 14, 1933:

> There could have been a decent, just, *imperial*, solution. The solution that has been opted for stems from hate, and it almost necessarily generates counter-hate. It will require a long, strenuous effort on my

part to be able to deal with what has been inflicted on me and my kind. (SKC 61)

Those who have sought to demonize Strauss have seized upon these pronouncements as firm evidence of his secret anti-liberal, anti-democratic tendencies, and his alignment with the very forces he exoterically appears to repudiate: Nietzscheanism, fascism, and amoralism. Given Strauss's account of esoteric writing, these private writings seem to expose him to just such a characterization. Students and other supporters of Strauss have provided various interpretations and explanations of these writings. Part of their difficulty is in their private and personal character. Beyond this, if these texts can be said to register a sympathy with right-wing "solutions," with "fascistic, authoritarian, *imperial* principles," do these alignments attach to Strauss for the whole of his scholarly life?

My own tentative sense of what is at work in these letters is that it is clear that Strauss was not sympathetic to liberalism prior to his migration to England and, later, to the United States. There is considerable evidence for his contempt for liberalism, especially as embodied in the "weak" Weimar Republic. Strauss's interest in Carl Schmitt, as well as his critique of Schmitt as remaining in the grip of liberalism, point to his critical relation to liberal modernity as a whole. Strauss's engagement with Schmitt's critique of liberalism inspired his interest in and study of Hobbes, whom he saw as the originator of liberalism and modernity. Strauss turned from liberalism to ancient non-liberal regimes as exemplary of the best regime. In this sense, he was and remained neither liberal nor fascist in his judgment of what was the best regime. This turn to the ancients arose as well because it belonged to the earlier Strauss to associate modernity – liberal, egalitarian, rights-of-man modernity – with Christianity, through modernity's being entangled by its efforts to refute Christianity. There is in the letter to Löwith, quoted above, a deep refusal of the assimilation that Strauss sees foisted upon him by a need to oppose the rise of the Nazis. His turn to "fascistic, authoritarian, *imperial* principles" can then be read as providing a solution to the crisis of Weimar liberalism – a solution that brings justice and order, that spares the vanquished and humbles the proud, without requiring the kind of assimilationist (Christian) standpoint implicit in a liberal, rights-of-man opposition. In short, Strauss is looking to a solution from what he calls the "Right," from authority, in accord with natural *right*, and not natural *rights*.

Further, I would agree with Steven Smith and others that it is reasonable to assume that Strauss's experience of the response of English-speaking liberal democracy to Hitler altered his judgment about the practical capabilities of those liberal democracies, and the continuing presence in them of classical sources. Strauss had a very great admiration for Winston Churchill and the Aristotelian greatness of soul he displayed in the face of Nazi Germany. Strauss had a less robust, but similar, admiration for Franklin Roosevelt. None of this is to deny that Strauss continued to have an ambivalence toward liberal democracy and its modernizing tendencies. What I am suggesting is that the "smoking gun" perceived in these letters Strauss wrote in the shock and heat of 1933 is not a direct reflection of his principles but rather an expression of his practical judgment in the face of worldly politics and the possibilities of liberalism as a political reality in 1930s Germany.

Straussians

The very use of the term "Straussian" has been something that students and admirers of the thought of Leo Strauss have struggled with. It has often been used in a detrimental way. It has also created problems for those seeking to articulate Strauss's own thought: a number of commentators have cited Marx's famous statement that he was not a Marxist – suggesting, equally, that Strauss was not, or would not have been, a Straussian. In fact, the very presence of a "school" identified with Strauss has a certain ambivalence. It seems clear that Strauss did strive to find students who would be shaped or informed by his distinctive standpoint, a standpoint that involves not only a certain set of philosophical claims and claims about the history of philosophy, but a distinctive and deeply controversial claim about how the texts that form that history were written, and how they are to be read (the exoteric/esoteric distinction). As we have already noted in chapter 3, this hermeneutic led to charges that Strauss's standpoint has an inherently circular and insular character that functions like an ideology: it makes sense of the world from within but resists critical or external input. To the extent that these charges are true, this feature of Strauss's thought has reinforced the sense that Straussians are, indeed, a school or even a cult or sect.

At the same time, that Strauss should be seen as responsible for the emergence of a "school" at all stands in contrast to his call to break down dogmatisms, above all the dogmatisms of modernity and historicism. The notion of a "school" seems to stand in opposition to Strauss's portrayal of philosophy as the "knowledge of ignorance" or as the open pursuit of knowledge in contrast to the closed world of the city, the world of opinion that must police its boundaries. So Straussians struggle both with accepting that designation and with resisting it, seeing it as a betrayal of the whole Straussian or Socratic project, which is meant to be a liberation from a closed world of opinion.

Even so, it seems reasonable to use "Straussian" as an adjective in a descriptive and not prescriptive form to speak of the many students of Strauss, who often identify themselves as such. However, over time it has become more and more difficult to give any stable sense to the term "Straussian," as the followers of Strauss themselves have become divided in their understandings of Strauss, or have developed positions in some contrast to his even while remaining indebted to his thought. Further, as Strauss's thought and influence have entered into American political and public life, various figures have been described as "Straussian" whose actual relation to Strauss or his students has ranged from significant to non-existent. This is especially the case when the terms "Straussian" and "neo-conservative" are used in confusing interchange with one another. All of this has attached to "Straussian" a number of associations that have little, or only a tangential, relationship to Strauss's own thought or opinions.

In 1987, one of Strauss's earliest students, Harry Jaffa, published an essay entitled "The Crisis of the Strauss Divided: The Legacy Reconsidered."[1] As Jaffa's somewhat playful title suggests, after Strauss's death serious divisions appeared among his students, who fell into various camps or schools. A number of articles and exchanges in the 1980s and 1990s brought to light a significant rift within the Straussians, above all between the "East Coast" and the "West Coast" Straussians.[2] Of course, all important thinkers inspire different – and sometimes sharply opposed – interpretations, and often these differences point to tensions or problems within the thinker. In the later appropriation of a thinker's standpoint, aspects

---

[1] Harry Jaffa, "The Crisis of the Strauss Divided: The Legacy Reconsidered." *Social Research*, 54, 1987, pp. 570–603. The article's title is a play on the title of Jaffa's most important book, *The Crisis of the House Divided*, a book dealing with the Lincoln–Douglas debates.

[2] For an excellent account of these schools, see Zuckert and Zuckert, *The Truth about Leo Strauss*, 228–59.

that are "in play" in the original thinker can take on a rigid and oppositional form. It is no different with Strauss: a rift among his students that is suggestive of tensions within Strauss's thought has resulted in more rigid positions among students on both sides of the divide.

In his contribution to *The Cambridge Companion to Leo Strauss* (2009), Michael Zuckert usefully outlines two substantive issues that Straussians commonly debate: (1) the relation of reason and revelation ("Athens and Jerusalem") in Strauss's thought; and (2) the validity or worth of the moral and civic virtues of the political life, in contrast to the philosophical life. This latter concern is helpfully restated by Zuckert as the question of the relative merit of the Platonic standpoint (which tends to derogate the moral life relative to the philosophical) and the Aristotelian standpoint (which tends to treat the moral life as having inherent worth, largely independent of philosophy). As we have seen, Strauss himself continually both emphasizes opposition and refuses synthesis as a way to mediate oppositions: the problematic and heterogeneous nature of his thought is fundamental to it and ties into his claim that there are permanent, fundamental, and irresolvable problems. At the same time, Strauss also modifies or attenuates opposition: for him, Athens and Jerusalem are irreconcilable – but in their mutual incapacity to refute each other, there is room for mutual respect and, indeed, a recognition of a whole series of commonalities. So also for the city and philosophy: there is both an irreconcilable opposition and then a series of interconnections (and, indeed, a need for the other) from within the standpoint of both city and philosophy.

The positions of East Coast Straussians and West Coast Straussians both trace themselves back to Strauss and his writings, but the East Coast tends to emphasize the oppositional moments, and the West Coast the reconciling, modifying moments. Both positions can be seen to be a partial account of Strauss but, in general, I would argue that the East Coast emphasis is closer to Strauss's own most basic intellectual commitments. Both go beyond Strauss to develop his position in relation to American politics, history, and cultural life. The West Coast Straussian position, especially as exemplified by its leading figure, Harry Jaffa, emphasizes the nobility of the American political project and the mutually sustaining roles of civic excellence and religious, biblical formation. In this sense, the West Coast Straussians may be seen as more conventionally conservative: they find support in aspects of Strauss that recognize American liberal democracy as both modern and open to ancient sources, religious and philosophical (above all, Aristotle). The East Coast Straussians tend to display a more ambivalent relation to the American regime, affirming its foundation in natural rights, but seeing even in that founding the seeds of tendencies toward conformity, leveling, and ultimately nihilism; they often look to Tocqueville's concerns about the dangers of soft despotism inherent in American egalitarianism and democratic principles. The West Coast Straussians will accuse the East Coast of Nietzschean tendencies in their denial of the ultimate validity of the moral and religious life in the face of a zetetic philosophical life. The East Coast Straussians, in turn, will accuse the West Coast of replacing philosophy as the quest for knowledge with edifying moralization. Commenting on Hegel's famous claim that philosophy must avoid being edifying, in *Thoughts on Machiavelli* (1958) Strauss himself writes:

> It would seem that the notion of the beneficence of nature or of the primacy of the Good must be restored by being rethought through a return to the fundamental experiences from which it is derived. For while "philosophy must beware of wishing to be edifying," it is of necessity edifying. (TM 299)

It would seem, then, that Strauss's own standpoint can be seen to comprehend both the East and West Coast positions. At the same time, as both schools emphasize different, but defensible, aspects of Strauss's thought, the clash between them brings to light genuine difficulties within Strauss's position.

The Cultural and Political Impact of the Straussians

The most notable student of Strauss is undoubtedly Allan Bloom (1930–92), who was very much an East Coast Straussian. Bloom rose to national prominence in 1987 with the publication of *The Closing of the American Mind*, a book that sold over a million copies and made its author both wealthy and famous. Perhaps Bloom's highest accolade was given posthumously when Saul Bellow, the Nobel and Pulitzer Prize-winning novelist, wrote his final novel, *Ravelstein*, as a *roman à clef*, with Ravelstein as the stand-in for Bloom. *The Closing of the American Mind* was a critique of contemporary American culture, particularly as exemplified in the American university, especially as it was transformed by the 1960s. While Bloom hardly refers to Strauss in *The Closing of the*

American Mind, the book is clearly informed by Strauss's critique of modernity and his concern about the radicalization of modernity. Bloom is very much declaring that America has been deeply corrupted by its coming to adopt the relativism and nihilism that Strauss associates with the third wave of modernity. Bloom writes of "nihilism American style," and speaks of the "flattening of the soul" affecting American youth as they take up the cultural legacy of the 1960s. His polemic follows a largely East Coast Straussian reading of the American founding that emphasizes its modernity and the lowered horizons that give life to a consumerist, relativist, empty liberalism. For Bloom, the pre-modern and religious aspects of American life are sadly vanishing in the face of the trajectory of modernity.

Bloom's book clearly struck a chord in 1980s America, seeming to reinforce the pushback against the 1960s found in the Reagan revolution and the Moral Majority movement. It was widely seen as a central text in the culture wars of the 1980s and 1990s, as battles raged over the proper content of American higher education, especially in the humanities. In the growing power of the American right, perhaps more significant was the emergence of a new political force within these political and cultural movements: the rise of the neo-conservatives. It is the apparent connection between Strauss, the Straussians, and neo-conservativism that has generated the most public and heated controversy about the (malign) influence of Strauss's thought. This concern came to a head when the decision was made by the George W. Bush White House to invade Iraq in March 2003. To get a sense of the role and place of Strauss in American public life, we need to give this incident some consideration.

In the wake of the invasion of Iraq, various articles in a number of leading newspapers, magazines, and journals – including *The New York Times*, *Le Monde*, *The New Yorker*, and *Harper's* – made the surprising claim that the response of the Bush White House to the events of 9/11 was deeply connected to the thought of Leo Strauss. The notion that George W. Bush would consult the writings of Strauss or Plato – neither of whom said a great deal about international affairs, or anything about Islamic terrorism – in order to sort out how to respond to the events of September 11, 2001, seems to require a suspension of disbelief usually called upon only by readers of pulp fiction. Yet many important and established media outlets drew a very strong connection between Leo Strauss and the Bush White House. The BBC aired a three-hour documentary series,

The Power of Nightmares, to give wider awareness to the idea that such a connection existed. Actor and writer Tim Robbins produced and directed *Embedded* – a play critically panned but publicly well received – which toured a number of major American cities and included scenes with characters clearly drawn from the Bush White House inner circle worshipping and shouting "All Hail Leo Strauss" before an image of Strauss and, later, coming to a state of sexual frenzy at the invocation of Strauss's name in Latin.

The explanation for the unlikely claim of an alliance between Strauss and the George W. Bush White House lies in the emergence of neo-conservativism, which played a mediating role. The neo-conservatives form a loosely connected movement – or, as the godfather of neo-conservativism, Irving Kristol (1920–2009), preferred to call it, a "persuasion" – that was seen as very influential in formulating the White House's response to 9/11. The argument for connecting Strauss to the Bush White House suggests further that the neo-conservatives were influenced by the thought of Leo Strauss; indeed, a number of them are former students of Strauss, or students of students of Strauss. Those who see a Straussian conspiracy or neo-conservative "cabal" at work in the formulation of the White House response to 9/11 generally, and particularly in the decision to go to war in Iraq, claim that these individuals, operating in the context of support from friendly think tanks and institutes on the one hand and the right-wing media on the other, were able to "hijack" the Bush White House foreign policy to fulfill their own ideological (Strauss-inspired) objectives.

We are faced with the claim, then, that Leo Strauss has, posthumously through his teaching and his students and their role in the Bush White House, brought about a transformation of American foreign policy. This transformation was seen as an ideological shift from the post-1945 orthodoxy of multilateral containment, diplomacy, and support for international law and institutions, to a foreign policy that is resolutely nationalistic, imperialistic, unilateral, pre-emptive, and militaristic in orientation, and whose first clear result was the Iraq War (2003–11). But beyond this, the claim was made that Strauss's influence, through his neo-conservative acolytes, altered not only the character of American foreign policy, but also the very way the American government understood its relation to the American people. Strauss's position, and his turn to Plato and the ancients, was understood to mark a radical break with the ideals and principles of modern liberal democracy. The core of this claim lay in features of Strauss's standpoint with which we are already familiar: (1) his critique of modernity as leveling and nihilistic and his turn to the ancients; (2) the centrality of the distinction between philosophy and the city, which then undergirds the distinction between esoteric and exoteric teachings; and (3) his discussion of the necessity of the "noble lie" in Plato's *Republic*. All of this suggests to critics an erosion of modern democratic principles and the encouragement of manipulation of the many by the elite. In Shadia Drury's view, the Straussian neo-conservative influence is to be seen not simply in the fact that the Bush White House took up a new foreign policy, but in the way it was perceived to have done so – through the manipulative use of dishonesty, misrep-resentation, and a whole array of practices and policies aimed at undermining the principles, procedures, and safeguards of liberal democracy. From this point of view, the Bush White House, insofar as it engaged in untruth and incomplete disclosure of information, was not just carrying on with the follies and foibles of government-as-usual, but was actually doing so deliberately, out of ideological principle – self-consciously, and with a good conscience.

The alarm of those times has long since faded. The claims of Strauss's influence on the White House of the early 2000s can seem now as much a part of that historical moment as any number of other past ideological pronouncements. It is, however, still worth pausing to investigate this case in some detail, as it goes to the heart of the question of Strauss's influence on American conservative thought. Irving Kristol, whom we have already mentioned, recog-nized Strauss's influence upon his own thought and on American conservative thought generally. In 1996, Kristol wrote: "Strauss's analysis of the destructive elements within modern liberalism, an analysis that was popularized by his students and his students' students, has altered the very tone of public discourse in the United States" (Kristol, *Reflections of a Neo-Conservative*, 16). At the heart of the critique of Strauss's influence on the neo-conservatives is the notion that he teaches hypocrisy: that rulers can and should be deceptive in invoking moral virtues, a sense of nobility, or a sense of piety. But – as we saw in chapter 4 – these virtues and sensi-bilities according to Strauss answer to natural wants and needs of the soul, and indeed apply to the philosopher insofar as he is a citizen and moved not only by a love of what is good, but also by a love of his own city and its well-being. Strauss was, however, equally clear that these virtues are limited to the horizon of the city during periods of normalcy. The philosopher must detach himself from his love of his own and from the "spiritedness" necessary to moral virtue, in order to pursue his fearless quest for the truth. The philosopher must break through the horizon of the city in order to pursue the natural horizon of the permanent problems. Equally, in extreme situations, the city must be able to abandon its virtues for the sake of the city itself, whose survival is necessary for the existence of these virtues: "in extreme situations the normally valid rules of natural right are justly changed, or changed in accordance with natural right; the exceptions are as just as the rules" (NRH 160). This sense of the limited character of the moral virtues can appear to be a justification for all manner of Machiavellian actions. But Strauss addresses this concern directly: "Machiavelli denies natural right, because he takes his bearings by the extreme situations ... and not by the normal situations in which the demands of justice in the strict sense are the highest law" (NRH 162).

Strauss's explanation of natural right as he discovered it in the texts of Plato and Aristotle does not, then, provide a justification for lying or manipulation in order to avoid electoral defeat. In a democracy, the defeat of one party is hardly an extreme situation. The concepts of natural right and the noble lie do not justify undermining the political order or violating the constitution, except to save that order or constitution. They do not justify consciously governing for the sake of one's own interests or the interests of some, and not for the common good. All these, Strauss would say, the ancients characterized as actions of a corrupt government, and ultimately belong to tyranny.

Even more directly relevant to those who see Straussianism in the perceived lies and manipulation in the Bush White House's efforts to draw America into war with Iraq is that Strauss does not present the doctrine of natural right as justification for ignoring ordinary moral and political virtues, to create the impression of an extreme situation where in fact none exists. This seems to be the heart of the issue. If the Bush White House did have to respond to an extreme situation for the United States, then Strauss's account of the ancients would provide principles of justification for necessary measures that are not in accord with normal civic or moral virtue. But in the absence of this condition – in the absence of the extreme situation – such actions are open to condemnation on those very same principles.

For Strauss, there was something deeply ambiguous and vulnerable about American liberal democracy. Its institutions simultaneously make room for and depend upon an older sense of the liberal or aristocratic soul, and yet those self-same institutions have within them tendencies that would undermine the inequalities necessary to standards of excellence and of virtues (LAM 3–25). By contrast, the neo-conservatives, especially in the early twenty-first century, had a much less fragile sense of this; rather, they demonstrated a confidence that American liberal democracy would not only retain but indeed cultivate and develop a sense of the pre-modern moral personality. The neo-conservatives of the 1960s and 1970s wrote about the cultural contradictions of capitalism in a spirit similar to that of Strauss, but this sense of vulnerability about the moral dimension of the American economic system disappeared in the next generation. Indeed, among the second generation of neo-conservatives – those associated with the Bush White House – one finds a confidence and optimism about the United States that is lacking in Strauss. The neo-conservatives assert that Americans can and must be both ancient and modern, and that Americans are able simultaneously to affirm aspects that for Strauss were fundamentally opposed: religion and secularity, virtue and freedom. This confidence underlies the most notable area of difference between Leo Strauss's teaching and the viewpoint of second-generation neo-conservatives: that of foreign policy.

It is ironic that Leo Strauss came to be identified in the popular press with the neo-conservatives in relation to the one aspect of their position – their imperialist, idealistic foreign policy – which is most clearly where he would be deeply critical. Certainly, there are general aspects of Strauss's position, especially the notion of "regime" and the use of moral categories to characterize and understand the action of regimes, that neo-conservatives have explicitly adopted from Strauss (NRH 136–40). It is not clear whether Strauss can be credited as the source for the use of the term "regime" in George W. Bush's now-famous phrase "regime change," but clearly this aspect of Strauss's thought was important to the neo-conservative way of understanding the political world. However, although they share at least some common background assumptions, Strauss and the neo-conservatives come to opposed conclusions.

Strauss's own statements about foreign affairs are singularly critical of idealistic or imperialist foreign policy. He viewed the primary aim and purpose of any regime to be excellence: all regimes "look up" to something, as he put it. The regime informs the whole life of a city, and so most fundamentally determines the city's character and essence. Strauss viewed it as a failing of modernity that its political theorists tend to downplay the formative role of the regime in setting a city or state's character. Hobbes, for instance, was fundamentally indifferent to the type of regime in place in any given state. The ancient concentration on the internal excellence of the city, for Strauss, meant that foreign policy was only an external and derivative concern. In a discussion of the fourth book of Plato's *Republic*, Strauss argues that the good city is not guided in its relations to other cities:

> the size of the territory of the good city is determined by that city's own moderate needs and by nothing else; the relation of the city to the other cities belongs to the province of wisdom rather than of justice; the good city is not a part of a community of cities or is not dedicated to the common good of that community or does not serve other cities. (CM 100)

There are two aspects of this quotation that must be noted here: (1) that Strauss rejected a central role for foreign affairs in defining the city, and, in particular, rejected the subordination of the city to an international league of nations; and (2) that, equally, he rejected imperialism. Let us discuss these points in turn.

Strauss's skepticism about (and indeed opposition to) the notion of a community of nations may well have influenced or at least provided support for similar tendencies in the neo-conservatives and the Bush White House. Strauss's essential argument here was developed in his introduction to *The City and Man*. In that work, he was writing in the context of the Cold War. Fundamentally, Strauss responded to what he saw as an international liberalism at work in the notion of a community of nations or an international law absolutely binding on all parties irrespective of their type of regime or intentions. Strauss saw this as an expression of the Kantian vision of a community of nations moving to a "perpetual peace," and at its heart he saw two kinds of untruth: a denial of the ineradicable character of evil, and a denial of the regime as the space and context of civic loyalty and authority.

Strauss wrote in *The City and Man* that "no bloody or unbloody change of society can eradicate the evil in man" (CM 5). This claim has implications not only for the internal requirements of any regime, but also for international relations. The indelible presence of evil in international affairs means not only that there is an ineradicable need to be wary of other regimes, but also that, inevitably, there will be worse and better regimes. For Strauss, the notion that there is a legal equality and legitimacy of all nations that belong to the "international community" is a "pious fraud" (CM 6).

Notions that a body like the United Nations could have overriding moral authority, or that international law has binding legitimacy, can for Strauss be necessary, and even useful, pieties – but they should not actually be believed or assumed. Behind the claim of an international law or a community of nations, Strauss detected a progressive, secular humanism fully implicated in modernity and its break with nature.

For Strauss, the most compelling exponent of this viewpoint was his friend Alexandre Kojève, who, on the basis of an interpretation of Hegel, argued that the end point of history is the Universal and Homogeneous State (UHS). Strauss, however, argued that the truth of the UHS is not freedom and the fulfillment of humanity, but necessarily a tyranny that must eradicate all the intimations of a nature related to human excellence. For Strauss, the international system, insofar as it is grounded in the ideal of the UHS, is not in accord with natural right, but rather presupposes the replacement of natural right by ideology. Following his interpretation of the classics and especially of Plato, Strauss reckoned foreign affairs to be essentially amoral (CM 100, WIPP 84–5). What provides limit and order is not an overriding principle of international law or a presumed community of nations, but the internal character of nations: their regime.

Strauss wrote in the face of what appeared to be an intransigent divide during the Cold War: "all this amounts to saying that for the foreseeable future, political society remains what it always has been: a partial or particular society whose most urgent and primary task is its self-preservation and whose highest task is its self-improvement" (CM 6).

For Strauss, the problem with a notion of international law and a community of nations (in contrast to alliances) was that this subordinates the regime and its self-improvement to a spurious ideal that implicitly points to the dissolution of all regimes into the UHS. But, according to Strauss, the implication of this seeming amoralism and realism was not a defense of expansionism and imperialism (except where strictly necessary). Rather, Strauss drew upon both Plato and Thucydides in his recognition that imperialist, expansionist foreign policy tends to undermine the moral and political order at home. Strauss's byword in politics, both domestic and international, is moderation. For him, the good city is not a danger to its neighbors, as its end is not wealth and power, but virtue. Instability and danger in foreign policy have their roots in corrupt regimes. The goal of international peace, then, is achieved less through international institutions and laws (though these may have their uses) than through the presence of good regimes.

This is where Strauss parts company with the neo-conservatives. For him, the great example of democratic folly in international affairs was the Sicilian expedition that Athens undertook in the disastrous Peloponnesian War, promoted by Socrates' most extravagant and politically effective student, Alcibiades. It is not clear that there was an Alcibiades among the neo-conservatives who joined the Bush White House, but the extravagant and idealist language of "hegemony" and "empire" that the neo-conservatives used seems to provide a strange parallel between some of Strauss's students and this particular student of Socrates. Strauss wrote in his commentary on Thucydides, in seeming repudiation of empire and hegemony: "generally speaking, even the lowliest men prefer being subjects to men of their own people rather than to any aliens" (CM 239).

So while Strauss may well have been a crucial source for the neo-conservatives in their move to a post-liberal analysis of foreign policy involving a release from the moral demands of international law, nonetheless a liberal idealism re-emerges in the neo-conservative position in the ends their post-liberal means are intended to pursue. There are, of course, those who questioned the benevolence in the "benevolent hegemony" recommended by neo-conservatives or doubted the claim that the goal was ever to bring "democracy," rather than simply American control, to the Middle East. However, even if the ends were more material and realist than ideal, it is imperialism itself that Strauss would have criticized as destructive of the American regime. But this point about the material interests in the Middle East of the United States, as a capitalist consumerist society, also reconnects us to a more fundamental point of distinction between Strauss and the neo-conservatives. Strauss remained deeply apprehensive of the release of the acquisitive passion that belonged to the United States as a modern regime. The neo-conservative confidence that capitalist consumerism need not be destructive, and indeed may be positively supportive of virtue and the well-being of the American regime, parallels a similar confidence in the positive rather than negative effects of a new, idealistic, imperial American foreign policy. The neo-conservatives suppressed Strauss's deep opposition to claims to reconcile opposites such as modern capitalism and ancient virtue or a healthy regime and imperial ambition.

One can say that Strauss's critique of modernity, and his revival of what he took to be the standpoint of Plato and antiquity generally, provided a crucial background for neo-conservatism. Students brought up in the age of ascendant liberalism who came to Strauss, or to one of his many followers, would have found in their teaching a release from liberal moralism and idealism. This is the Nietzschean moment of revolt against secular humanism that we saw in chapter 1. But together with this release – embodied in the philosopher's break from the city – those students would equally have discovered a retraction of this release in the name of nature and of natural right. It is this retraction of Nietzschean will in the face of an always- and already-existing natural order that returns those students to political life – but now from a standpoint of already having transcended it. For Strauss, these two moments must be kept carefully apart: the philosopher may be given to divine madness in his philosophizing but remains moderate and promotes moderation in political life. The spirit of an Alcibiades is of one who has sought to tear down the sacred veil that separates philosophic immoderation from practical moderation. In the neo-conservative rationale for the war in Iraq that emanated from within the administration of George W. Bush, Strauss would likely have detected more the spirit of Alcibiades than of Socrates.

With the failures of the Iraq War and a growing consensus surrounding the limitations of American power, the influence and role of neo-conservativism in American foreign policy have dissipated. This was confirmed with the election in 2008 of Barack Obama as President. Strauss's public prominence, limited as it was, has now largely disappeared, even while his reputation and place in the scholarly and academic world have grown; this can be gauged not only by the number of publications produced about Strauss, but also by the substance of those publications. For several years after the first widely publicized exposés of the Straussian influence in the early 2000s, books continued to appear developing the critique, but also challenging it and defending Strauss. But the deeper tendency of recent Strauss scholarship has been to liberate Leo Strauss from these partisan wars. In this sense, Strauss is finally emerging not just as a focus of controversy, but as a significant intellectual figure comparable to, and in conversation with, other prominent thinkers of the twentieth century.

The presidency of Donald Trump was, in general, not associated with the influence of Strauss – nor really with any significant intellectual figure, even though a number of actors who were part of the George W. Bush White House also served in the Trump White

House, and some of these have (largely tangential) connections to Strauss. The one notable exception was the role of some figures connected to Claremont College, an institution connected to the West Coast Straussians where Strauss himself taught after his retirement from the University of Chicago. Charles R. Kesler and some of his students provided some intellectual argumentation supporting the Trump presidency. The most notable of these is Michael Anton, who wrote an infamous article, "The Flight 93 Election," which appeared just prior to the 2016 presidential election under the pseudonym Publius Decius Mus, in the *Claremont Review of Books*. In the article Anton compares Hillary Clinton to the terrorists who piloted the plane that was to crash into the Pentagon as part of 9/11. Trump is then somehow identified with the passengers who, although not trained in flying, broke into the cockpit and managed to prevent the most terrible outcome. Anton subsequently joined the Trump administration for fourteen months and, in a subsequent book (*After the Flight 93 Election*), explained the kind of vision for America that he saw in Donald Trump's election. In so doing, Anton explicitly draws upon the thought of Strauss (Anton, *After the Flight 93 Election*, 16–20, 58). Anton's critique in both the book and the earlier article is directed against his fellow conservatives, precisely for their indifference to the threat posed by Hillary Clinton's potential presidency and for their opposition to Trump. So while there was a Strauss-inspired defense of Trump's presidency, a number of the neo-conservatives who supported George W. Bush engaged in a conservative critique of Trump's presidency. For many, Trump was in no way a conservative figure, and clearly his foreign policy, while very different from Barack Obama's internationalist approach, was as complete a repudiation of the imperialist ambitions of the Bush White House neo-conservatives as was that of Obama.

Leo Strauss Today

Now, approximately a half-century since he died, Strauss is emerging less as a figure of partisan contestation and political conspiracy and more as a fundamental figure of twentieth-century intellectual life. A developed field of Strauss scholarship has arisen, not only in the United States or among "Straussians," but among scholars of all stripes communicating in a variety of languages. All of Strauss's books are still in print – primarily through the University of Chicago Press – and a multivolume complete works, a *Gesammelte Schriften*, is being published by the German publisher J. B. Metzler. Perhaps most significant for Strauss's legacy has been the establishment of the Leo Strauss Center at the University of Chicago, which has made available online a large number of audio recordings and transcripts of his lectures given at the University of Chicago, so that those who could never attend a class led by Strauss can have direct access to that experience.

The body of Strauss scholarship – some of which can be found in the "Further Reading" section that follows the Conclusion – has allowed important works by Strauss to be translated from German and French and made available to English speakers, including valuable correspondence between Strauss and his intellectual contemporaries. The journal *Interpretation*, which Strauss was involved in founding, is the most significant scholarly vehicle for Strauss studies, often publishing previously unavailable writings by Strauss. Scholars have made use of these and other scholarly sources to investigate the life and intellectual development of Strauss. Together this has allowed a more objective and multi-sided approach to Strauss that has drawn him into a whole series of debates and exchanges that widen and deepen his influence in Jewish studies, in theories of modernity, in hermeneutics, in medieval studies, in political science, and in any number of other fields. Strauss has joined the pantheon of thinkers that he dedicated his life to bringing so powerfully to bear upon the deep tensions and problems of the contemporary world, problems that may point us toward the "fundamental and permanent problems."

Conclusion

As a way of concluding, I would like to recall the thesis that I outlined in the Introduction. My claim is that Strauss is indeed a key contemporary thinker and, as such, cannot be seen to be – as he described himself – a mere scholar. I suggested that Strauss made this self-identification not out of modesty, but as in fact connected to his entire project of recovery, specifically recovering the standpoint of classical political philosophy.

As we have seen over the course of this book, Strauss understood the nihilism of the contemporary world as fundamentally a result of historicism. In Strauss's view, the way to escape from this standpoint rests not in trying to get historically "beyond" nihilism, but, rather, in a return to a world prior to historicism. Insofar as "originality" is tied to something historically new, Strauss's whole work depended upon him being radically unoriginal: only this could allow a genuine return to the origin of Socratic political philosophy in its own terms. Nietzsche's and Heidegger's attachment to originality, which for Strauss was a form of historicism, kept them trapped in the very nihilism they sought to move beyond.

My claim in this book has been that Strauss is in fact an original contemporary thinker, with a distinctive and specifically contemporary standpoint. His debt to Husserl is especially important, but so also are the influences of both Nietzsche and Heidegger. My argument has been that, in order to understand Strauss, it is necessary to see the emergence of his thought in the context of the Weimar Republic. His work of historical recovery is everywhere informed by this beginning point: this means that he reads history from out of the assumptions that belong to this standpoint. The challenge of Strauss's position is that his originality lies in the way that, through his work of historical recovery (through his readings of Plato, Aristotle, Machiavelli, and so on), he has constructed an ahistorical phenomenological stance. He discovers either this stance (ancient) or its negation (modern) in the various thinkers he reads.

Strauss's central claim is that this ahistorical phenomenology – what he calls Socratic political philosophy – can and does escape from the hold of historicism, and thereby from nihilism. This is true from within Strauss's position – and, in fact, that position is constructed or discovered with precisely this end in view. The presentation of a standpoint that is of a nature or "whole" – humanly available as a realm of permanent problems in which history takes place but unaffected by that history – does present exactly such a standpoint. As we have seen, Strauss takes enormous care to establish this position, and to show by careful exegesis (relying on his rediscovery of the exoteric/esoteric distinction) the presence of this standpoint in the pre-modern world, and above all in Socratic political philosophy.

Nonetheless, Strauss's position – against Strauss's own deepest intentions – is a contemporary standpoint, and so is inscribed by the very history it seeks to be free from. As a contemporary phenomenological standpoint, it is a remarkably powerful and interesting position that stands in relation to other contemporary positions. My basis for making this claim here is that Strauss's account remains marked and inscribed both by a contemporary problematic (nihilism) and by a contemporary response to that nihilism (phenomenology). Strauss certainly develops and alters that phenomenology through his brilliant readings of texts by Plato, Xenophon, Aristotle, and others. However, his work remains determined by its phenomenological assumptions. Strauss's efforts to discover a non-metaphysical teaching in classical political philosophy is one indication of the presence of those assumptions.

A way to think about the continuing hold of contemporary assumptions within Strauss's position is to consider his lifelong reflection on Plato's cave. Strauss ties this image to the phenomenological term "horizon" that is so important to Husserl. Strauss's account of historicism is that historicism claims we are trapped by history and historical consciousness in our various caves. Historical consciousness then functions as a "cave beneath the cave" of Plato. Strauss's effort is to move us out of this "second cave" to the original cave, so that we (or at least the philosophers among us) can ascend from that cave to encounter nature or the whole. But, as we have seen, it is fundamental to Strauss that we cannot really leave this original cave because (as he consistently argues) we need to stay in contact with the opinions of the city. To do more, to enter into a thinking beyond the cave as that is humanly available, would be for Strauss to enter into metaphysics, a realm that he assumes exceeds our humanity. Nature can, then, only ever be an absolute horizon of permanent problems, and our access to it remains fundamentally tied to the opinions of the city. For Strauss, this is precisely the self-awareness of political philosophy. In order for philosophy to remain a quest – to remain with the permanent problems – thought cannot rise to a higher, more independent position: such independence of thinking and its objects of thought is the very position that a more traditional reading of Plato suggests is the object of Platonic dialectics.

So, for Strauss, the only difference between this cave (the horizon of the fundamental and permanent problems) and the historicist caves is the claim of Strauss's cave to be non-historicist. The argument of this book has been that such a stance is itself historically marked and determined. All of Strauss's wonderful readings are, then, made from out of this contemporary standpoint. As with other contemporary readings – one thinks of Heidegger here – there is what Hans-Georg Gadamer called a "hermeneutical circle." For those who share Strauss's standpoint, his readings are enormously compelling; for those external to it, the readings appear forced and problematic. This is why to recognize Strauss as an original and important contemporary thinker is also, fundamentally, to criticize him.

Strauss would have a perfectly reasonable response to this criticism. His originality or distinctiveness, he would argue, is purely local: he is only bringing to light things to which modern assumptions have blinded others. He would say that his originality lies purely in the conditions, and not in the substance, of his thought. Strauss points not to himself, not to Leo Strauss, but to Socrates and Plato. But for Strauss, even Socrates and Plato are not original in anything but a conditional sense; they are original only in being the first to realize the possibility of a political philosophy that is coeval with humanity.

In other words, in the end we are left with an opposition not unlike the many other oppositions we find in Strauss. There is no simple refutation of the Straussian claim to access nature through Socratic political philosophy, nor is there a Straussian refutation of the claim that Strauss's position, rather than getting beyond history, falls within it. We are left, then, with what could be called "the Straussian/non-Straussian problem." And this is, perhaps, a fitting conclusion for an introduction to Leo Strauss.

Further Reading

For further reading in the secondary literature on Leo Strauss, what follows is by no means a comprehensive list, but it will suggest some good places to start. For full bibliographical information on each author, see the section on "Works by Authors Other than Strauss" in the "Works Cited" list that follows this section.

For overviews or general introductions, especially useful are both the books by Catherine and Michael Zuckert, and the ones by Steven B. Smith (both his own book and the *Cambridge Companion* volume he edited). To look further into Strauss's intellectual biography, the first thing to read is Daniel Tanguay. Further information and assessment of Strauss's formation in the Weimar Republic can be found in Heinrich Meier, Eugene R. Sheppard, David Janssens, and, more controversially, William H. F. Altman. For contributions to and assessments of the debates about Strauss's politics and accusations of his holding a secret Nietzschean or anti-democratic position, see Shadia Drury, Peter Minowitz, Nicholas Xenos, Robert Howse, Stanley Rosen, and Laurence Lampert as well as some of the books listed above. I should also mention some articles that were especially helpful to my understanding of Strauss, though they are often more difficult: Seth Benardete, Victor Gourevitch, Richard Kennington, Robert Pippin, and Christopher Bruell.

On more specialized topics, just a few suggestions to get you started: on the exoteric/esoteric distinction the clear place to go is Arthur M. Melzer. There are some interesting critiques of Melzer published in the journal *Perspectives on Political Science* (2015). On Strauss's contributions to Jewish thought, see Kenneth Hart Green,

Jeffrey Bernstein, Leora Batnitzky, Joshua Parens, and Sharon Portnoff. These authors also consider Strauss on the theological-political problem, but see too Heinrich Meier and Susan Orr. A very helpful collection for Strauss's understanding of classical philosophy is Timothy Burns, and useful – but more critical of Strauss – on early modern thought is Winfried Schröder. Strauss's relation to Husserl is discussed by Rodrigo Chacón, and his relation to Heidegger is the topic of a very interesting book by Richard Velkley. Strauss's relation to Carl Schmitt was the subject of Heinrich Meier. Strauss's debate with Alexandre Kojève is considered in George Grant, Victor Gourevitch, and the volume edited by Timothy Burns and Bryan-Paul Frost.

Beyond these suggestions, there is a large and growing scholarship on Leo Strauss to explore. This includes a number of collections – both books and journals – of articles and chapters dedicated to the thought of Leo Strauss.

Works Cited

Works by Strauss

The Argument and Action of Plato's Laws. University of Chicago Press, 1975.

The City and Man. University of Chicago Press, 1964.

"The Crisis of Our Time." In *The Predicament of Modern Politics*, ed. Harold J. Spaeth, University of Detroit Press, 1964, pp. 41–103.

"Correspondence Concerning Modernity: Karl Löwith and Leo Strauss." *Independent Journal of Philosophy*, 4, 1983, pp. 105–19.

"Correspondence Concerning *Wahrheit und Methode*: Leo Strauss and Hans-Georg Gadamer." *Independent Journal of Philosophy*, 2, 1978, pp. 5–26.

"Correspondence: Karl Löwith and Leo Strauss." *Independent Journal of Philosophy*, 5/6, 1988, pp. 177–92.

Faith and Political Philosophy: The Correspondence Between Leo Strauss and Eric Voegelin, 1934–1964. Trans. and ed. Peter Emberley and Barry Cooper, University of Missouri Press, 2004.

"Farabi's Plato." In *Louis Ginzberg: Jubilee Volume on the Occasion of his Seventieth Birthday*, English section, American Academy for Jewish Research, 1945, pp. 357–93.

"German Nihilism." *Interpretation: A Journal of Political Philosophy*, 26 (3), 1999, pp. 353–78.

Hobbes's Critique of Religion and Related Writings. Trans. and ed. Gabriel Bartlett and Svetozar Minkov, University of Chicago Press, 2011.

An Introduction to Political Philosophy: Ten Essays by Leo Strauss. Ed. and intro. Hilail Gildin, Wayne State University Press, 1989.

Jewish Philosophy and the Crisis of Modernity: Essays and Lectures in Modern Jewish Thought. Ed. and intro. Kenneth Hart Green, SUNY Press, 1997.

Leo Strauss: The Early Writings (1921–1932). Trans. and ed. Michael Zank, SUNY Press, 2002.

Leo Strauss: Liberalism Ancient and Modern. 1968. With a new Foreword by Allan Bloom, Cornell University Press, 1989.

"The Living Issues of German Postwar Philosophy." In Meier, *Leo Strauss and the Theologico-Political Problem*, pp. 115–39.

"Natural Law." In *International Encyclopedia of the Social Sciences*, ed. David L. Sill, Macmillan, 1948, vol. 11, pp. 80–5.

Natural Right and History. 1953. University of Chicago Press, 1965.

"Notes on Carl Schmitt, *The Concept of the Political.*" Trans. J. Harvey Lomax, in *The Concept of the Political*, Carl Schmitt, trans. George Schwab, University of Chicago Press, 1964, pp. 81–107.

On Tyranny: Corrected and Expanded Edition, Including the Strauss–Kojève Correspondence. Ed. Victor Gourevitch and Michael S. Roth, University of Chicago Press, 2013.

Persecution and the Art of Writing. 1953. University of Chicago Press, 1980.

Philosophy and Law: Contributions to the Understanding of Maimonides and His Predecessors. Trans. and intro. Eve Adler, SUNY Press, 1995.

The Political Philosophy of Hobbes: Its Basis and Genesis. Trans. Elsa M. Sinclair, 1952. University of Chicago Press, 1963.

"Reason and Revelation." In Meier, *Leo Strauss and the Theological-Political Problem*, pp. 141–80.

The Rebirth of Classical Political Rationalism: An Introduction to the Thought of Leo Strauss. Selected and intro. Thomas L. Pangle, University of Chicago Press, 1989.

"Relativism." In *Relativism and the Study of Man*, ed. Helmut Schoeck and James W. Wiggins, Van Nostrand, 1961, pp. 135–57.

Reorientation: Leo Strauss in the 1930s. Ed. Martin D. Yaffe and Richard S. Ruderman, Palgrave Macmillan, 2014.

"Restatement." *Interpretation: A Journal of Political Philosophy*, 36 (1), 2008, pp. 3–100.

Socrates and Aristophanes. University of Chicago Press, 1966.

Spinoza's Critique of Religion. Trans. E. M. Sinclair, Schocken, 1965.

"The Spirit of Sparta or The Taste of Xenophon." *Social Research: An International Journal of the Political and Social Sciences*, 6 (4), 1939, pp. 502–36.

The Strauss–Krüger Correspondence: Returning to Plato through Kant. Ed. Susan Meld Shell, Palgrave Macmillan, 2018.

Studies in Platonic Political Philosophy. Intro. Thomas L. Pangle, University of Chicago Press, 1983.

Thoughts on Machiavelli. 1958. University of Chicago Press, 1978.

Toward Natural Right and History: Lectures and Essays by Leo Strauss 1937–1946. Ed. J. A. Colen and Svetozar Minkov, University of Chicago Press, 2018.

What Is Political Philosophy? And Other Studies. 1959. University of Chicago Press, 1988.

Works by Authors Other than Strauss

Altman, William H. F. *The German Stranger: Leo Strauss and National Socialism.* Lexington, 2011.

Anton, Michael. *After the Flight 93 Election.* Encounter Books, 2019.

Batnitzky, Leora. *Leo Strauss and Emmanuel Levinas: Philosophy and the Politics of Revelation.* Cambridge University Press, 2006.

Batnitzky, Leora. "Leo Strauss and the Theologico-Political Predicament." In Smith, *Cambridge Companion to Leo Strauss*, pp. 41–62.

Benardete, Seth. "Leo Strauss' *The City and Man.*" *Political Science Reviewer*, 8, 1978, pp. 1–20.

Benardete, Seth. "Strauss on Plato." In *The Argument of the Action*, ed. Ronna Burger and Michael C. Davis, University of Chicago Press, 2000, pp. 407–17.

Bernstein, Jeffrey Alan. *Leo Strauss on the Borders of Judaism, Philosophy, and History.* SUNY Press, 2015.

Bruell, Christopher. "The Question of Nature and the Thought of Leo Strauss." *Klesis-Revue Philosophique*, 19, 2011, pp. 1–10.

Burns, Timothy W., ed. *Brill's Companion to Leo Strauss' Writings on Classical Political Thought.* Brill, 2014.

Burns, Timothy W. and Frost, Bryan-Paul, eds. *Philosophy, History, and Tyranny.* SUNY Press, 2016.

Chacón, Rodrigo. "Strauss and Husserl." *Idealistic Studies*, 44 (2–3), 2015, pp. 281–96.

Descombes, Vincent. *Modern French Philosophy.* Cambridge University Press, 1980.

Drury, Shadia. *The Political Ideas of Leo Strauss.* St. Martin's Press, 1988.

Gourevitch, Victor. "Philosophy and Politics." *Review of Metaphysics*, 22, 1968, pp. 58–84 and 281–328.

Gourevitch, Victor. "The Problem of Natural Right and the Fundamental Alternatives in *Natural Right and History.*" In *The Crisis of Liberal Democracy: A Straussian Perspective*, ed. Kenneth L. Deutsch and Walter Soffer, SUNY Press, 1987, pp. 30–47.

Grant, George. "Tyranny and Wisdom: A Comment on the Controversy Between Leo Strauss and Alexandre Kojève." *Social Research* 31 (1), 1964, pp. 45–72.

Green, Kenneth Hart. *Jew and Philosopher: The Return to Maimonides in the Jewish Thought of Leo Strauss.* SUNY Press, 1993.

Green, Kenneth Hart. *Leo Strauss and the Rediscovery of Maimonides.* University of Chicago Press, 2013.

Howse, Robert. *Leo Strauss: Man of Peace.* Cambridge University Press, 2014.

Janssens, David. *Between Athens and Jerusalem: Philosophy, Prophecy and Politics in Leo Strauss's Early Thought.* SUNY Press, 2008.

Kennington, Richard. "Strauss's *Natural Right and History.*" *Review of Metaphysics*, 35 (1), 1981, pp. 57–86.

Kristol, Irving. *Reflections of a Neo-Conservative.* Basic Books, 1983.

Lampert, Laurence. *Leo Strauss and Nietzsche.* University of Chicago Press, 1996.

Lampert, Laurence. "Strauss's Recovery of Esotericism." In Smith, *Cambridge Companion to Leo Strauss*, pp. 63–92.

Levine, Peter. *Nietzsche and the Modern Crisis of the Humanities.* SUNY Press, 1995.

Mahoney, Daniel J. "L'Expérience du totalitarisme et la redécouverte de la nature." *Revue des Deux Mondes*, Jan. 1997, pp. 109–25.

Meier, Heinrich. *Carl Schmitt and Leo Strauss: The Hidden Dialogue.* Trans. Harvey J. Lomax, University of Chicago Press, 1995.

Meier, Heinrich. *Leo Strauss and the Theological-Political Problem.* Trans. Marcus Brainard, Cambridge University Press, 2006.

Melzer, Arthur M. *Between the Lines: The Lost History of Esoteric Writing.* University of Chicago Press, 2014.

Minowitz, Peter. *Straussophobia: Defending Leo Strauss and Straussians Against Shadia Drury and Other Accusers.* Lexington Books, 2009.

Orr, Susan. *Jerusalem and Athens: Reason and Revelation in the Works of Leo Strauss.* Rowman & Littlefield, 1995.

Parens, Joshua. *Leo Strauss and the Recovery of Medieval Political Philosophy.* University of Rochester Press, 2016.

Pippin, Robert. "The Modern World of Leo Strauss." *Political Theory*, 20 (3), 1992, pp. 448–72.

Portnoff, Sharon. *Reason and Revelation Before Historicism: Strauss and Fackenheim.* University of Toronto Press, 2011.

Rosen, Stanley. *Hermeneutics as Politics.* Yale University Press, 2003.

Rousseau, Jean-Jacques. *The Social Contract and Other Political Writings.* Trans. and ed. Victor Gourevitch, Cambridge University Press, 1997.

Schaar, John H. and Wolin, Sheldon S. "Review Essay: Essays on the Scientific Study of Politics: A Critique." *American Political Science Review*, 57 (1), 1963, pp. 125–50.

Schröder, Winfried, ed. *Reading Between the Lines: Leo Strauss and the History of Early Modern Philosophy.* De Gruyter, 2015.

Sheppard, Eugene R. *Leo Strauss and the Politics of Exile: The Making of a Political Philosopher.* University Press of New England, 2006.

Smith, Steven B. *Reading Leo Strauss: Politics, Philosophy, Judaism.* University of Chicago Press, 2006.

Smith, Steven B., ed. *The Cambridge Companion to Leo Strauss.* Cambridge University Press, 2009.

Spinoza, B. *Theological-Political Treatise.* Trans. Samuel Shirley, Hackett, 2001.

Storing, Herbert J., ed. *Essays on the Scientific Study of Politics.* Holt, Rinehart and Winston, 1962.

Tanguay, Daniel. *Leo Strauss: An Intellectual Biography.* Trans. Christopher Nadon, Yale University Press, 2007.

Xenos, Nicholas. *Cloaked in Virtue: Unveiling Leo Strauss and the Rhetoric of American Foreign Policy.* Routledge, 2008.

Velkley, Richard. *Heidegger, Strauss, and the Premises of Philosophy: On Original Forgetting.* University of Chicago Press, 2011.

Zuckert, Catherine H. and Zuckert, Michael P. *The Truth about Leo Strauss: Political Philosophy and American Democracy.* University of Chicago Press, 2006.

Zuckert, Catherine H. and Zuckert, Michael P. *Leo Strauss and the Problem of Political Philosophy.* University of Chicago Press, 2014.

Zuckert, Michael. "Straussians." In Smith, *Cambridge Companion to Leo Strauss*, pp. 263–86.

Index

Alcibiades, 191, 192
Alfarabi, 12, 56–8, 62, 70, 75, 82
Altman, William H. F., 177–8
America
 foreign policy of, 185, 188–9,
  191–2, 193
 liberal democracy and, 2, 170–80,
  182, 187–8
 political thought of, 6, 7, 171,
  174–6, 177, 181, 182
ancients, return to, 21, 23–4, 26,
 32–3, 37, 42–3, 55, 87, 113, 137,
 147
"anti-theological ire," 20, 143, 147n,
 151, 152, 155–6, 158
Anton, Michael, 193
Aquinas, Thomas, 56, 122, 125,
 130–2
Archimedean standpoint, 155–6,
 166
Aristophanes, 12
Aristotle, 12–13, 86, 125
 Metaphysics, 26
 on esoteric writing 75
 on natural right 130–2, 137, 183,
  196
 Plato and, 26, 39, 55, 70, 175,
  187

atheism, 10, 23, 52–5, 66–7, 71, 77,
 93, 98
 of probity, 53–5
 political atheism, 159
"Athens and Jerusalem," 2, 10,
 58–64, 65–8, 70–2, 79, 152, 154,
 182
Avicenna, 54–6, 62, 63

Bellow, Saul, 183
Benardete, Seth, 39, 120
Bloom, Allan, 183–4
Burnyeat, Myles, 97
Bush, George W., White House of,
 2, 171, 184–9, 191–3

Cambridge School of
  interpretation, 96–7
Cassirer, Ernst, 5, 24
"cave beneath the cave," *see*
  "second cave"
"change of orientation," 5, 6, 9–10,
 33–4, 41–4, 45, 52–6
Chicago, University of, 5, 6, 172,
 193, 194
Christianity, 20, 22, 30, 41, 50, 55,
 56, 61, 63, 139, 146–7, 155, 179
Cicero, 111, 136